PRAEGER LIBRARY OF CHINESE AFFAIRS

China's Cultural Legacy
and Communism

PRAEGER LIBRARY OF CHINESE AFFAIRS

General Editor: Donald W. Klein, Columbia University

China is one of the world's oldest civilizations and one of the least known or understood. Its rich history has much to contribute to our understanding of man; its experiences in modernization are relevant to other developing nations; its crucial role in Asian and world politics makes imperative a fuller comprehension of the Chinese past and present.

The volumes in this multidisciplinary series will explore central issues of China's political, social, and economic structure, its philosophy and thought, and its history, civilization, and culture. The contributors to the series represent a wide variety of approaches and attitudes, and all are specialists in their respective fields. Included in the series are the following works:

Ralph C. Croizier, ed., *China's Cultural Legacy and Communism* (1970)

Donald G. Gillin, *History of the Chinese Civil War, 1945–50* (1971)*

James P. Harrison, A *History of the Chinese Communist Party* (1971)*

Michel Oksenberg and Frederick C. Teiwes, eds., *The Chinese Communist Bureaucracy at Work* (1971)*

Theodore Shabad, *China's Changing Map: A Political and Economic Geography of the Chinese People's Republic*, rev. ed. (1971)*

William W. Whitson, with Chen-hsia Huang, *The Evolution of the Military High Command in China, 1928–68* (1970)*

* Title and publication date are not yet final.

CHINA'S CULTURAL LEGACY AND COMMUNISM

EDITED BY

RALPH C. CROIZIER

PRAEGER PUBLISHERS
New York · Washington · London

For Marion,

companion of my "husks and bran" days

PRAEGER PUBLISHERS
111 Fourth Avenue, New York, N.Y. 10003, U.S.A.
5, Cromwell Place, London S.W.7, England

Published in the United States of America in 1970
by Praeger Publishers, Inc.

Library of Congress Catalog Card Number: 77–83334

Printed in the United States of America

Contents

List of Illustrations

Acknowledgments

An anthology is of necessity the product of many persons' thought and labor. Some of the contributors I know personally or by reputation; others, especially in Communist China, remain anonymous. But I am indebted to them all and to all others who have studied or sustained China's cultural legacy.

My deepest gratitude, however, is reserved for my teachers and colleagues, who have developed my interest in modern China's cultural and intellectual history. Foremost among these is my late teacher Joseph Levenson, who encouraged me to proceed with the anthology and several of whose articles grace this collection.

Several publishers and organizations generously let me use their materials without charge. I am, accordingly, grateful to *The China Quarterly*, The Asia Society, The American Consulate General in Hong Kong, The University of California Press, and The China Policy Study Group. I also wish to express my thanks to the University of Rochester for financial and secretarial assistance in preparing this manuscript and, finally, to my editor, Miss Mervyn Adams, for so cheerfully putting up with my procrastinations.

China's Cultural Legacy
and Communism

Introduction

It can hardly be claimed that Communist China is a neglected subject. The recent proliferation of scholarly and journalistic writings, ranging from superficial "I was there" accounts to formidable sociopolitical treatises, has made China better known, if not better understood, in the United States than almost any other Asian country. As a sure sign of the arrival of contemporary Chinese studies, a good number of anthologies have been appearing. Why, then, one more book that says nothing essentially new, and an anthology at that? My justification is that one corner of the contemporary China garden has been very sparsely cultivated by Western scholars and deserves more care. I refer to traditional Chinese culture in the People's Republic or what the Communists themselves call "the cultural legacy."

The importance and interest of this subject for both China and Chinese Communism is readily apparent. So far, however, it has received relatively little attention from Western scholars. The reasons are not hard to find. Most of our China watchers have social-science backgrounds and are naturally more interested in political, social, and economic developments in the People's Republic. Those who might be expected to take an interest in cultural trends—literary historians, art critics, students of Chinese philosophy—have frequently been repelled by the violent changes forced upon the traditional culture they have studied and loved. Hence, taking the traditional Chinese scholar's refuge from an unpleasant and degenerate present, they have tended to confine their studies to the past. Perhaps on purely aesthetic grounds they cannot be blamed for their retreat, but it has left vital questions about the recent past and the present and future of China relatively neglected.

Of course, there have been notable exceptions among Western scholars, without whom the selections in this book could not have been compiled. But the fact remains that not only is there no comprehensive treatment of China's cultural legacy but the several recent anthologies on Communist China give little space to the purely cultural field. Hence, the appearance of one more anthology, its object not to celebrate, much less to eulogize, but to show what has happened to the indigenous tradition of Chinese culture during the twenty-year history of the Chinese People's Republic. This means that I am dealing entirely with cultural subjects and, for the most part, deliberately eschewing the vague but tantalizing question of how Chinese tradition has influenced Communist policies and ideology.[1] The compensating advantage of this approach should be a clearer focus on culture. I should also add that not all culture in Communist China is covered—only the indigenous tradition, the "cultural legacy."

In one sense, Chinese culture—the self-contained and self-sufficient cultural entity of traditional China—is already dead; indeed, it has been dead for more than half a century. But "cultural legacy" is something else again. What needs to be preserved is not an ancient but still-living culture but rather what China's old culture, now dead and gone, has passed on to its descendants. It is up to those descendants (the Communists being very anxious to place themselves at what they consider the inevitable end of China's historical development) to select and develop what from this legacy is useful for their own purposes. That their purposes are very different from those of their ancestors bears remembering; that the new culture they seek to produce must differ from the old is obvious.

Yet, when building, even revolutionaries must work with material at hand. In China, the cultural material comes from two broad sources—the Western borrowings that have poured in during the last century and the ancient indigenous cultural tradition. It is a mark of the Chinese Communists' nationalism and suspicion of things Western that much of what they have chosen has been of native origin. To be sure, they have also had their suspicions about traditional Chinese culture (these suspicions are currently at their sharpest), but this has not prevented large-scale preservation of traditional cultural forms and, more significantly, their adaptation to serve the goals of the new society. For the masters and molders of the new China, the paramount task has been to create a vital, contemporary Chinese culture. It must

[1] For a recent attempt in that direction, see Ho Ping-ti and Tang Tsou (eds.), *China in Crisis*, vol. I (Chicago: University of Chicago Press, 1968).

serve the present but still be recognizably Chinese, not just a pastiche of Western influence.

"Cultural legacy," therefore, has been a much-used phrase in Communist China, and how properly to inherit this legacy is a much-discussed question. In a sense, the problem transcends specifically Communist concerns, for how to be modern and still Chinese has been a dilemma for all Chinese since the end of the last century. To preserve the old culture inviolate, as true Confucian conservatives wanted, was to condemn China to backwardness in a modern world; to abandon all the old culture in favor of Western borrowings was offensive to nationalistic sensibilities. The result has been deep tension between new and old, foreign and Chinese.

Indeed, the cultural question—and even "cultural revolution" —long predates Communist China. Fifty years ago, the majority of China's new intellectual leaders had already lost confidence in the old culture's ability to sustain itself. In the intellectual ferment out of which the Chinese Communist Party was born in 1921, these men sought a new culture for modern China. Only a minority immediately chose Marxism as the guideline to China's future, but almost all the significant figures of the May Fourth Movement[2] considered traditional Chinese culture to be bankrupt and in need of Western-inspired rejuvenation. Though the rabid iconoclasm of this generation did not obliterate the old culture, it did shake it fundamentally, along with the assumptions upon which it had rested. The vexing problems of what the new culture would be and how the old might contribute to it were only raised, not solved, by the May Fourth Movement. But China and Chinese culture were never to be the same again.

Attempts to resolve this cultural tension were numerous and, at times, ingenious. Some Westernized liberals, like Hu Shih,[3] saw the solution in a Chinese renaissance to be based on a critical re-evaluation and "putting in order" of the traditional culture. The emphasis here was on "critical," for the admirers of modern Western culture were determined to root out everything that con-

[2] The student-led protest movement of May 4, 1919, against the Versailles Treaty and the warlord rulers of China gives its name to the larger cultural and intellectual revolution that swept educated Chinese youth around the end of World War I.

[3] Student of John Dewey and one of the leaders of the cultural revolution of the late 1910's and 1920's.

flicted with Western culture in content or spirit. The valuable part of China's cultural legacy was that which could sanction or buttress such modern values as rationalism, democracy, and progress; the rest (in a formula quite similar to what Mao Tse-tung would prescribe twenty years later) was dross to be discarded.

There were also contemporary conservatives who, out of either alarm at the rapid pace of change or nationalistic fear that it would blanch all the Chinese quality out of Chinese culture, recoiled from the proposals of the "Westernizers." Sometimes this took the form of a stubborn obscurantism that pretended that there was no cultural choice—Chinese was self-evidently better than Western. But the West and its culture were increasingly difficult to ignore for any Chinese thinker who wanted to be relevant to the twentieth century. A few modern conservatives tried to resolve the dilemma by interpreting the essence of Western culture as reaffirming rather than negating the value of traditional Chinese culture. Of course, this required a selectivity just as biased as that which Hu Shih applied to his re-evaluation. Moreover, it was even less workable, for it was impossible to pretend that classicism, morality, and religion were really at the heart of the modern West. And it was the modern West, not the classical or the medieval, that threatened and enthralled modern China.

The only conservative defense left, then, was one very untraditional by Confucian standards—cultural particularism. Chinese culture was best for Chinese, not because it was the best of all possible cultures, but because it was Chinese. Here is the premise behind much of modern Chinese cultural nationalism, light years removed from the blandly confident assumptions of cultural superiority in Confucian China and an integral part of the new sense of a particular identity that is central to modern Chinese nationalism. Much of the quasi-traditional ideology of the Chinese Nationalist Party rests on this, and, though complicated by other factors, it is not absent from Chinese Communism.

Of course, not all Chinese intellectuals in the three decades before 1949 were either cultural conservatives or iconoclasts. The majority were somewhere in the middle, caught by the conflicting claims of old and new, with all the implications about modernity, progress, nationalism, and cultural loyalty involved in their choices. Most tried to compromise or to blur the choice through eclecticism: Ibsen in the afternoon and Peking Opera at night for a well-rounded day, or Van Gogh on one wall, Mi Fei on the other, the height of cosmopolitan sophistication. But, though such décor might work on Park Avenue, cosmopolitan eclecticism did not solve the dilemma of how to produce a vital Chinese culture. It did not solve the malaise over what it meant culturally to be Chinese in the twentieth century.

That required some sense of Chinese identity without a lapse into cultural obscurantism or chauvinism. In 1936, a group of prominent university professors issued a Manifesto for Cultural Construction on a Chinese Basis, which called for progress and innovation without negating China's unique heritage. The proposition was rejected by the more militant Westernizers, but it was significant of the widespread desire for a middle ground. The more general idea of some kind of cultural synthesis—the "best" of East and West—was enormously popular. The vagueness of such a proposition was probably its main asset. "Best" could be subject to widely differing interpretations; the precise nature of the syncretic new culture was seldom spelled out. In practice, attempts to fuse specific cultural elements in art, literature, or philosophy were not notably successful. But the impulse toward change and the hope for a meaningful synthesis were undoubtedly present in pre 1949 China. That such ambitious cultural synthesis was not accomplished in so short a time is not surprising. The continued separate existence of both Chinese and Western theater, painting, and even medicine up to and after 1949 simply points to the cultural problem inherited by the People's Republic.

If the Chinese Communists face this problem as modern men and modern Chinese, they also face it as Marxists with a particularly clear view of the values they want to inculcate in the society they seek to build. This vision, ideology if you like, is far from irrelevant to their policies and attitudes toward China's cultural legacy. For one thing, it gives them no compunction about deliberately shaping the cultural "superstructure" to suit the needs of the socialist society. They may not be unique in this, since previous modern Chinese governments, notably the Nationalists, also attempted to disseminate new values through old cultural forms. But the People's Republic has been far more thorough and effective. This does not mean that the Chinese Communists have been simply emotionally detached cultural engineers. As Chinese, they too are involved in the culture they are remolding but, as Marxist revolutionaries, they are determined to remold it in a specific fashion. This has led to a great ambivalence: pride in Chinese accomplishments plus appreciation of the popular appeal of traditional cultural forms in gaining mass support versus suspicion that the reactionary feudal content of the old culture might poison the new society. Several solutions have been attempted. One tries to separate content from form or to make the old cultural forms carry a new content. This is most evident in the reform of Peking Opera, as are the inherent difficulties and frequent incongruities of such an operation. Old bottles, it seems, are not always the best containers for new wine.

A class analysis of Chinese culture has been more promising for the Communists' purposes and more dialectically Marxist. This divides the cultural legacy into a feudal aristocratic culture belonging to the oppressive ruling class and a popular democratic culture belonging to the people. The latter, as "people's," must be above reproach; but this popular democratic "essence" in the cultural legacy must be separated from feudal "dross." Ever since the Yenan period of 1935 to 1947, the Communists' cultural line has been neither wholesale acceptance nor complete rejection of China's past but rather "critical inheritance." The other slogan they have commonly used in trying to express the proper dialectical relationship between past and present is "develop the new out of the old" (*"t'ui ch'en ch'u hsin"*). Neither repudiating nor accepting the past, Mao and the Communist Party thus in good old Confucian parlance opted for the golden mean between cultural iconoclasm and conservatism, or, in more fashionable Marxist terminology, took the correct line between leftist nihilism and rightist revisionism. Old and new, Chinese philosophers are fond of the middle ground.

Although Mao Tse-tung's statements during the Yenan years have provided the theoretical basis for all arguments over the cultural legacy ever since, intentionally or unintentionally, they were general enough to provide great flexibility in subsequent policy. The major ambiguity, over just how much of the cultural legacy can be included in the democratic "essence," has fluctuated considerably over the years. Initially, during the Yenan period and the first few years of the People's Republic, a fairly rigid definition of "people's culture" was applied, one similar to Robert Redfield's distinction between the little and the great traditions in peasant society. Woodcuts and peasant folk dances were in; landscape painting, classical opera, and other art forms of the old high culture were out, or at least eclipsed by the deluge of Soviet-inspired socialist realism. With minor exceptions, mainly from folk arts and popular culture, it appeared that there was no room for much of the old culture in the new China.

Within a few years after the revolution, however, there began to appear signs of a more favorable attitude toward the cultural legacy, a more flexible interpretation of what was essence as opposed to dross. The fanfare greeting the World Peace Council's 1953 selection of the ancient poet Ch'u Yüan as one of the giants of human thought was a significant harbinger. More conclusively, when cultural commissar Chou Yang addressed the Second National Conference of Writers and Artists that September, his remarks about the cultural legacy were considerably softer than they had been at the First Conference in 1949. While maintaining the familiar division of feudal and democratic culture, he noticeably relaxed the criteria for inclusion in democratic culture. With the inclusion of such factors as "realism," "patriotism," and "progressivism," strictly defined class connections were no longer the chief grounds for judging a particular figure or cultural element. After all, the frustrated feudal courtier Ch'u Yüan had hardly been a peasant and his poetry had hardly been folk songs. Adding historical relativism—"it is important that we consider the concrete historical conditions under which the figures in question lived and not just present-day conditions"—the theoretical barriers to embracing almost everything in the cultural legacy were removed.

Nevertheless, the rehabilitation of large sections of the cultural legacy proceeded slowly and unevenly during the middle 1950's. If theoretical barriers had been lowered, there were still formidable psychological obstacles derived from decades of iconoclasm plus practical difficulties from the lingering association of certain cultural elements with objectionable social and intellectual traditions. But the way had been opened to assimilation of more of China's traditions than just folk culture—all in the name of the people but also all in the name of China.

The strong nationalist appeal in this policy, to non-Party intellectuals and dedicated Communists alike, is unmistakable. It accounts in part for the surprising vitality of many traditional cultural forms after their former sources of social support had been wiped out in the revolution. Paradoxically, the very destruction of the old social and political order seems to have made traditional arts more acceptable to the Communist revolutionaries. No longer facing traditional culture as a living whole, one against which they were engaged in a life-and-death struggle, the Communists could now afford to be more tolerant and to give more rein to their cultural and nationalist proclivities. They could now regard the old culture as simply legacy—their legacy—elements of which could be discriminately rehabilitated. These, in turn, could be used to castigate Western-influenced intellectuals for their unpatriotic bourgeois cultural tastes. With feudalism apparently dead, it seemed safe enough to redeem a good part of what had been considered feudal culture for service in the struggle against still dangerous bourgeois influences. Though not socialist, a good part of the cultural legacy was judged "progressive" or "patriotic." And for much of the late 1950's and early 1960's, this seemed good enough to insure its survival.

During the liberalization of the Hundred Flowers Movement in 1956–57, there was a remarkable upsurge in traditional cultural activities. Among other manifestations, classics that had been burned in 1949 reappeared in new editions. For the first time since the revolution, articles were published that lauded Confucius as a great progressive figure in Chinese history. A national conference on archaeology suggested more intensive study and protection of the relics of China's past. All such activities received a setback with the strict enforcement of Communist orthodoxy in the anti-rightist campaign of the latter part of 1957 and the subsequent emphasis on all-out socialist construction of the Great Leap Forward. Yet, even while historians in particular and scholars in general were being instructed "more present, less past," there were also determined attempts to portray socialist reality through national forms. Reliance exclusively on foreign art forms, even Soviet inspired, was still eschewed as unpatriotic.

The grim years of economic retrenchment following the Great Leap were enormously complex. There was no outburst of cultural and intellectual activity comparable to the Hundred Flowers period, but, from 1959 on, there was a remarkable revival of interest in traditional arts and scholarship. The Communist Party applauded this for the nationalistic and antibourgeois reasons mentioned earlier, but some aspects of the revival evidently aroused deep misgivings among at least some of the Party leaders.

Increased freedom for and patronage of traditional cultural elements was probably seen as a safe and prudent concession to disgruntled intellectuals following the rigors of the Great Leap and the disillusionment in its aftermath. But the ardor with which intellectuals, Party as well as non-Party, turned to the cultural legacy provoked suspicions that, instead of following the approved slogan of "using the past to serve the present" (*ku-wei chin-yung*), they were escaping from a dreary present into a more attractive past. This could hardly be reassuring to the builders of the future. Even more serious were signs that the past was being used to criticize the present, that the cultural legacy might be involved with the nemesis of revisionism.

By late in 1962, after the worst years of economic hardship were over, the Party started to restore ideological discipline over study of the cultural legacy. Apparently the leadership itself was badly split on this issue and others, however, so that there is a curiously inconclusive quality to the campaigns and struggles launched in the next several years. Official policy toward the cultural legacy continued to be one of critical acceptance. State patronage and increasingly qualified praise for the traditional arts continued. But a storm was brewing over the cultural legacy that was to be unleashed with cataclysmic force in the Great Proletarian Cultural Revolution.

We shall deal with that storm, since late in 1965, in the final section of the book, but first it is necessary to see the development of policy toward the cultural legacy. Chapter I explores the over-all question systematically; the other chapters deal with specific cultural fields. I have attempted, in my chapter-by-chapter commentary, to give coherence without imposing my own conclusions. Accordingly, the selections that form the bulk of the text are drawn from a wide variety of sources with a wide variety of viewpoints. These include studies by Western scholars, reactions of visitors to China, statements by Chinese Government spokesmen, and the works of Chinese scholars, artists, and writers. It is my hope that the result is a book useful to students of Chinese Communism and to everyone interested in Chinese culture.

I

Policy Toward the Cultural Legacy

1. THE NEW *Locus Classicus:*
SELECTIONS FROM MAO TSE-TUNG

Much in the fashion of traditional Confucian scholars citing the classics for authority, every discussion of the cultural legacy in Communist China refers to Mao Tse-tung's statements from late in the 1930's and early in the 1940's, especially his "Talks at the Yenan Forum on Literature and Art."

Here are excerpts from two early essays, "Study" (1938) and "On New Democracy" (1940), along with the relatively brief sections of the Yenan "Talks" (1942) that deal directly with the cultural legacy.

In these years, against the background of a patriotic war effort and a struggle against Moscow-trained elements in the Party who had little experience with Chinese conditions, Mao repeatedly emphasized the need to Sinify Marxism. In culture, this meant emphasis on a Chinese national form, "the fresh, lively Chinese style and spirit which the common people of China love."

He makes it clear, especially in the Yenan "Talks," that the inheritance of the cultural legacy must be critical and must lead to a new culture in the service of the revolution. But all these discussions are brief and general enough to permit considerable variation in interpretation. In this, too, there is a resemblance to China's Confucian classics.

STUDY

MAO TSE-TUNG

Another of our tasks is to study our historical heritage and use the Marxist method to sum it up critically. Our national history goes back several thousand years and has its own characteristics and innumerable treasures. But in these matters we are mere schoolboys. Contemporary China has grown out of the China of the past; we are Marxist in our historical approach and must not lop off our history. We should sum up our history from Confucius to Sun Yat-sen and take over this valuable legacy. This is important for guiding the great movement of today. Being Marxists, Communists are internationalists, but we can put Marxism into practice only when it is integrated with the specific characteristics of our country and acquires a definite national form. The great strength of Marxism-Leninism lies precisely in its integration with the concrete revolutionary practice of all countries. For the Chinese Communist Party, it is a matter of learning to apply the theory of Marxism-Leninism to the specific circumstances of China. For the Chinese Communists who are part of the great Chinese nation, flesh of its flesh and blood of its blood, any talk about Marxism in isolation from China's characteristics is merely Marxism in the abstract, Marxism in a vacuum. Hence to apply Marxism concretely in China so that its every manifestation has an indubitably Chinese character, i.e., to apply Marxism in the light of China's specific characteristics, becomes a problem which it is urgent for the whole Party to understand and solve. Foreign stereotypes must be abolished, there must be less singing of empty, abstract tunes, and dogmatism must be laid to rest; they must be replaced by the fresh, lively Chinese style and spirit which the common people of China love. To separate internationalist content from national form is the practice of those who do not understand the first thing about internationalism. We, on the contrary, must link the two closely. In this matter there are serious errors in our ranks which should be conscientiously overcome.

FROM Mao Tse-tung, "Study," *Selected Works of Mao Tse-tung* (Peking: Foreign Languages Press, 1965), II, 208–9.

ON NEW DEMOCRACY

MAO TSE-TUNG

New-democratic culture is national. It opposes imperialist oppression and upholds the dignity and independence of the Chinese nation. It belongs to our own nation and bears our own national characteristics. It links up with the socialist and new-democratic cultures of all other nations and they are related in such a way that they can absorb something from each other and help each other to develop, together forming a new world culture; but, as a revolutionary national culture, it can never link up with any reactionary imperialist culture of whatever nation. To nourish her own culture, China needs to assimilate a good deal of foreign progressive culture, not enough of which was done in the past. We should assimilate whatever is useful to us today not only from the present-day socialist and new-democratic cultures but also from the earlier cultures of other nations, for example, from the culture of the various capitalist countries in the Age of Enlightenment. However, we should not gulp any of this foreign material down uncritically but must treat it as we do our food—first chewing it, then submitting it to the working of the stomach and intestines with their juices and secretions, and separating it into nutriment to be absorbed and waste matter to be discarded—before it can nourish us. To advocate "wholesale westernization" is wrong. China has suffered a great deal from the mechanical absorption of foreign material. Similarly, in applying Marxism to China, Chinese Communists must fully and properly integrate the universal truth of Marxism with the concrete practice of the Chinese revolution, or, in other words, the universal truth of Marxism must be combined with specific national characteristics and acquire a definite national form if it is to be useful, and in no circumstances can it be applied subjectively as a mere formula. Marxists who make a fetish of formulas are simply playing the fool with Marxism and the Chinese revolution, and there is no room for them in the ranks of the Chinese revolution. Chinese culture should have its own form, its own national form. National in form and new-democratic in content—such is our new culture today.

FROM Mao Tse-tung, "On New Democracy," *Selected Works of Mao Tse-tung* (Peking: Foreign Languages Press, 1965), II, 380–81.

TALKS AT THE YENAN FORUM
ON LITERATURE AND ART

MAO TSE-TUNG

We have said that China's new culture at the present stage is an antiimperialist, antifeudal culture of the masses of the people under the leadership of the proletariat. Today, anything that is truly of the masses must necessarily be led by the proletariat. Whatever is under the leadership of the bourgeoisie cannot possibly be of the masses. Naturally, the same applies to the new literature and art, which are part of the new culture. We should take over the rich legacy and the good traditions in literature and art that have been handed down from past ages in China and foreign countries, but the aim must still be to serve the masses of the people. Nor do we refuse to utilize the literary and artistic forms of the past, but in our hands these old forms, remolded and infused with new content, also become something revolutionary in the service of the people. . . .

In the last analysis, what is the source of all literature and art? Works of literature and art, as ideological forms, are products of the reflection in the human brain of the life of a given society. Revolutionary literature and art are the products of the reflection of the life of the people in the brains of revolutionary writers and artists. The life of the people is always a mine of the raw materials for literature and art, materials in their natural form, materials that are crude, but most vital, rich, and fundamental; they make all literature and art seem pallid by comparison; they provide literature and art with an inexhaustible source, for there can be no other. Some may ask, is there not another source in books, in the literature and art of ancient times and of foreign countries? In fact, the literary and artistic works of the past are not a source but a stream; they are created by our predecessors and the foreigners out of the literary and artistic raw materials they found in the life of the people of their time and place. We must take over all the fine things in our literary and artistic heritage, critically assimilate whatever is beneficial, and use them as examples when we create works out of the literary and artistic raw materials in the

FROM Mao Tse-tung, "Talks at the Yenan Forum on Literature and Art," *Selected Works of Mao Tse-tung* (Peking: Foreign Languages Press, 1965), III, 76 and 81.

life of the people of our own time and place. It makes a difference whether or not we have such examples, the difference between a low and a high level and between slower and faster work. Therefore, we must on no account reject the legacies of the ancients and the foreigners or refuse to learn from them, even though they are the works of the feudal or bourgeois classes. But taking over legacies and using them as examples must never replace our own creative work; nothing can do that. Uncritical transplantation or copying from the ancients and the foreigners is the most sterile and harmful dogmatism in literature and art.

2. THE CULTURAL LEGACY UNDER SUSPICION

On the eve of national victory, Party cultural spokesman Chou Yang explained to writers and artists at their First National Conference what would be expected of them under the new order. He said very little about traditional culture, except for folk art. From his remarks, it is clear that the division between acceptable popular culture and noxious feudal culture was drawn generally along the line of folk art versus high culture, hence the praise for popular literary forms, yangko peasant folk dances, woodcuts, and folk songs as vehicles for carrying themes of class struggle and national resistance. "Bourgeois culture of the West" is scorned along with "feudal literature and art," but the Chinese quality of the new national forms scarcely transcends the village. In the first flush of revolutionary victory, the glories of old Chinese high culture remained in eclipse as faithful copies of Soviet socialist realism dominated the arts.

THE PEOPLE'S NEW LITERATURE AND ART

CHOU YANG

Because the literature and art of the liberated areas are new in content, there are, correspondingly, many innovations in form. This was evident first in the language. After the May Fourth Movement, progressive and revolutionary writers and artists were discussing the question of adopting a popular and national form but were unable to find a practicable, thoroughgoing solution. After Comrade Mao Tse-tung's talks at the Yenan Forum on Literature and Art, the problems of "popularization" and "national forms" came to be solved naturally, or, at least, the correct road was found to their solution, because the writers and artists made great efforts to mingle with workers and peasants and studied their language and budding literature. A unique feature of the literature of the liberated areas is that its language is fairly popular in form. Language is the major element of literary works and the primary indication of national forms. Chao Shu-li's outstanding success is, on the one hand, due to his deep understanding of rural life and rural class relationships and of the complexity of the struggle between the various classes in the countryside, an understanding that makes his works highly realistic and vivid. But, on the other hand, his success is also due to his language, which is truly the language of the masses, and has been worked over and polished into such simplicity and naturalness that it does not have a trace of artificiality. In his works, artistic form and ideological content are integrated to a rather high degree. Many other writers, too, especially those who have worked with the masses, have done no little to improve the language.

Another important characteristic of the literature and art of the liberated areas is that they preserve close ties with the national and particularly the people's traditional literature and art. In fiction, there is *Rhymes of Li Yu-tsai*; in poetry and song, we have *Wang Kuei and Li Hsiang-hsiang*; and in drama, *The White-haired Girl* and *Bloody Tears of Vengeance*. Works that prove most popular with the masses are all of this nature.

Why are new dramas like *The White-haired Girl* and *Bloody*

FROM Chou Yang, "The People's New Literature and Art, Report to First All-China Conference of Writers and Artists, July 1949," *China's New Literature and Art* (Peking: Foreign Languages Press, 1954), pp. 60–64.

Tears of Vengeance record-breaking in their popularity, and why have they had such a deep influence? The main reasons are these: During the people's war against the Japanese invaders, such works presented the theme of class struggle in bold relief and with a strong, romantic color. At the same time, they were presented in forms which the masses were familiar with and could readily accept. *The White-haired Girl* was a further attempt to create a new type of drama on the foundation of folk opera after the success of the first *yangko* drama, *Brother and Sister Pioneers*. After Comrade Mao Tse-tung's talks at the Yenan Forum on Literature and Art, our writers and artists did considerable research and constructive work in popular literary and artistic forms. Their major achievement was the promotion of the *yangko* form. We have created a new popular *yangko* on the old rural basis. Its influence has spread all over China.

The liberated area woodcuts, New Year's pictures, picture story books, etc., are all rich in Chinese style and flavor. We all know the woodcuts of Ku Yuan, Yen Han, Li Chun, and the cartoons of Hua Chun-wu and Tsai Jo-hung. In music, many new songs have been produced which are widely popular and retain the flavor of folk songs.

We make use of the old forms not simply by "pouring new wine into old bottles" but rather by "deriving the new from the old." This is entirely according to the laws of development usual with a national literature and art. Lu Hsün said, "In adopting old forms, some things must be excised. Since it is so, other things must be added in. The result is the appearance of a new form, and that is change." Lu Hsün's forecast has already begun to be realized in the liberated areas. Now no one can say that *Rhymes of Li Yu-tsai* or *Wang Kuei and Li Hsiang-hsiang* or the *yangko* dances are of the old form. On the contrary, they are the new forms for which we have been searching. Formerly, we only considered Western forms of bourgeois literature and art as new. This point of view was based on blind worship of the bourgeois culture of the West, which was, in essence, a reflection of semicolonial ideas. So far as the people's literature and art are concerned, the forms of both feudal and bourgeois literature and art are, in a certain sense, all old forms. We do not refuse to make use of them, but they must be revised. We shall revise them from a national, scientific, and popular viewpoint so that they can be used to serve the people. This is our basic attitude toward all old forms, including folk forms.

Writers and artists of the liberated areas have learned much from folk forms and will undoubtedly learn still more from them in future. However, this is not the same thing as saying that, apart from folk forms, we do not want any other forms or regard them as unimportant. No, that is definitely not the case. We highly respect and wish to learn what is useful from the fine heritage of all native and foreign traditional forms, especially from Soviet socialist literature and art.

3. REVIVAL OF CHINESE CULTURAL FORMS

By 1956, the revival of many previously ignored or proscribed cultural forms was well under way. The old plays were again on the Peking stage, Chinese-style paintings were being given national exhibitions, and historians were finding new virtues in ancient national heroes. Moreover, previous neglect of these national glories was being criticized from the highest Party sources. We can see this in the following passage from Lu Ting-yi's important speech "Let a Hundred Flowers Blossom, a Hundred Schools of Thought Contend." Delivered on May 26, 1956, by Lu, the Director of the Party's propaganda department, it marked the beginning of the famous experimentation in relaxing ideological control over intellectuals that was known as the Hundred Flowers Movement. The title itself, an impeccable classical phrase describing China's golden age of philosophical development, indicates a much more favorable appraisal of the cultural legacy in its entirety, not just folk culture.

The unmistakable echoes of national pride in China's cultural achievements, however, should not blind us to its continued purpose of producing a new culture for the new socialist man and society. In the selection following Lu's speech, a sensitive French journalist sees the Communist sponsorship of traditional culture not as its preservation or revival but as its death through a kind of "museumification." Although not all Guillain's predictions have materialized (the abolition of the ideographic script notably has not), his metaphor of the museum still seems appropriate for much of what has happened to the cultural legacy in the decade since he wrote. We shall return to this metaphor later.

LET A HUNDRED FLOWERS BLOSSOM

LU TING-YI

In medical science, agronomy, philosophy, history, literature, drama, painting, and music, etc., China has a rich heritage. This heritage must be studied seriously and accepted critically. The point is not that we have done so much in these fields but that we have done too little and have not been serious enough in our approach. There is still this attitude of belittling our national heritage, and in some spheres it is still a really serious problem.

What kind of heritage are we to accept and how?

If we were to accept only what is perfect by present-day standards, there would be nothing left for us to take over. On the other hand, if we were to accept our cultural heritage uncritically, we should simply be taking the attitude summed up in the phrase "everything Chinese is best."

We suggest that in dealing with our cultural heritage the principle should be: Carefully select, cherish, and foster all that is good in it while criticizing its faults and shortcomings in a serious way. At present, our work suffers because we do neither well enough. There is a tendency to reject offhand even what is good in our cultural heritage. At present, that is the main trend. The recent performance of the Kunshan opera Fifteen Strings of Cash shows how wrong it was to say there was nothing good in Kunshan opera. And if there is such a tendency in the theater, what about other branches of art, literature, and scientific research? We must admit that there are similar tendencies in them too, and we must do something about it. At the same time, we can also see a tendency not to criticize or even to gloss over shortcomings in and blots on our cultural heritage. This attitude is neither honest nor sincere, and that we must alter, too.

Workers in art, literature, and science need to learn from the people. The wisdom of the people is inexhaustible. There are still many treasures among the people that have not yet been dis-

FROM Lu Ting-yi, Let a Hundred Flowers Blossom, a Hundred Schools of Thought Contend (Peking: Foreign Languages Press, 1964), pp. 27–29.

covered or, though discovered, not made good use of. Take medical science, for instance. In the past, needling and cautery and
special curative breathing exercises were scorned; only now are
they being taken notice of. But other "popular" healing methods
such as osteopathy, massage, and herbal medicines have even now
not received the attention due to them.

Then take music and painting. Not enough attention has been
paid to our national heritage in these two spheres of creative
activity. Wherever there are such tendencies, they must be
corrected.

As they come from the people, things are often not systematically developed or are crude or lack theoretical explanation. Some
of them have more than a bit of the "quack" about them, or a
taint of the superstitious. There is nothing surprising about that.
It is the duty of our scientists, artists, and writers not to despise
these things but to make a careful study of them, to select,
cherish, and foster the good in them, and, where necessary, put
them on a scientific basis.

SIX HUNDRED MILLION CHINESE

ROBERT GUILLAIN

But New China, people will object, is giving unprecedented
encouragement to culture, in particular to the arts, literature, and
the theater. Better than that, she is bringing culture to the people
and is saving ancient China by repairing her ruins, preserving the
artistic treasures, multiplying archaeological researches. . . . That
is devastatingly true, and this cultural effort is remarkable from
every point of view. But it refers to new culture quite divorced
from the old. The ancient culture is honored as it had not been
for many years but as one honors only the dead—it has been
admitted into the museums.

And where *could* ancient Chinese art find a place in the culture of today except in the museum? The bamboo and the bird,
painted on silk with Chinese ink, are unemployed. The same
situation holds true for all the themes of an art that was essentially idealist and "detached"; the sage in the mountain or the lake
in a mist have no meaning in the world of collectives. Art, sub-

FROM Robert Guillain, *Six Hundred Million Chinese* (New York: Criterion
Books, 1957), pp. 265–69. Copyright © 1957 by S. G. Phillips, Inc.

jected to the universal political law, now has to be utilitarian to
contribute to the spreading of socialism and Marxist materialism.
The new themes include the factory and the machine, the peasant
at the wheel of his tractor, the class struggle in the village, and
socialist construction in a town. Studies of a work hero or a factory chimney do not lend themselves to Chinese ink sketches in
the traditional style.

The new culture further demands from the past that it should
conform whenever possible to socialism. It ransacks history and
literature to "liberate" and celebrate little-known Marxist heroes
while rejecting the enemies of the people. Reforming and re-
educating even the past, it tampers with folklore to disinfect it of
all trace of feudalism. Kuo Mo-jo, the high priest of culture, pre-
sides over the "reform of the ancient arts" and encourages the
"examination and correction of the old dramas and songs." He
announces with satisfaction that "hundreds of ballads, operas,
and other works of popular art have been rewritten." Today, the
Chinese opera is one of the rare products of the ancient culture
that has preserved its indestructible vitality. After proposing to
ban it, the Party decided to preserve and even to encourage it, so
that it might be used in the service of propaganda. This began
with the "remolding" of all actors and a purging of the texts,
which have since been amputated and revised. In the theater, as
in real life, feudalism must always be punished and the hero of the
play must always be a man of the people.

Culture and art are therefore in full revolution, seeking to create
a new world profoundly different from the past. And they turn to
Russia to find models and masters for this great renovation. In
this respect, too, the mimicry is incredible. Thousands of pictures
and images present to the people the work and struggle of New
China, her men and trades. Every detail conforms strictly to the
models of current Russian art. The subject—peasants in the fields,
heroes of labor, soldiers on the frontiers, or Mao Tse-tung meeting Stalin—is invariably executed in execrably bad taste and style,
copied from Soviet art. This is even more depressing, since it is
impossible to escape the imagery of this *art nouveau*. It is found
everywhere, from the anterooms of public offices to the walls of
the peasant cottage, because art is now one of the great mediums
of propaganda.

Never have I seen such a heartbreaking bankruptcy of good
intentions. The purpose of this ubiquitous art is to extol the fine
and the beautiful, but, unfortunately, the artistic quality is al-

most invariably lamentable. The beginnings of the new culture have placed art in a serious crisis. The foremost victim of the cultural revolution is taste. It is quite appalling. The whole of China has been invaded by art objects of socialist realism, Russian style. Even in remote Lanchow, the visitor is taken to some art shop to look at the souvenirs; from paintings to porcelain, everything is hideous. The invasion has become more general since the cheap articles have been put within reach of the people's purse. But whereas in neighboring Japan poverty and cheapness are the sources of a pure and austere popular art, in China they produce nothing but ugliness, even in articles of everyday use. The cup is ugly, the curtain is ugly, and so is the cushion, the painting on the wall, and the ceiling decoration. It seems that artistically nothing rises from below, from the people itself. What emptiness compared with the lively popular art of, for example, Mexico, Indonesia, Africa, or India! On the other hand, the government has flooded the people with a spate of artistic horrors, designed to corrupt forever its artistic sense, if any remains.

No doubt it has been possible, for a long time, to observe in China a certain degeneration of taste typified by certain *chinoiserias* of the worst type. But at least the sense of the pure object or of beauty remained very much alive among the top levels of the old society. The revolution has swept away these last vestiges of traditional art. The new men who come from the proletariat are no longer given the art and taste from the culture of other days. Even the country districts have been invaded by the new culture. They had remained the refuge of a kind of natural civilization, founded on the ancient Confucian order, which made the lowest Chinese peasant a man of subtlety. What will remain of this after the "socialist flood," which completely uproots rustic tradition and replaces it in the village by the Marxist catechism and collective thought?

A supreme revolution is taking place in the alphabetization of the Chinese script. This decision was taken by Mao Tse-tung himself, in 1951; the change therefore is now assured. "How long will it take? Will it be a matter of some twenty years?" I asked a competent authority whom I met in Peking. "Twenty years is too long," he replied. "Ten, then?" "Yes, I suppose ten would be about right." The stages of the alphabetization were fixed at a grand conference taking place in the capital while I was there. The work of simplification and rationalization of the characters has already begun: China is revising her script before finally rejecting it. What better proof of a completely new deal for China could there be than this reform?

Someone asked Kuo Mo-jo at this Peking conference if it was not to be feared that the Chinese characters would soon be completely forgotten. He replied with assurance, in a major speech: "There will always be scholars to study the language just as certain of them today study the ancient inscriptions on stones or metal." In other words, out of 600 million Chinese, only a handful will be able to read the ancient ideograms which record China's whole past. With the passing of the ideogram, a whole world will have vanished.

The world being born in its place is already visible and could already be given a name: Eurasia. Eurasia, a halfbreed product of Asia and Russo-Marxist Europe. I saw the first images of this all over China. As a start, I met Eurasia in Manchuria, which, though the head of China, today is not Chinese. This land of pioneers, which originally took shape under the Japanese and developed later with Russian help, has at once sought the formulas of a country which tomorrow will be nearer to America or Russia than to the China of yesterday. The current language in Manchuria is that of a new man who is impatiently calling for the new alphabetic writing. Here, steel and factories, techniques and statistics, are the subjects of conversation. All the lessons learned here—and the whole of Manchuria goes to school—are Russian and Western lessons. Here, faster than anywhere else, they progress toward kolkhozes and mechanized agriculture. The Manchurians are already completely immersed in the ways of life, thought, work, and amusement of a civilization which is no longer Asian but mingled with European innovations—Eurasian. And all China is following Manchuria's example.

The Chinese is in the course of becoming to ancient Asia what the American is to Europe—a man who has placed an ocean between himself and the past. The astonishing feature in his case is that he has not had to cross the ocean, has not moved from the spot. It is on the soil of his ancestors that he will have rejected the past and embarked upon the adventure of recreating his race.

4. PROBLEMS IN BALANCING PAST AND PRESENT

In the second half of 1957, following the outburst of unwanted criticisms during the Hundred Flowers liberalization, the Party tightened control over study of the cultural legacy, along with all other areas of intellectual activity. During the next year, as the Great Leap Forward got under way, the zeal for socialist construction left little room for cultivating traditional culture. On June 11, 1958, Kuo Mo-jo, the doyen of Communist China's cultural spokesmen, laid down the injunction to a meeting of prominent historians that their work must more directly serve current socialist construction. The slogan, a phrase out of pure classical Chinese, was "more emphasis on the present, less emphasis on the past."

Within a year, however, the Party was having second thoughts about this utilitarian dictum, as it was about many aspects of the Great Leap strategy. At another such meeting in 1959, Ch'en Po-ta, a close associate of Mao and a vice-director of propaganda, tried to modify the policy without abandoning it entirely. He was still suspicious of scholars who did not show sufficient Marxist critical spirit in approaching the cultural legacy and even hinted at an unhealthful tendency for scholars to escape into study of the past—those who "going in do not know how to come out." But his main criticism was levelled at people guilty of leftist infantilism in taking "a crude and scornful attitude toward the cultural legacy."

Citing Lenin and Mao, he forcefully reminded everyone that Marxists are historical materialists who realize that the present is built on the past. Nevertheless, Ch'en Po-ta was obviously uneasy about how to strike the proper balance between annihilating and preserving the past. This problem continued to trouble Party cultural spokesmen in following years.

CRITICAL INHERITANCE AND A
NEW INVESTIGATION
CH'EN PO-TA

Last year, in a scientific planning conference, I talked about the problem of more emphasis on the present and less on the past, provoking some discussion. Some essays on the subject, such as those by Comrades Kuo Mo-jo and Fan Wen-lan, were very good —better than what I had said. But there were also people who misunderstood, emphasizing the present over the past, and were a little confused in their thinking. For instance, some people believed that, since we advocate more emphasis on the present than on the past, we can adopt a crude and scornful attitude toward the historical and cultural legacy. This is completely contrary to our original idea.

As for us Marxists, whether or not to accept the historical and cultural legacy in principle is already settled. As everyone knows, the three sources of Marxism were English political economy, German classical philosophy, and French socialism. Lenin explained this very clearly in his essay "The Three Sources and Three Components of Marxism." He said:

> There is nothing like "sectarianism" in Marxism. It definitely is not a narrow, petrified doctrine that arose away from the main paths of development in world civilization. Just the opposite, Marx's genius lies in his providing answers to questions raised by the greatest of human minds. His theories were produced in direct and immediate continuation of the greatest representatives of philosophy, political economy, and socialism.

Marxism is a great creative science, but this great creative science was inherited from the past. It certainly did not come out of nothing. . . .

In the problem of accepting the historical legacy, Mao Tse-tung gave us Chinese Communists the same kind of clear directions. In his speech on the problem of correct study, given at the Sixth Plenary Session of the Sixth Central Committee in 1938, he said:

> Another of our tasks is to study our historical heritage and use the Marxist method to sum it up critically. Our national history goes back several thousand years and has its own characteristics and innumerable treasures. . . . We should sum up our history from

FROM Ch'en Po-ta, "Critical Inheritance and a New Investigation," *Hung-ch'i* (*Red Flag*), 13 (July 1, 1959), 36–39 and 43. Translated by the editor.

Confucius to Sun Yat-sen and take over this valuable legacy. This is important for guiding the great movement of today.

No clearer explanation of Chinese Marxist attitude toward the cultural legacy could be given. Furthermore, the charge enjoined by Comrade Mao twenty years ago is still relevant to academic circles today.

It is just as the proverb says: "Looking at the present, we should also delve into the past; without the past, there can be no present." Since we want to inherit all valuable things from history and sum up its legacy, why then do we raise the question of "more emphasis on the present and less on the past?" Moreover, since research on practical problems is proceeding with a lively spirit within our academic circles, why is it necessary to raise this question at this time?

I think raising the question is still proper. Why? As I said the last time, the reason lies in the fact that among academic, cultural, and educational circles there is an inclination to emphasize the past more than the present. Moreover, there still are two different opinions on the question of inheriting the historical legacy. One is Marxist, the other non-Marxist.

"More emphasis on the present and less on the past" is nothing but stressing, in academic and cultural work, creative activity and the daring to break the fetters of old traditions. During the past century or more, many enlightened persons have raised this thought. The slogan "Break the Nets" of T'an Ss'u-tung and "Down with Confucianism" of Wu Yü both had as their object people breaking free from the fetters of traditional concepts in the pursuit of new knowledge. What is the difference between these earlier persons and ourselves? The difference lies in the fact that they viewed the problem with the world view of the bourgeoisie, but we view it with the world view of the proletariat.

The limitations of the Chinese bourgeoisie's world view and their weakness in the anti-imperialism–antifeudalism struggle made it impossible for those enlightened figures to solve thoroughly and historically the relationship between past and present. . . . The proletarian world view and Marxist-Leninist world view have broken the limitations of the bourgeois world view. As Lenin has explained, Marxist dialectical materialism is "the most complete, penetrating, and unbiased theory on development." The proletariat uses this world view to see the history of development in nature as well as in human society. Guided by this world view, the Chinese proletariat has carried out the most penetrating criticism of the old society, twice hoisted the flag of social revolution, awakened the entire people, realized this great historical change, and basically ended the "prehistory of human society" in China. . . . The new great era needs many, many brilliant stars, persons of great talent, and new great knowledge. This new knowledge is not the learning of Confucius or Lao-tzu, not that of the philosophers Ch'eng Tzu and Chu Hsi, not that of any other old thinkers. It must be knowledge surpassing all the achievements made by previous men in China, combining theory and practice under the direction of the proletarian world view.

Just as Comrade Mao Tse-tung said, our revolution and socialist system require a rapid change in old China's economic poverty and cultural blankness. Could this academic blankness possibly be eliminated by merely taking excerpts from piles of old papers? Could it be solved by relying only upon old historical knowledge? Of course not! Old materials and old knowledge (no matter whether they deal with economics, politics, philosophy, literature, or art) are useful for developing new learning and new culture. But we certainly cannot adopt a self-satisfied attitude toward these materials. On the contrary, we should use them to "develop the new out of the old," letting them serve as fertilizer for our new learning. . . .

We are fortunate that our country has an ancient culture, but, if we do not treat it properly, it will be to our misfortune. Mounting volumes of historical documents and ever increasing numbers of newly discovered ancient relics—these are full of fascination. Naturally, we and our descendants must put forth effort to study, straighten out, and sum up all these so as to promote creative activities in the new era. However, if too many people go into this work, and especially if going in they do not know how to come out, so that it becomes the dominant trend, it will become a problem. This will not be right and proper. . . .

The struggle is on two fronts. One is against the rightists who revive the old. This rightist deviation is to consider everything that is old as good and deny it proper criticism. The other is against leftist infantilism. This leftist deviation is to adopt coarse, simplified methods in denigrating all history while condemning ancient people according to the standards of today's revolutionary proletariat, regarding past history as just an accumulation of mistakes, and refusing to inherit the legacy of human civilization. It is correct for Marxists to struggle along these two fronts, because Marxists have a historical perspective and analyze everything according to concrete historical conditions. As for the essence of the legacy (such as ancient materialism, simple dialectics, and various other progressive elements in thought and culture), Marxists also treat this historically, recognize its position in history, distinguish correct parts from incorrect parts, and neither exaggerate nor minimize its historical function.

5. GROWING CONCERN OVER CULTURAL LEGACY

From 1959 through 1962, all aspects of the cultural legacy, from painting to philosophy, increasingly flourished. The regime, beset by economic problems, seemed inclined to give much more freedom to the study of the national past so long as it avoided bourgeois influences. The promotion of national cultural forms also accorded well with the nationalist assertion of independence from the Soviet Union. But there were still doubts about maintaining the proper attitude of critical inheritance, as is shown by Wu Chiang's article in the leading Party theoretical journal, Red Flag. Appearing at the height of the revived interest in the cultural legacy, it is basically positive in tone, with only minor misgivings.

After 1962, such misgivings became more serious, as we see in Kung Tun's article also from Red Flag. The cultural legacy is not condemned, but the fears about elements of it "poisoning the minds of the people" are much sharper, especially since the aesthetic appeal of traditional art and literature is fully recognized.

ON THE QUESTION OF STUDYING AND CRITICIZING THE CULTURAL LEGACY
WU CHIANG

Side by side with the study of various practical problems, the study of cultural legacy has also been undertaken on quite a sig-

FROM Wu Chiang, "On the Question of Studying and Criticizing the Cultural Legacy," *Hung-ch'i* (*Red Flag*), 6 (March 16, 1961). Translated in American Consulate General (Hong Kong, B.C.C.), *Extracts from China Mainland Magazines*, 255, pp. 33 and 36–38.

nificant scale in our cultural and academic circles in the past several years. In the fields of philosophy, history, economics, medicine, and literature and the arts, there have been raised some problems regarding how to criticize and inherit the cultural legacy, discussions have been conducted, and definite achievements have been gained. All this is very helpful to promoting contention among all schools of thought, to activating· the academic atmosphere, and to the development of cultural enterprises. . . .

With regard to the cultural legacy that either has class nature or has no class nature, we must distinguish between the essence and dross in it in order appropriately to absorb the essence and discard the dross. But, on many occasions, essence and dross are mixed up and cannot be distinguished easily. Under such conditions, we must conduct a concrete analysis of concrete problems, and, in some cases, we must also conduct analysis repeatedly and with different approaches. Feudal culture is not entirely feudalistic. Apart from things which are feudalistic, it also contains popular, democratic, and antifeudalist things, and these two things—feudalist and antifeudalist—must be separated. Even feudalist things must be distinguished, too. When feudalism was still emerging and developing, it had certain things which had a definite value. Culture in the capitalist era should also be distinguished. Essence in the legacy, such as old materialism and simple dialectics, fine Chinese and foreign classical products, and various popular and democratic ideas must be treated historically; we must not use them wholly uncritically because they always have the localized nature of a given era. In past eras, popular literary works also often carry the influence of certain exploiting and ruling classes. With regard to these, we must also carry out concrete analysis in order to distinguish between the correct elements and incorrect elements in them, scientifically and appropriately give them definite positions in history, and neither reduce nor magnify their values. As regards dross, we do not simply reject it. This is because, on the one hand, "announcing that this philosophy is wrong does not mean that this philosophy is subdued." It is only through necessary scientific criticism and analysis that we can overcome it and reach the goal of "disinfection." On the other hand, by carrying out necessary analysis of the erroneous things in history, we shall be able to gain certain experience in thought and absorb certain useful ideological material in them. This is an example of how bad things can be turned into good things.

In the sphere of legacy, we are often confronted with various sorts of contradictions, the contradiction between essence and dross, the contradiction between the democratic nature and feudalist nature, the contradiction between the scientific nature and nonscientific nature, the contradiction between the ideological nature and academic nature in literary and artistic products, etc. We must conduct concrete and all-round analysis of these contradictions. For instance, in judging a literary or artistic product, we advocate politics as the first criterion. But it does not mean that political and ideological analyses are enough and that artistic analysis has ceased to be necessary. We carry out correct analysis of literary legacy not only in ideological terms but also in artistic terms. Through this analysis, we inherit all fine, useful things of the artistic legacy, including artistic forms. Comrade Mao Tsetung said: "We do not refuse to make use of the artistic and literary forms of the past, but in our hands these old forms, remolded and filled with new content, also become things which are revolutionary and serve the people." Undoubtedly, we should absorb and make use of all good and useful things in the world. However, we should devote more attention to the study of the fine things of our nation in the fields of painting, music, and literature with regard to the artistic forms and the methods of creation, so that the ideological content of socialism and communism can be manifested in fine national forms loved by the people. The people will welcome this, and at the same time many valuable things will be added to world literature and art.

From the above, one thing is certain: It is necessary to adopt an extremely delicate and prudent attitude toward the cultural legacy. No problem can be solved if we fail to conduct a concrete analysis of concrete problems and do things in summary fashion. And even if problems are solved, they are solved in form only. In this respect, we must reject two tendencies toward oversimplification: One is simply to inherit the cultural legacy uncritically and advocate that it should be accepted on a wholesale basis. This is the rightist one-sidedness. The other is to regard criticism as simply obliterating everything in the cultural legacy, to deny the necessity of, or refuse to pay attention to, the study and inheritance of the cultural legacy. This is "left" one-sidedness. In criticism of many leaders of the May Fourth Movement, Comrade Mao Tse-tung said:

> With regard to the existing conditions of that time, to history, and to things foreign, they lacked the critical spirit of historical mate-

rialism and regarded what was called bad as absolutely, totally bad and what was called good as absolutely, totally good. This formalistic approach to problems affected the subsequent development of the movement.

Such a formalistic approach to problems must be rejected. What we need is the critical spirit of Marxism-Leninism, which enables us to conduct scientific analysis of ancient thoughts and culture.

It is a good thing that China has a culture with a history of several thousand years. Nevertheless, it is a heavy task to undertake a successful study of such a huge cultural legacy. It is never easy to grasp the historical conditions in which ancient thoughts were born as well as the original historical face of these thoughts, for many problems cannot be solved and conclusions reached within a short time. Engels said:

> The whole of history should be studied afresh now. In the first place, we should make a detailed study of the conditions for the existence of various forms of society before we should attempt to find out the corresponding political, legal, aesthetic, philosophical, religious, and other viewpoints.

We are now faced with this task: We must carry out a long-term and serious search. In various spheres of legacy, economic, political, philosophical, and artistic and in ancient literary products, we must assist one another, supply material and fruits of study to one another, and cooperate in this effort to the fullest possible extent before we can gradually obtain more reliable results.

Comrade Mao Tse-tung has called on all members of the Chinese Communist Party to study history and legacy. In the final analysis, the objective is to push forward unceasingly the great undertaking, integrating the universal truths of Marxism-Leninism and the concrete practice of the Chinese revolution, and to apply and develop incessantly Marxism-Leninism in accordance with the concrete historical conditions in China and the characteristics of China. As Comrade Mao Tse-tung has said, we obviously cannot do this if we know only how to copy things foreign and fail to understand China itself or know only the China of today and not the China of yesterday and the day before yesterday. The series of creative Marxist-Leninist works written by Comrade Mao Tse-tung are a brilliant example of the full use of all fine legacies, both Chinese and foreign, and the attainment of originality. This example, without doubt, will continue to inspire our academic and cultural circles to march forward with more fruitful results.

DREGS MUST NOT BE TAKEN FOR ESSENCE

KUNG TUN

In order to appraise correctly China's ancient literary legacy and distinguish clearly between its democratic essence and feudal dregs, we must necessarily follow the direction of policy laid down by Comrade Mao Tse-tung, namely, to "place the political criterion first and the artistic criterion second." He says: "We must treat the art and literature of the past according to their attitude toward the people and judge whether they are progressive in the light of history."

When it comes to analyzing and criticizing literary works of the past, we would neither be able to appraise them correctly nor find out about their democratic essence and feudal dregs if we do not attach first importance to their ideological tendencies but measure them by their artistic forms of expression. If we see only their good points with regard to artistic technicalities but are blind to their basic tendentious defects, we would possibly make the mistake of passing off fish eyes for pearls and grains of sand for gold, and in that way, we would make the wrong start in studying and inheriting our literary legacy. As Engels once pointed out, if we accept a product and shower lavish praise on it on account of its artistic technicalities, then "there is practically none who has not written a good work, none who has not produced a masterpiece, and none who has not made certain literary achievement." . . .

Comrade Mao Tse-tung once told us: "We must take a sniff at a thing to distinguish the good from the bad before we decide to accept or reject it." We should, of course, follow this instruction in dealing with China's ancient literature. It is naturally wrong to regard the good works of ancient literature as absolutely good and the bad works as absolutely bad, instead of making a concrete analysis of concrete works. But if we think that all ancient works have essence as well as dregs, fine points as well as shortcomings, namely, that they are mixtures of good and bad things, when it comes to concrete assessment of them, if we do not take the trouble to distinguish clearly what is their principal

FROM Kung Tun, "Dregs Must Not Be Taken for Essence," *Hung-ch'i* (*Red Flag*), 1 (Jan. 5, 1963). Translated in American Consulate General (Hong Kong, B.C.C.), *Selections from China Mainland Magazines*, 350, pp. 1 and 2–4.

aspect, or if we only talk about the principal and secondary aspects of these works without actually finding out the principal and secondary aspects, and without studying the main currents, then the likely result is that we would lose our direction in the study of China's ancient literature.

Some people in their articles have advanced the following view: Due to various complicated reasons, China's feudal society continued for more than 2,000 years with its social system unchanged. Therefore, if we regard literature and art as part of the superstructure during this long history, there would not have appeared large quantities of basic reactionary things. Such a view has no basis.

Such a view regards the history of the feudal society, which lasted for more than 2,000 years in our country, as a history in which tranquillity prevailed and in which there were no social contradictions and changes. But, in reality, in the prolonged feudal society, the class struggle between the feudal ruling class and the broad masses of the laboring people went on unceasingly in various forms, and at times was very acute. . . .

Some people in their articles hold the belief that our ancient reactionary works mostly do not have any artistic quality to speak of. It seems as if few of the works that have artistic quality would be reactionary products. True, the reactionary products that defended the feudal reactionary rule and publicized feudal ethical and moral concepts are for the most part rotten and objectionable, and today they are particularly disgusting. However, it is not consistent with facts to think that any reactionary product of the feudal period did not have bewitching and deceiving artistic skills. Did not the "court style poems" of the Six Dynasties . . . bewitch some people?

Comrade Mao Tse-tung says: "A product whose content is more reactionary and that has more artistic quality is more capable of poisoning the minds of the people and should therefore be rejected more quickly." In rejecting these feudal reactionary literary products, we must analyze and criticize them and allow them to play the role of teacher by negative example so as to let "poisonous weeds" become "fertilizer for the soil." As these reactionary works which have reactionary ideological content but which have artistic quality are criticized more deeply and thoroughly, we shall find it easier to strip them of their cloaks so that they may not again deceive and benumb the readers and may be disinfected in the end.

We must apply the spirit of scientific analysis of Marxism-Leninism to our research work on China's ancient literature. We must of course resolutely oppose the erroneous tendency of treating roughly the useful parts of our ancient literary legacy and obliterating them at one stroke. But if we only inherit, and fail to criticize, our ancient literary legacy; if we consider all things that had been praised by our forefathers as good; if we energetically laud those works that have some commendable artistic skills without regard for their ideological nature; and, above all, if we treat the dregs of our ancient literature as precious things, then would we be essentially different from those who talk a great deal about "ancient saints and emperors of ancient dynasties, "inherited rules and traditions," prose of the Ch'in and Han dynasties, poetry of the T'ang dynasty in its golden years, and sayings of the Three Periods (Hsia, Shang, Chou). Such a wrong tendency of uncritically affirming our ancient literary legacy must be firmly opposed. In an article entitled "What Legacy Should We Reject After All?" Lenin points out: "To preserve legacy is to preserve heaps of old paper." One should, he says, find out what should be preserved and what should be discarded. In criticizing and studying our ancient literature, we must bear this instruction in mind.

II

Museums and Monuments

Even hostile observers of the People's Republic have been impressed with the care and expense it has lavished on the physical monuments to China's past greatness. Both in the construction of museums housing the flood of relics being uncovered in archaeological work and in the physical restoration of historic monuments, the new regime has shown itself the proud inheritor of China's past. As has already been suggested by Robert Guillain and as will be developed by Joseph Levenson in Chapter V, the Communists may feel much safer with the past put into museums. Nevertheless, the restoration of the symbols of the revolutionaries' very recent opponents—Buddhist temples, imperial palaces—is a significant indicator of this national pride and confidence that the past has really been left behind.

1. THE MUSEUMS

In this brief description of museum-building activity, the author shows characteristic pride in contrasting the People's Republic's loving care of historical relics with the physical neglect they suffered under previous conservative governments.

MUSEUMS IN BUILDING
ANONYMOUS

Before liberation, China had not a single museum worthy of the name. The Palace Museum in Peking was famous, not because of its contents, but as a magnificent piece of ancient architecture. According to Tang Lau, an archaeologist who now is its chief custodian, nobody used to bother how the items on hand could be shown to best advantage. The Hall of Supreme Harmony was the main exhibition hall; in it were two enamel pagodas, two huge mirrors, and several Buddha statues. The Palace Museum in those days was disappointing, even to the most ardent sightseer. With hardly any funds at its disposal, admission tickets were rather expensive, with the result that most of the working people could not afford to pass through its gate.

Apart from the Palace Museum in Peking, the country had only a few museums in coastal cities. Such regional museums fared even worse. The museum in Nanking, for instance, under Kuomintang rule was never open to the public. The Shanghai Museum was situated on the second floor of a three-story building, sandwiched in between an opera school and a primary school! Practically no Shanghailander knew it even existed.

Today, there is an endless stream of visitors at the gate of the Peking Palace Museum, especially on Sundays and holidays. A large number of them are workers and peasants bringing their families. In 1954 and 1955, more people visited the museum than there had been in 24 years before liberation. Tickets now are cheap and easily obtainable. For a few cents, the visitor can spend a whole afternoon in the halls that show Chinese sculptures and *objets d'art*, paintings and porcelains; in the Hall of International Friendship, they can view the gifts from more than forty countries.

After the liberation, the museum in Nanking was enlarged and opened with an exhibition on the life of China's national minorities in the Southwest. The Shanghai Museum has moved to a grand building on People's Square in the center of the city.

New museums are now being opened all over the country. Almost every province and region—including the Uighur Autonomous Region in Sinkiang and the Inner Mongolian Autonomous Region—has its own museum to explain to people their topo-

FROM "Museums in Building," *Chinese Literature* (Jan., 1957), pp. 198–200.

graphical environment, the historical background, and the present-day socialist construction going on in these areas. Most of these regional museums are quite new. The Anhwei Provincial Museum has a floor space of 15,000 square feet.

2. MONUMENTS, NATIONAL AND PROVINCIAL

The first of the two items that follow are European journalists' impressions of two great imperial monuments, the Forbidden City in Peking and the Ming Emperors' Tombs near the capital. The third item, a provincial travel account by the expatriate New Zealander Rewi Alley, who has lived in China for more than thirty years, shows that China's history permeates its vast landscape, not just Peking. Chingchow is not one of the foremost national historical sites, but there, too, the past obtrudes into the present, and its relics are well taken care of.

THE NEW FACE OF CHINA

PETER SCHMID

Today, the Forbidden City is forbidden no longer. On the contrary. Even under the Republic it had still been confined to the fortunate few who could afford the high admission fee, and hence it had been deserted most of the time. Today for a mere five fen—which is less than a penny—the coolie can partake of the splendor and the marvels of his former rulers. For, although it was built by the "feudal" rulers with the sweat of their subjects, the new rulers are nevertheless proud of this splendor as a manifestation of the national genius, and every moron is invited to stroll about the Forbidden City, feeling himself as a fellow-creator, as part of that inspired collectivism which has created these treasures. And thus every Sunday a swarm of blue-clad ants descends upon the enormous site, losing itself in the vast courtyards, crowding on the steps: blue termites, male and female, with funny little children (who are still allowed colorful clothes) wel-

FROM Peter Schmid, *The New Face of China* (London: George G. Harrop, 1958), pp. 28–31. Reprinted by permission of the publisher.

comed by young girls who act as eager guides, and everybody
listens and learns.

The Chinese spirit is strangely reflected in these edifices. Europeans strive for variety: They try, whenever their buildings are
grouped together, to invest them with individual features. Every
little Gothic church and every Renaissance palace seeks its own
physiognomy. But here the law is a cosmic symbol: Axes and
symmetries impose their stranglehold on every building, and there
is no room even for a tower. The vertical is avoided as though it
were sacrilege. Breadth is everything, massively horizontal halls.
In the Tai-ho Tien, the emperor used to hold his New Year
reception; the Chung-ho Tien was used for religious ceremonies;
the Pao-ho Tien was the scene of a vassals' banquet on New Year's
Eve; in the Chien-ching Kung, the highest officers of the state
were received. And thus it continued, with grandiose generosity,
one sacred place for every imperial function, and every one of
them—no matter whether used for banqueting, praying, sleeping,
or merely passing through—almost totally identical with every
other. Yet, with all its monotony, the Forbidden City is one of the
world's greatest architectural wonders. Beauty is created here
not by any originality of forms, but by their interrelation, just as
one spider's web is much like another, without any special individual distinction and yet beautifully and wonderfully devised.
Wherever one stands in this city of golden roofs, one feels
embedded and included in a harmony of carefully attuned proportions. The gentle curve of the double roofs, the cadence of the
columns which bear them, the marble balustrades whose white
posts rise up like stalagmites to meet the descending wood—all
these are just right and could not be otherwise, just as each golden
vessel, every shrine, and every fabulous beast occupies in this
secret system of co-ordinates the place where it belongs.

Whereas the Forbidden City is situated, as a meaningful hub,
right amid the homes of the common mortals, I had to have myself pedalled a long way through the streets of the Tartar City before reaching the remote neighborhood of the Temple of Heaven.
While the Imperial City is dominated by the red hue of active,
throbbing life—the red of its walls and the rust of its timbering
—the Temple of Heaven is lifted by the blue and green of its
dome into a more abstract, spiritual world. From outside, the
gate through which the sacred precincts are entered glows rose-
colored. But the moment you have passed under its arch you are
part of a different world. You feel, upon entering the numinous,

that you want to halt at every step, retrace it, and advance more slowly, so as to savor to the full the harmony of the proportions of this symphony in space. The Temple of Heaven, of course, entirely lacks the impressive ostentation of the Forbidden City. [Seated] on its white, circular base [and] surrounded [by] buildings, [it seems] to become a symbol of loneliness, of the loneliness of the Most Exalted, the emperor, who used to repair here for prayer to Shang Ti, the highest god, in times of drought and famine. As in the pyramids of the Egyptians and the Mayas, this encounter is woven about with a mystery of numbers. The floor is composed of nine marble circles, the innermost consisting of nine and the outermost of eighty-nine slabs, around the circular block on which the emperor would kneel, girdled, as an ancient sage has put it, "by the circles of the terrace and beyond it the circle of the firmament."

But, alas! little is felt today at this spot of those mysterious cosmic bonds of power. The Temple of Heaven, too, has become a historical monument, the object not so much of devotion as of national pride. The endless stream of blue-uniformed visitors is, moreover, channelled into a useful purpose: The adjoining buildings now house exhibitions illustrating the country's economic development and the queue of those waiting to be admitted never comes to an end.

RED CHINA TODAY

HUGO PORTISCH

As an expression of its bond with tradition, the government also gave orders that the secret of the Ming emperors, hidden for many generations, should be revealed: the secret of the Ming tombs.

At the end of the fourteenth century, the first of the Ming dynasty emperors commanded that the construction of grave sites for the Chinese rulers be started near Peking. Those who were sent out to find a suitable place chose one of the most beautiful valleys of China.

FROM Hugo Portisch, *Red China Today* (New York: Fawcett Books, 1966), pp. 269–72. Copyright © 1965 by Verlag Kremayr & Scheriau, Vienna; English translation copyright © 1966 by Quadrangle Books, Inc. Reprinted by permission.

I have seen that valley. It is enclosed on three sides by wooded hills, divided by a stream; a broad road winds through the bottom of the valley. This is the road along which the funeral processions of the Ming emperors once made their way. Pictures of it are often seen in the West. At its beginning stands a large imperial gate, beyond which lies the first stone temple. In its center stands a large marble turtle about 10 feet long and almost as tall as a man. On its back a marble tablet 16 feet high records in hundreds of characters the names, dates, and deeds of the Ming emperors.

From the temple the crooked road runs into the hills. Along both sides of the road stand gigantic stone figures: kneeling camels, standing camels, kneeling elephants, standing elephants, horses, unicorns, and other fabled creatures. These statues stand in long rows at intervals of 50 to 65 feet. They are followed by more-than-life-size mandarins, soldiers, and other types of that time. "All the world lined the road when the emperors were borne to the grave."

Nowadays this region is known as the Valley of the Tombs. On each of the hills stand main temples and antetemples, indicating the grave site of an emperor. Most of these are built of wood with large round columns, lacquered red. "The columns are of one piece. Such large trees grow only in the south of China. They were brought here over a distance of about 1,300 miles. This could have been done only during the winter, when snow covered the roads. The columns were pulled on sleds and transported on rollers through the cities. Thousands of people were required to haul these gigantic trees."

In this valley are buried thirteen Ming emperors with their wives and concubines. In keeping with the ancestor cult, the tomb of the first emperor is the largest and most beautiful, and that of the last and youngest is the smallest. Sons must always be more modest than their fathers.

Although the sumptuous temples and palatial structures in the Valley of the Tombs were known for almost six centuries, no one knew the exact location of the tombs themselves. According to Chinese custom, they would be dozens if not hundreds of feet underground for safety from robbers and vandals. It was partly assumed and partly known from ancient manuscripts that innumerable treasures were hidden in the tombs. Archaeologists from many nations have tried to find them. When the Japanese occupied Peking they made an all-out effort to open the Ming tombs. They, too, failed to locate them.

It was only in the 1950's that Chinese archaeologists succeeded in locating one of the burial sites, commissioned by the new government and using methods which have not been divulged to this day. They managed to penetrate the tomb of the Emperor Chu-I-chin, who was the fourteenth emperor of the Ming dynasty. It is one of the smallest graves and lies buried about 1,400 feet deep in the middle of a hill.

But if finding it was difficult, opening it was even more difficult. It was supposed, rightly, that the emperors had safeguarded themselves against intruders and that any careless penetration would cause the tomb to collapse. Months were spent studying the mechanism of the doors to the grave. Then the explorers burst in, only to find themselves in an antechamber.

They stood before two more huge doors, each cut from a single slab of white marble. These could be opened—but only from the inside. They were equipped with a mechanism that caused an immense bolt to fall into place on the inside when the doors were slammed from the outside, thus locking them.

Weeks were required to reconstruct this mechanism, invisible from the outside, and to reverse its motion. When the marble doors opened, the archaeologists entered a marble hall, in which stood three thrones: two for each empress and the third, much larger and decorated with marble dragons, for the emperor. In front of it were huge vessels filled with precious stones, vases, and implements used in sacrifices.

The largest of the vessels contained oil. Here, in honor of the emperor, an eternal flame should have burned. The supply of oil would actually have been sufficient for many years; what had not been considered was that the flame would also need oxygen. Deep in the earth the light soon died, and the oil remained.

But the dead were not in this marble hall, nor in the two side chambers that were opened next. Here, too, were found only funeral offerings of rare value.

Then the third door, behind the marble hall, was opened. The sight that presented itself to the archaeologists must have been overwhelming. Three large red sarcophagi stood on a platform surrounded by innumerable treasures—gold and silver bars, ceremonial objects of precious metals studded with hundreds of gems, jade figures of singular beauty, and jewelry of all kinds, especially diadems.

Yet all that was as nothing compared with the treasures found in the caskets. The bodies of the dead had not been embalmed, or the embalming had been done badly. But, in the headdresses of the empresses, there were dozens of gems of almost unimaginable splendor and, in addition, wigs made entirely of jewels.

And that was one of the smallest Ming graves! I visited that grave, named "the subterranean palace." Today it is lighted by electricity. One descends into its depths by a broad, circular flight of stone stairs, enters the antechambers, goes through the marble gates, and stands before the thrones. In the sepulchral chamber itself, the sarcophagi have been reconstructed, because the originals disintegrated when they were opened.

The treasures were divided among several museums. Some can be seen in a museum standing at the foot of the hill at the grave site. Whatever was transferred to museums in Peking has been replaced here by copies, so that one can see what the precious objects looked like.

Driving back to Peking from the valley of the Ming tombs, one comes to a reservoir. The dam, which holds back the water of the river, was built . . . at the beginning of the Great Leap Forward. In the center of the dam, a pavilion has been erected, from which the lake and the dam can be seen in tranquillity. The pavilion was designed in the style of the ancient imperial structures. Instead of the usual Communist slogans, one finds miniatures of the traditional Chinese paintings: mountains, streams, valley, trees, people, and animals.

At the edge of the artificial lake stands a monument dedicated to the workers who built the dam in a few months. It bears an inscription in the imperialist manner, but in the handwriting of Mao Tse-tung.

A column bearing a decorated marble hook stands in front of the monument. Identical columns stand before the hills containing the tombs of the emperors. The emperors had them erected so that important news and announcements could be hung on them, and they have been considered tokens of imperial might since time immemorial. But the column with Mao's signature was erected in 1958.

This seems to be in contrast to the newest slogans of the Party according to which China has to break completely with her past. Many old monuments, statues, and imperial edifices were damaged and even destroyed during the Cultural Revolution, and this after years of careful renovation of these very same art treasures. Obviously, a sacrifice to be offered in order to stir up the revolutionary movement. But, on the other hand, most of the really valuable treasures of old China were very well protected even during this revolution, among them the Forbidden City and the Temple of Heaven in Peking, the Ming tombs, and many more which were in time occupied by troops of the regular army to keep the Red Guards out. And, in a sense, the Cultural Revolution even stressed the fact that the regime has always been conscious of the past and still is: Symbolically the Red Guards replaced the images of the old emperors by plaster busts of Mao Tse-tung.

OLD CHINGCHOW

REWI ALLEY

"Returning to Chingchow, eh?" I smiled as I turned to look at the speaker who stood behind me in the saloon of the S. S. Chiangling. It was my second trip up the Yangtze in one autumn, and the last time I had come I had met him in Chingchow. The allusion was to the cry of Kuan Yü, after he heard of the fall of Chingchow and put all his last efforts to get back there and retake his fief. He was, with his son Kuan Ping, captured by the soldiers of Wu on the way, executed, and his head sent as an offering from Wu to Ts'ao Ts'ao of Wei in Loyang.

Chingchow was the key city between North and South, capital of an area bigger than a modern province, famous already for 1,000 years prior to the beginning of our era, when the Han Empire was split into three kingdoms—Wei, Wu, and Shu—famous still today because of the exploits of heroes who have been popularized over the centuries. The three poor men who founded the kingdom of Shu—Liu Pei, seller of sandals, Kuan Yü, a rebel turned pusher of handcarts, and Chang Fei, a butcher—surely these have had their story romanticized, have been used by feudalists to inculcate loyalty to the emperor—yet again their oath of brotherhood, their fighting against great odds, and their contempt for death have their own appeal. The answer of Kuan Yü to offers of preferment and power when he was in hard straits still lives on: "Maybe our city will fall, and I die. You can smash a block of jade, but its purity remains; you can burn bamboo, but even as it burns its joints stand out. You can destroy my body, but for long

FROM Rewi Alley, "Old Chingchow," *Eastern Horizon*, 3, 3 (March, 1964), 29–35.

people will like to hear my name." And so it has been. Not only around modern Chingchow but in many other parts of Central and South China, you may see pictures of his battles painted up over house doors. Actors depict him nightly on a thousand opera stages.

Chingchow city today is one of the few remaining in China that retains its city wall. It is of Ming dynasty construction, built on the old Han base. In the Manchu period, it was garrisoned by Manchu bannermen, who after the 1911 revolution had to learn how to become farmers and work for their living. In the War of Resistance, it was heavily bombed by the Japanese Imperial Army, and on the site of its ruins an airfield used for bombing Chungking was constructed by the Japanese after they had occupied the city. Still, it is the seat of the Chingchow prefecture, and also that of the Chiangling country. Wide, treelined boulevards run through it, but most of its land is farmed by local communes whose crops grow well among shards and bits of old brick the plows upturn. Only one of the original gate towers is left, below which is one of the old streets which escaped bombing. . . .

Also escaping the bombing was the old Taoist temple by the west gate, which is now used as a museum. A beautiful old building with colored tiles and quiet courtyards, it serves as a place where relics of the Ch'u kingdom (of the Warring States period), and those of later historical periods, can be kept.

A morning spent in this museum is a fascinating experience. Quite a few Ch'u graves have been excavated and some of the specimens are kept here, while others have gone on to Peking or Wuhan. But here is the wooden feline animal with a big red tongue lolling out, deer horns covered with early designs protruding from its back, which came from a Ch'u tomb. It is an amazing piece, and I could not help thinking how much the late archaeologist Mr. Salmony, who wrote a book on the antler and the tongue as fertility symbols, would have liked to have seen it.

Here in the museum are quite a number of Ch'u bronzes and a wealth of Han material; the big pot in which political offenders were boiled in oil and the stone manger of Kuan Yü's horse "Red Hare." There are many house models taken from graves that run from Han to Sung, and among the fragments a small gilded bronze of Han, of a man wearing the same kind of coat as a court jester of medieval Europe. Most fascinating to me, however, were some of the bronze fragments of Ch'u, especially one of a design that reminded me of some Polynesian carving.

A good deal of research has been done into the Ch'u and Han cities, remains of which are near Chingchow. We went out to the first Ch'u city—then called Yintu, and later Chinan—south of the Chi Mountain. Then to the remains of the city called Ying-chieng, which was the next one, smaller, and probably built after a change in the course of the Yangtze, which again possibly accounted for the final change to Chingchow and the modern removal of the commercial center from Chingchow to Shashih, only a few miles distant, but on the river bank.

We did not go to the Wu city of Fancheng, later called Wang-ch'eng, which is some fifty li away by road and has nothing but the remnants of a wall and one tower remaining. At Chinan and Yingch'eng, there were bits of broken Han dynasty brick everywhere. At Chinan, there had been the usual tower and five beacons below it, remains of which are familiar to any who have been through Kansu and Sinkiang. But here, only the mounds and brick remained of them. Commune farmers till the soil of the interior of both cities.

At Yingch'eng, there is a huge memorial stone—that of a Manchu who was born in Chingchow, but who achieved fame as the commanding general of Heilungkiang in the early Ch'ing period when that province included the portion later seized by the Tsar and made into the Far Eastern Region of Russia. The space enclosed by the walls, still quite high, is much smaller than that enclosed in Chinan. The river flowed past its walls once, and the Chingchow of the Three Kingdoms period may have been the landing place south of the river, then, with a change of course, becoming the border city on the north bank, and consequently soon achieving great importance. Looking across at it today from the wall of Yingch'eng, one can see the remaining tower rising over the rich fields of cotton and grain.

Modern Chingchow is almost a suburb of Shashih, the big, rapidly industrializing river port. The river has raised its bed over the centuries, and the big Chinkiang dike has grown higher to keep it back. The old pagoda on the dike top in the Ming period has about a quarter of its height buried in the present dike. Around Shashih and through the Chingchow prefecture, not so many ancient relics have survived the successive floods of the centuries. The bronze or iron cows, which were held to be able to assist in flood prevention, however, seem to have mostly survived. Between Shashih and Chingchow by the highway are two tall iron temple poles with dragons encircling them. They are massive, weighty entrance poles for a big temple which has long ceased to exist.

Around Chingchow, the river moat is still used by local shipping, and one can anchor by any one of the gates. There are old maps in the museum which show the city at various periods and its position in relation to the three other ancient city sites not far away.

Around it, life goes on quietly, with crops that are probably the best in its long history being harvested. Rice and cotton are the main ones, with beans, wheat, millet, and sorghum as strong supporters. Shashih has a growing industry, its knitted goods and its thermos bottles now being used throughout Hupei.

Chingchow has been a magic name for the thirty centuries it has existed. Now the prefecture gains fame from the massive harvests it produces and from its new industrial products. T'ienmen, one of its counties, is the old home of many overseas Chinese who emigrated in the bad days. Hung Hu, another, gained much fame through its struggles in the revolution. The great success of *ho-wang-hua*—total rearrangement of farming land into large fields bounded by canals straight as a line, with controlled ingress and egress of water—gives the country a new look. Around the walls of its old city a new generation rises, with new tools in its hands, new ideas fermenting in many minds. More will be heard of Chingchow in the days yet to come.

3. SUSPICION OF PAST MONUMENTS

Starting in the mid-1950's, loving care of historical monuments was the order of the day, but it was based on the assumption that the past can no longer harm the present. By the early 1960's some Party spokesmen were not quite so sure of that. We see a small sign of the growing suspicion of the cultural legacy in this article. Imperial tombs of long-dead emperors were safe; ancestral temples in living villages were something else again.

REPAIR OF TEMPLES AND PRESERVATION
OF CULTURAL OBJECTS

TING CHUNG

In a number of areas in the countryside recently, temples and ancestral halls were repaired on a large scale, involving the use of a great deal of money, materials, and manpower, and affecting agricultural production. Not long ago, a reader in Lech'ang *hsien* wrote that a production brigade also repaired a "Pao-kung Temple" (Pao-kung, a legendary figure in ancient China who administered justice with strict impartiality, was much revered by the people), that several production brigades of Yunyen commune were repairing ancestral halls and painting "ancestral tablets," and that, in one production brigade, members were involved in quarrels over the repair of ancestral halls.

Speaking of cultural objects, ours is a country with a long history, rich in revolutionary traditions and fine heritage. It abounds in historical spots and sites and relics which are preserved above and under the ground. In preliberation days, many of these historical objects were lost or heavily damaged due to plundering and vandalism by imperialism and the reactionary ruling class. Since the founding of the People's Republic of China, however, a series of measures have been taken under the Party and People's government's leadership to launch activities for preserving cultural objects, and exhibitions have been held as part of the education of the broad masses of the people in revolutionary traditions and patriotism, and also as part of the effort to provide rich data for scientific research. This never once happened before in our history. Protection of cultural objects is indeed an extremely important work.

However, we should not look upon temples and ancestral halls as cultural objects and "protect" them with lots of money. Although the reader of Lech'ang *hsien* did not say which category of "cultural objects" to which the temples and ancestral halls under repair by the several production brigades belonged, yet according to my conjecture I am afraid that these can hardly be described as

FROM Ting Chung, "Repair of Temples and Preservation of Cultural Objects," *Southern Daily* (Canton) (May 3, 1962). Translated by American Consulate General (Hong Kong, B.C.C.), *Survey of China Mainland Press*, 2742 (May 21, 1962), 19–20.

structures having historical, artistic, and scientific research values. This being so, how can they be included in the list of cultural objects for protection and preservation? If a small number of people raise a demand for repair of temples and ancestral halls, in which case much money and material would be used, the cadres concerned should seriously consider it, and it is not right to adopt the attitude of giving the people a free hand in this. If the masses do have superstitious ideas and carry out superstitious activities in connection with the repair of temples and painting of "ancestral tablets," then what should we do? I think that this is a problem of ideological understanding among the people, and the only way to solve it is by conducting persuasions and education among the masses for the purpose of helping them raise their ideological understanding. It is impermissible to try to solve them with administrative orders. At this time of the year, there is a special need for the rural Party members, League members, and cadres to be brave in convincing the masses, breaking old taboos and conventions, carrying out persuasion and explanations patiently among the masses, and carefully proceeding with ideological and educational work.

III

History and Archaeology

1. TOWARD A NEW CHINESE PAST:
HISTORIOGRAPHY OF THE 1950'S

In traditional China, history was the Confucian scholarly discipline par excellence. Ever since the sage himself compiled The Spring and Autumn Annals "to terrify rebellious ministers and unfilial sons," history had been an essential moral guide for maintaining the proper social order. The Chinese Communists have a very different view of history and a very different idea of what constitutes that proper social order, but history plays a no less exalted role in the Marxist scheme of things. As both Marxists and inheritors of the deep tradition of historical consciousness in China, the Chinese Communists have been vitally concerned with finding an interpretation of Chinese history that satisfies them both as Marxists and as Chinese.

During the first decade or so of the People's Republic, Chinese historians, under the watchful eye of Party ideologues, struggled manfully to produce this new interpretation—one that would satisfy all commitments to Marxist historicism, Chinese nationalism, and present political exigencies. In the following essay, Joseph R. Levenson examines what this new historiography had to say about China's past and what it revealed of China's present. In the second selection, Albert Feuerwerker discusses the efforts of Chinese Communist historians to deal with the threat of a meaningless past.

THE PLACING OF THE CHINESE COMMUNISTS
BY THEIR STUDIES OF THE PAST

JOSEPH R. LEVENSON

There is a theory abroad—partly sentimental (China is "forever China," the cliché has it) and partly skeptical of dynamic potential in Chinese society—that the Chinese Communist is not really a new man. Part of a dominant bureaucracy in a centralized state committed to public works, and with a set of classics to swear by, he plays a role, allegedly, that Confucianists played for centuries. One of the things that might seem to support this is the dedication of Confucianists and Communists alike to the study of history. But the central concern of Marxist historical thinking, of course, is with linear development through stages, while Confucian thinking was ordinarily concerned not with process but permanence, with the illusion of the fixed ideals of the Confucian moral universe. The Communist idea of progress, like Liao P'ing's and K'ang Yu-wei's, is both a break with conventional Confucian conceptions and a means of explaining the break away.

In other words, to put it flatly, traditional Chinese civilization has not been renewed in modern times but unravelled. The intelligentsia, though accordingly losing its Confucian character, naturally repelled any inference that Chinese history was running dry or was simply being diverted into the Western stream. And many of its number, therefore, developed a taste for Communist views on history. For, the latter, without implying an impossible loyalty to systems thought passé, yet provided for continuity with the Chinese past; and, at the same time, it gave assurance of development parallel to Western history, not just an unnerving confrontation in modern times. Communist historical premises anywhere are developmental. It was not simply a Communist dictatorship which established these premises in China, but the appeal of the premises particularly in China which helped to establish the dictatorship.

FROM Joseph R. Levenson, *Confucian China and Its Modern Fate*, vol. III, *The Problem of Historical Significance* (Berkeley: University of California Press, 1965), pp. 47–60. Reprinted by permission of the publisher.

Equivalence and Periodization

That is why periodization on universal Marxist lines came to seem, in the 1950's, the favorite task of Communist historians. On a world scale, periodization is what they saw as the great theoretical issue engaging capitalist and Communist historians in combat. For China alone, it engaged their attention in the highest degree. In monographs, in the three main periodicals (Peking monthlies) devoted to problems of teaching history, and in the scholarly journals, problems of adjusting the outer limits of primitive, slave, feudal, and capitalist society predominated. In December, 1956, a Peking National University seminar made a critique of a new book by Shang Yüeh, *Essentials of Chinese History;* the discussion centered on points of view about transition from slave to feudal society and from feudal to capitalist. That these topics should be singled out from a book of that title shows what such a group regarded as the stuff of Chinese history.

Paradoxically, this passion for equating Chinese history with the West's periodization, and thus denying to China any highly individual character, was combined with insistence that all the transitions were essentially internal to China. It was not to be supposed that foreign tribal conquest in the second millennium B.C. ushered in the slave-society of the Shang era, nor that Chou conquerors brought in a feudalism not potentially there with Shang. Most important, it must not be thought that capitalism depended on the incursions of the modern West. The "shoots of capitalism" question was raked over and over again, with constant quoting of Mao Tse-tung's ruling, in 1939, that indigenous capitalism was beginning to grow before the Opium War and that a Chinese capitalism would still have emerged had there been no influence of foreign capitalism. Late Ming–early Ch'ing (sixteenth to nineteenth centuries) weaving, mining, and shipbuilding—characteristic, according to Marx, of burgeoning capitalism—as well as porcelain-making and other handicrafts, overseas trade, urbanization, division of labor, etc., came frequently under review, and early Ch'ing intellectuals of relatively unorthodox views, like Yen Yüan, Li Kung, and the textual critics of the "Han Learning," were said to reflect a rise of new, protocapitalist social forces. Chinese history *on its own* developed in a way *not just its own.* This was the basic Communist historical statement, with equal weight on subject and predicate; these together established the equivalence of China and Europe.

Open controversy was possible on the issue of whether slave society was Shang only or Shang and Hsia before it (Hsia, interestingly enough, being the Confucian-traditional "first dynasty," though archaeologically not yet identified) or Shang and its successor, western Chou, or even on through eastern Chou and Ch'in and Han. Evidently, no one had to agree with even great names, Fan Wen-lan or Kuo Mo-jo, that slave society began or ended just here or there. When Mao permitted "contradictions among the people" (as distinct from dangerous counterrevolutionary ideas), he was speaking primarily about political, social, and economic tensions. But intellectually, too, this was the sort of thing he meant. Chien Po-tsan, a most eminent Communist historian, granted that there might be a question as to when this or that historical stage existed; critics took him precisely at his word and rejected his finding of a slave basis for Han agriculture. However, when Chien went on to say that there could be no question *whether* a stage existed, no one seems to have demurred. "Slave society is a stage which human society must pass through": this was a flat imperative. And it was unequivocally emphasized that a slave-feudal sequence, however differently men might fix the dates, was not itself in dispute.

When the periodization controversy was set in motion, it was a refreshment, not a threat, to Marxism as "grand theory." Scope was given to dissidence and its appropriate emotions, all within the system. It made the latter more truly all-embracing than total authoritarianism, which would flood, chokingly, into every crevice. Here, intellectuals were allowed "freedom" within the maze. They should never emerge, but they could roam, in tonic exercise. It was hardly serious but a kind of sport, vital in the constraining Marxist framework. But if flexible boundaries of historical periods helped to make Marxism viable in China, the rigorous order of periods ("Oriental despotism," a disturbing joker, omitted) gave Marxism much of its explicitly Chinese appeal.

Parallel histories, Chinese and Western, with the same internal dynamic principle (though, of course, with short-run disparities) —this, then, was an article of faith which the literature labored but would not argue. . . .

"Feudalism" was the one permitted social tag for ancient down to modern times—Mao said, some 3,000 years, directly from Chou and Ch'in. And yet, while invoking the term was a matter of strict discipline, its definition was remarkably loose. It must be the connotation of process (with the European parallel) which the Communists sought in the term, for feudalism was qualified so broadly, with stages within the stage, that it hardly served an analytic purpose. It conveyed almost nothing of specific social character.

The characterization "feudal," that is, for Mao's 3,000 years, did not imply the homogeneity that one might expect. Mao might say "feudal from Chou and Ch'in" and others repeat it, but only the adjective—*not* the actual social · description— bracketed those eras, Chou and Ch'in, together. For the famous "first emperor" of Ch'in, in 221 B.C., consolidated the state which (in other hands) gave such novel scope to Confucian bureaucracy. Mao knew it, others knew it, they actually described these eras as vastly different, and only an *a priori* assumption made them paste the feudal label over the cracks.

Everything was feudal for a long time, but for Mao and his epigones pre-Ch'in feudal was aristocratic-autonomous, post-Ch'in feudal was autocratic-centralized. Somewhere under this verbiage lay a clear sense of essential transformation. "From the time that Ch'in Shih Huang-ti united China, it was a unified feudal state." And what had "Lord Shang" accomplished, the famous minister of the Ch'in state in the fourth century B.C., before Ch'in won the empire? He had "broken the economic influence of the hereditary ruling class"; he represented a "stage in the establishment of the *chün-hsien* system," a stage, that is, of rationalized local government by centrally appointed officials, no longer by regional magnates. Fan Wen-lan (b. 1891) described the repercussions of the Ch'in conquest in terms that would seem to exhaust the vocabulary of qualitative change—the great monarchs of Ch'in and Han unified, reduced the feudal lords, fixed the *chün-hsien* administrative system, organized vast public works, standardized weights and measures and script and system of laws. And yet all this centralization, hardly feudal in implication if the term implies anything at all, still added up to "feudalism." For here Fan explicitly disavowed analogy with the West. In Europe, it was early capitalism that he saw leading to centralized monarchies before the French Revolution. But with the strongest rose-colored glass, he could hardly spy a Chinese capitalism this side of eighteen centuries, so the Ch'in and Han empire must be feudal, "representing the landlord-class." Or—the reason why it was feudal is that, being feudal, it stood for the landed interest, which (everything else aside) made it qualify as feudal. Or, once more—if it was precapitalist and postslave, what else could it be but feudal? . . .

Equivalence and Modernization

When Communist historians shifted their sights to relatively recent times, the air of scientific detachment in their discussions of feudalism tended to be dispelled by the passion of involvement, and "feudal" became an epithet. The short span of history since the Opium War had stages assigned to it, too, by many historians. Most of them used the classic textbook topics—Opium War, Taiping Rebellion, Sino-Japanese War, Reform Movement, Boxer Rising, 1911, May Fourth—as markers, with appropriate references to foreign aggression, people's movements, feudal persistence, and revolutions old-democratic and new-democratic.

But periodization on this shrunken modern scale had quite another character from that of the over-all periodization. It was not assumed, for instance, that there must be Western counterparts to the modern Chinese substages. And, similarly, while in the grand design both China and the West were allotted an epoch of capitalism, imperialism, the "last stage of capitalism," was the West's alone, with China no more than a victim. Though there was considerable talk of rising *bourgeoisie* and nascent proletariat, Communist historians wrung little assurance of parallel development from the specifically modern record—at least, parallel with the West. If anything, China's modern history, its revolutionary record, was offered as a prospective parallel to other peoples, *non*-western peoples, seeking liberation. Thus, for the continuum of the recent past, the present, and the future, the gaze was not on a Western model for China but on a Chinese model for the nations which the West had long exploited. They "will expect to find in Chinese history the key to the solution of their own problems."

Yet, despite this different approach to modern history—an understandably special, sensitive area—the interest of historians was the same. When feudalism was more a Chinese blemish than a ubiquitous type of society, when imperialism was more a Western crime than a universal stage, one could still, with these ingredients and a Marxist flair, create a sense of confidence of equivalence with the West.

What was it in modern history that had jeopardized such confidence? Clearly, the crisis grew out of a subjugation of the literati's China, which began as political and economic and came to be intellectual as well. Intransigent traditionalism could not stand, and no eclectic apologetics could mask the Confucian retreat before foreign standards of value. Where once new ideas had had to face tests of compatibility with received tradition, now Chinese tradition faced tests of compatibility with independently persuasive ideas.

But the tradition was Confucian—or, in the Communist lexicon, feudal. Then a Chinese might cut himself away from the doomed tradition by calling it class, not national. He might identify the nation as a "people's China," quite uncommitted to the feudal culture of landlords, hence emotionally uninvolved in its debacle. So much for one side of the Western-Confucian imbalance.

Yet, the other side, carrying the preponderance of Western intellectual influence, had to be righted. In itself, the simple abandonment of Confucianism by an antifeudal "people" could never restore the equilibrium implied in self-respect. There was, however, a still point in the center. For the West, instead of being left in solitary eminence, could be scored off as imperialist, and the last century of Chinese history, with all its invasions and revolutions, could most solacingly be contemplated in a dialectical way.

Antifeudal and anti-imperialistic, between a rejected Confucian China and a resisted modern West, the Communists located themselves in synthesis. Historically, the iconoclastic May Fourth Movement of 1919 remained a great tradition. But one heard it said that its revolutionary thought must be distinguished from its reactionary thought, such as Hu Shih's and Ts'ai Yüan-p'ei's ideas. These were liberal intellectuals, and liberalism seemed culturally off-balance in China, leaning to Europe and America. Communism, on the other hand, was nicely centered between moribund Confucianism and the non-Communist West which had discomfited Confucianists in the first place. So Communists could denounce liberalism as cultural colonialism, even while they matched liberals in cold scrutiny of the Confucian past. If antiimperialism was not enough to make a Communist (see the limitation of Liao Chung-k'ai), antifeudalism was not enough either. One needed to fill it out with an anti-imperialist complement.

This could be seen in cultural terms. After World War I, the "new literature" in Western vein might seem to be revolutionary. But in Communist eyes, it was basically unpopular, in the fullest sense of the word. A learned, exclusive, hyperaesthetic character was attributed to it. Thus, in its Western ("imperialist") form, it had the same essential content as the traditional literature of the feudal gentry in periods of decline. So much for resistance to the West: now for rejection of Confucian standards.

Mao could continue to write poetry in the classical style—to the pure all things are pure. But generally, Communist poets were warned off the ancient literary forms and foreign forms as well. They were led to adopt the "median" form of the Chinese popular songs.

Historical writing had its median, too. For the red thread running through the whole Communist version of modern history was the charge that feudal China and foreign imperialism inevitably came together, each a support for the other against the Chinese people rising against them both. These "twin enemies" rode with all the Communist historians, who wrote of the 1860's, "Foreign capitalism and the feudal landlord power, which was represented by Tseng Kuo-fan, Li Hung-chang, and Tso Tsung-t'ang, joined forces to press down the Chinese people," or of the 1900's, "The Ch'ing government and imperialism had a tight alliance, imperialism and feudalism laid heavy oppression on the Chinese people," and "The abortiveness of 1911's anti-imperialism and antifeudalism marked out the area of the revolution's failure." These simplicities from run-of-the-mill historians could be easily matched in the modern studies of Fan Wen-lan or Hua Kang. They colored all the introductions to the new, rich, multivolume collections of modern source materials—on such central subjects as the Opium War, the Taiping and Nien and Muslim rebellions, the French and Japanese wars, the Reform Movement, the Boxers, and the revolution of 1911.

Thus, social protest and patriotism were held to belong together, residing in the people, for the feudal oppressors were, first, inept, then, unwilling in the fight against foreign pressures. If the imperialists outraged Chinese nationalism, and the feudalists, desperate for succor domestically, connived at the outrage, then their common foe, the people, stood for absolute morality. Under the spell of this conception, Communist historians often departed from Marxist historical relativism. That is, while there was plenty of Communist emphasis on the historical limitations of the Taipings (and of other peasant rebels throughout Chinese history)— allegations, for instance, of internal corruption and eventual "separation from the masses," all for the lack of a proletariat—there remains also a vast, less technical literature, where the Taipings figure as "our side" in a paradigm of conflict. The same holds true

for Li Tzu-ch'eng (the "bandit Li" of the older accounts of the
fall of Ming) and other leaders of antidynastic risings.

Popular and Unpopular Themes

This variant of Communist historical insight, wherein the
people is seen as eternally poised against the antipeople, brought
certain motifs into prominence. Feudal China is literati-China, or
the China of formal intellectual expression. Then people's China
is the China of material culture—at least the way people lived and
the things they used were highly proper themes for the new intelligentsia. For the latter, whom the death of Confucianism or-
phaned, sought another line of ancestry in the nonliterati past;
and Marxist historicism, too, which also made the loss of Confucianism easier to take, confirmed by its very premises the right-
ness of the new line of research. The materialist assumptions of
the periodizers accorded rather well with a bias against the former
governing classes, the builders of the "superstructure," Confucianism. Against the latter's literary emphasis, Communist historians
weighed in heavily with studies of tangible stuff—artifacts from
the fascinating archaeological excavations, Chinese military weapons and their history, even something as homely as the use of
manure in the Shang period. The purpose was not antiquarian, it
was made quite clear, but study of the development of ancient
society; that meant unearthing materials which reflected the life
of the ancient workers. And it was not amiss to connect the study
with contemporary development—to point out that archaeological
discovery was coinciding with current economic construction. . . .

If material culture was a congenial theme, as a standing reproof
to the "idealism" which Communists freely diagnosed as the literati's flaw, natural science had this and more to recommend it.
Ancient Chinese inventions or suggestions of the future, like
versions of the compass, seismograph, distance-measurement
gauge, and armillary sphere, were proudly emphasized as national
achievements. The lore of Chinese medicine was especially
combed in both a historical and a practical spirit, for the enrichment of Western medical science. At an earlier day in the Communist movement, before its victory and identification with all
China dictated a certain delicacy in dealing with the Chinese
past, Taoism had been excoriated as superstition (by the Communists' favorite, Lu Hsün [1881–1936], for one), as a code of
mere escapism. But, later, its affinities with proto-science, as in
Taoist alchemy's place in metallurgy, came to occupy historians.

This was a people's tradition in the course of construction. For science, so little esteemed in the Confucian official tradition, was "people's" by default.

Indeed, the particular effect of victory on Communist assessments of the Chinese record is something to ponder. Not only "people" but certified literati, great names to long generations of Confucianists, were taken into the Communist pantheon, at least for a visit. Ssu-ma Ch'ien, "Grand Historian" of Han China and the whole great tradition, was praised for realism (a highly legitimizing quality in Communist judgments) and given outstanding bibliographical attention; Ssu-ma Kuang of the Sung, once consigned by Communists to the dustheap of orthodox historians, came back in 1957 as "surpassingly great," one who had the crucial realization that history is a matter of objective facts. Even K'ang Yu-wei, the "modern sage" of a reform Confucianism, who was a radical in the 1890's as a constitutional monarchist and then remained a monarchist, like Wang Kuo-wei, until his own death in 1925—even K'ang, assailed by Sun Yat-sen as a reformist diversionary before 1911 and written off as dead by most republicans well before his time, was forgiven his tie with counterrevolution and accepted (for his Confucian version of social stages) as a "progressive." The conclusive and fatal collapse of the old order had released its foes from some of the compulsion to attack, to see famous men of the past as living spokesmen for a still obstructive Confucian order. With the virtual end of that struggle, and also by virtue of the theory of stages, Ssu-ma Kuang and others of his traditional stature could be revitalized, as it were, into their own times, and redeemed from absolute censure.

For the near-contemporary scene, not many brands were plucked from the burning like K'ang Yu-wei. The polemical note sounds louder than the broadly theoretical in studies of the republican era, when Communists were themselves involved in the action, or at the very least were struggling to be born. For the more recent noncooperative non-Communists, the Liang Souming treatment was general. As for earlier figures like the sometime strong man and would-be emperor, Yüan Shih-k'ai, his death in 1916, some time before he could oppose the Communists as such, did him no good. Though certainly no Buddhists, Communists took him to be reincarnated as Chiang K'ai-shek; in tone, at least, it is more than doubtful that Ch'en Po-ta's early tribute (1946), *Introducing the Thief of the Nation, Yüan Shih-k'ai*, will ever be superseded.

On the subject of Chiang and the Kuomintang, there was plenty of opprobrium, but it is possible that the Communists wished to play down merely anti-Kuomintang muckraking, such as any reformist liberal might engage in. Turning from domestic opponents to foreign, Communist historians seemed more interested in blackening the United States than Japan or Great Britain, and they reached back for any likely ammunition. The editors of the Opium War source materials collection, while forced by the nature of the documents to give Britain its lion's share of censure, insisted that America had a hand in this aggression. The same point was made in the sister publication on the Sino-Japanese war. A book entitled *Battles of the Masses Before the Revolution of 1911*, dealing with post-Boxer "people's patriotic struggles" (while "the Ch'ing government sells the nation"), dwelt lovingly on the "anti-American patriotic movement," the boycott of 1905. And Hu Shih, indicted as a reactionary idealist in his approach to world history, was traced back to William James, "creator of American imperialist pragmatism," and to John Dewey, who dispensed, allegedly, a pluralistic idealism to counter the Marxist monistic materialism.

Communist publication on foreign history did not go much beyond this sort of reference to essentially Chinese concerns. A Szechwan University history group studied American China policy, 1945–50, and American "capitalist class use of scholars' writings on the China question." (The group did, however, investigate also the "capitalist historians' slanted misconstruction of the North American War of Independence.") Anti-imperialism, and the centennial year of 1957, inspired several articles and translations concerning the Indian Mutiny, and foreign policy requirements (at least, before the break on the Himalayan frontier) kept green the grand old subject of Sino-Indian contacts, though the purely religious story was varied with the less-developed and more congenial subject of commercial interchange. The twentieth-century Russian revolutions naturally claimed attention. Japanese research on China had long been all-embracing, but there was little reciprocity, limited mainly to Sino-Japanese relations and radicalism in Japan. For the "several thousand years old history of China"—not unique, but autonomous—was the real concern. Marxism-Leninism was supposed to assume Chinese features, to cease to be Western centered. Absorbed really in Chinese periodization, Communist historians kept their occasional treatments of such miscellaneous problems as ancient Babylonian society, medieval European taxation, and the industrial revolution in England very close to home.

Home, they say, is where the heart is, and, in this first decade or so, the hearts, the emotions, of historians in Communist China were very much engaged. Mao had laid down the law for China's modern history: Imperialism invaded China, opposed Chinese independence, obstructed the development of indigenous capitalism. All the rest was commentary. But where the mainland historians became so committed, outsiders, too, must comment. One may hold that so many Chinese felt so strongly about autonomous generation of their modern values because really this autonomy was doubted. For Chinese Communism came to the fore *because* of the foreign invasions—which broke the older civilization and set off the drive for compensation—and not in spite of them, in train of inevitable historical progress. There is a venerable tradition in Marxist matters of intellectual gymnastics. I think Mao should be turned on his head: Chinese history *not* on its own (in modern times, at least) developed in a way *just* its own.

The history that produced the Chinese Communist historians was not the history that these historians felt able to produce. History, the events of the past into which they inquired, and history, the inquiry they conducted, could not quite coincide.

CHINA'S HISTORY IN MARXIAN DRESS

ALBERT FEUERWERKER

My over-all characterization of Chinese Communist historiography, then, is that it is in danger of being meaningless. This is a fact of which even one who does not read Chinese may satisfy himself by a look at a recent English-language volume emanating from the Foreign Languages Press in Peking and entitled *An Outline History of China.* (Nothing much better in the way of an introductory general history written after 1949 is yet to be found in Chinese.) It reveals only a mechanically acted melodrama, culminating inevitably in "the great victory of the new democratic revolution" in 1949.

FROM Albert Feuerwerker, "China's History in Marxian Dress," *The American Historical Review*, 66, 2 (Jan., 1961), 347–53. Reprinted by permission of the author.

What way out of this state of affairs? One way was to "emphasize the present and de-emphasize the past" (*"hou-chin po-ku"*). The May, 1958, issue of *Li-shih yen-chiu*, the most important historical journal in the People's Republic of China, led off with a string of heavyweight editorials by Kuo Mo-jo, Fan Wen-lan, Ch'en Yuan, Hou Wai-lu, Lü Chen-yü, and Liu Ta-nien which proclaimed that slogan, a clear sign that the Party was unhappy about the condition of historical studies. *Hou-chin po-ku* had a double edge. On the one hand, it was meant to be taken literally as a guide to cutting up the pie of available historical manpower and other facilities. But it also indicated a tightening of the political screws so far as the historians were concerned. Fan Wen-lan, in an address to a symposium of historians and archaeologists in April, 1958, put it very neatly:

> The difference between placing more emphasis on the present than on the past and placing more emphasis on the past in preference to the present represents a struggle between the two paths of promoting the proletariat and demoting the bourgeoisie and of promoting the bourgeoisie and demoting the proletariat. We, of the new historians, should adhere to the Marxist standpoint and regard it as our responsibility to emphasize the present in preference to the past and to promote the proletariat and demote the bourgeoisie.

Running parallel with the *hou-chin po-ku* "line," so to speak, there has most recently appeared another candidate for the first string of Chinese Communist historiography, none other than the celebrated general and poet Ts'ao Ts'ao (155–220). The most prominent character in the exciting epoch of the downfall of the later Han dynasty, Ts'ao Ts'ao is known to every Chinese as the villain of the famous novel *Romance of the Three Kingdoms* (*San-kuo chih yen-i*), the tyrannic usurper who seized the last Han emperor, Hsien-ti, and in lifelong warfare contested with the heroic Liu Pei and his great minister Chu-ke Liang for universal dominion of the empire. The evaluation of Ts'ao Ts'ao among historians has more or less corresponded to that of the novel: able and crafty, but wicked and unscrupulous. In the traditional histories, this judgment depended in part on the fact that the Wei dynasty (220–65) of the Three Kingdoms epoch, which was established by Ts'ao and his son, was not a "legitimate successor to the Han, while Liu Pei who founded the Shu dynasty (221–64) was a distant relation of the Han ruling house, and his rule could thus be considered legitimate. For the modern "progressive" historians the principal blot on Ts'ao's record was his brutal suppression of the peasant uprising known as the "Yellow Turbans" during the last years of the Han. But, beginning with pronouncements by Ch'ien Po-tsan and Kuo Mo-jo early in 1959, and followed by intensive discussion in the newspapers and historical periodicals, the case of Ts'ao has recently been reopened and, it seems, the judgment of the past completely overturned.

The discussion has centered on three issues: Ts'ao's suppression of the Yellow Turban rebellion, the policy of land reclamation that he carried out with his troops (*t'un-t'ien*), and his ruthless military expedition against the Wu-yuan people. Ts'ao Ts'ao, wrote Kuo Mo-jo, in putting down the Yellow Turban rebellion did not violate the goals of that quite just peasant uprising. The Yellow Turbans were poorly organized and incapable of bringing about the improvement that they sought in the people's livelihood. When Ts'ao defeated them, many of the Yellow Turban troops voluntarily joined his forces. Would they have followed him if he were the vicious person that the historians have alleged? The *t'un-t'ien* policy, moreover, far from being in the interest of the great landlord families or contributing to Ts'ao's own enrichment, provided his troops and the civil population of northern China with the food and other agricultural products that had been in such short supply. Ts'ao himself led a spartan life, and with the popular support and military resources that the land reclamation policy ensured, he was able to defeat his enemies in battle and eventually to unify much of China. The suppression of the semicivilized Wu-yuan tribes was not an aggressive act against a weaker people but a defensive war against a backward barbarian invader, for which he had wide popular support. (It is of interest that on this last point Kuo quotes a poem by Mao Tse-tung, in which he finds a favorable reference to Ts'ao Ts'ao's expedition against the Wu-yuan—poet and military leader Mao bowing to poet and military leader Ts'ao!) Ts'ao, Kuo admitted, had often recklessly slaughtered his enemies, and his errors and shortcomings were not to be overlooked. Yet, his strong points outweighed his shortcomings. "In my opinion . . . Ts'ao Ts'ao made a greater contribution to the development of the nation and its culture than any of his contemporaries." Although there was some dissent from Kuo's call for a new estimate of Ts'ao Ts'ao, the consensus strongly supported the view that Ts'ao Ts'ao's contributions to enriching and strengthening the Chinese "nation"—the key word in Kuo's brief for the defense—warranted a reappraisal of his place in China's history.

Along with the refurbishing of the erstwhile villain Ts'ao Ts'ao has gone an appeal for the re-evaluation of many others, not popular heroes or leaders of peasant revolts, but emperors, generals, statesmen, and scholars of the feudal past, such as King Chou, the "licentious" last ruler of the Shang dynasty, the first Ch'in emperor (reigned 221–10 B.C.), Han Wu-ti (reigned 140–87 B.C.), T'ang T'ai-tsung (reigned 627–49), and the great Manchu emperors K'ang-hsi (reigned 1661–1722) and Ch'ien-lung (reigned 1736–1796).

These recent developments are potentially of great significance for the problems that the Chinese Communist historians face. Although there has been no Chinese equivalent of M. N. Pokrovsky, the approach to China's past through such topics as peasant rebellion, capitalist origins, and periodization is in a number of ways quite similar to the tendency in Soviet historiography associated with the name of that Russian historian. Pokrovsky, who dominated his profession until the 1930's, and his adherents presented their materials "in a theoretical and schematic form," writing an almost anonymous history of the movement and clash of social forces. They "portrayed all pre-Soviet institutions and personalities in a sarcastic vein. This did not meet the needs of a regime that wished to stimulate patriotism by rehabilitating selected personalities, and to present Russian history in an interesting narrative form suited to secondary school education." After his death, Pokrovsky was severely attacked, and Soviet historiography moved steadily onto a more nationalistic tack, which culminated in the near chauvinist output of the World War II period. I suggest that the rehabilitation of Ts'ao Ts'ao and the others is analogous to the post-Pokrovsky re-evaluation of Ivan the Terrible, for example, by Soviet historians. It represents a shift from an emphasis on the popular past to an emphasis on the national past. But, I hasten to add, neither need exclude the other, nor can one say with any assurance how far the change will go in China. Yet the context within which the Ts'ao Ts'ao discussion has occurred leads me to believe that it is part of the most recent attempt by the mainland historians to cope with the threat of a meaningless past.

About the same time that the matter of re-evaluating Ts'ao Ts'ao was occupying a prominent place in mainland publications, Ch'ien Po-tsan and others who had reopened the case of Ts'ao Ts'ao were also expressing their reservations about the manner in which the *hou-chin po-ku* "line" had been carried out. Writing in *Hung-ch'i*, the semimonthly theoretical organ of the Central Committee of the Chinese Communist Party and manifestly the most authoritative publication in the People's Republic of China, Ch'ien was highly critical of the fact that "some colleges have excessively reduced the proportion of ancient history in the general study of history." He thought it an error, too, that a number of schools, in response to "emphasizing the present and de-emphasizing the past," had turned their curricula upside down and were now teaching modern history before ancient history. This could only make it more difficult for the students to comprehend the laws of social development. Chien then proceeded to criticize those historians who taught an anonymous history—saying "the early Han" rather than "Ch'in Shih Huang" or "Han Kao-tsu"—and those who in their Marxist purity omitted all mention of the ruling class. "To sum it up, when teaching history, we must emphasize the explanation of the laws of social and economic development of each period, and the creative role of the masses, but we must also discuss the roles of individual historical personages." In a similar vein, Kuo Mo-jo was critical of historical research. It is correct, he asserted, to abandon court-centered history, but imperial dynasties nevertheless existed and cannot simply be ignored. He objected to those who omitted the *nien-hao* (reign title) and the customary honorific or temple names of the emperors and cited merely the Western calendar years and the rulers' personal names (*ming*), in the belief that to do otherwise would indicate deference or respect to these "feudal" rulers. And, like Ch'ien, Kuo took exception to the tendency to write only about the masses and to give short shrifts to the affairs of the ruling classes of the past.

This implied dissatisfaction with the cruder aspects of Marxist historiography, though of course not with Marxism-Maoism itself, seems to be related to the Ts'ao Ts'ao discussions in that both are part of an effort to patch up what I earlier described as the largest hole in the garment of Chinese Communist historiography, the two millennia of "feudal" void. It will doubtless remain "feudal," but it is possible that larger and larger portions of it will be re-evaluated from a viewpoint that is at least as much Chinese as it is Marxist. "One of the important meanings implicit in the discussions of Ts'ao Ts'ao," stated a report of a meeting of historians in Shanghai in the spring of 1959,

is that we know how to make a correct appraisal of the characters of history. In the course of the discussion, all participants agreed on the principles advanced by Kuo Mo-jo that we should judge a character in history from an over-all point of view and assess his place in history according to his major deeds. Particularly we should see whether he made any contribution to the people and to the development of the whole nation and to cultural development. We should make an over-all analysis of him and of the background of the times he was in, taking the role he played in historical development as the standard.

It is too early to say what the effects of these pronouncements will be. If, however, a re-evaluation of Ts'ao Ts'ao and the other "feudal" figures is in fact carried out on the basis of their "contribution to the people and to the development of the whole nation and to cultural development," the mainland historians will indeed have taken a long step toward replacing a Chinese meaning in their past. In the words of the report of the Shanghai historians' conference that I referred to earlier: If the problem of Ts'ao Ts'ao "is correctly settled, then we can gradually discover a correct attitude toward our cultural heritage, and find the solution to the questions of how to tackle present problems in the light of ancient, similar cases."

Chinese history will never be "bourgeois" history again. And it is equally unlikely that the Pokrovsky-like treatment of anonymous social forces will disappear from the scene in the People's Republic of China. It is, however, possible to conceive of (perhaps, better, to hope for) a time when the importunate demands of the real world, as interpreted by the Chinese Communist leadership, will have abated enough to permit the relinquishment of belief in a single source of evil in modern history. "Imperialism" will not be banished from the mainland historical workshops, but its dimensions may be reduced as the successful construction of a new domestic tradition proceeds apace. The result will still not be the kind of history that will satisfy the Western student of China, any more than the dominant Marxism of Japanese historiography can be taken as an adequate picture of Japan's past. But some of the emotion, and aggression, will have been wrung out of the Chinese fabric. And it may be that, on some matters, at least, the historiographical meeting of minds, East and West, will be feasible.

2. MARXISM, NATIONALISM, AND
THE GREAT NAMES OF THE PAST

By the late 1950's, the difficulties inherent in producing a new Chinese history that would satisfy the new China's various intellectual and emotional needs was becoming apparent. One of the major problems was that an over-reliance on Marxist historical determinism threatened to iron all the uniquely Chinese quality out of Chinese history. Historical "equivalence" with the West was desirable and necessary, but, when coldly impersonal historical forces and stages replaced living figures and events in Chinese history, there was the danger of its losing emotional appeal to modern Chinese nationalism.

During 1958, frustration with historical studies and the general Great Leap atmosphere produced the "more present, less past" directive for historians. Yet, as shown in the first chapter, downgrading the past was no substitute for finding meaning in it—hence, the deep concern over "evaluating historical figures" that came almost to pervade Chinese historiography by the end of the 1950's. The concern was both to rehabilitate great names of the past from their feudal associations and, in some cases, to recast stock Confucian villains as modern nationalist heroes.

Professor Levenson has noted this phenomenon in his description of Chinese historiography, earlier in this chapter and in the essay on Confucius in the next chapter. In the preceding selection, Professor Feuerwerker has analyzed Chinese efforts to counter what he sees as a threatening meaninglessness in their history by turning to concrete historical personages.

Following are two essays by very prominent Chinese historians. In the first, Hou Wai-lu, writing during the relaxation of 1956, rehabilitates the father of Chinese history, Ssu-ma Ch'ien. The note of national pride in ancient greatness is unmistakable and typical of articles on many other famous historical figures. The second essay, by Wu Han (who became a leading target of the Cultural Revolution), is part of a running debate early in the 1960's ostensibly on evaluating certain historical personages but going much deeper into the whole attitude that modern Chinese should take toward their past and the role it might play in the present. He makes a strong plea for a balanced and relatively tolerant evaluation, one which does not oversimplify history to prove Marxist lessons for the present.

SSU-MA CH'IEN: GREAT ANCIENT HISTORIAN

HOU WAI-LU

Ssu-ma Ch'ien (145–90? B.C.) was one of the greatest historians of ancient China. He was also one of its towering literary figures. Extending the achievements of previous scholars, he wrote the *Shih Chi* (*Historical Records*), popular in style and deep-going in their philosophy, which gave guidance to the Chinese people of his own and subsequent generations.

Throughout the 2,000 years since they were written, the fine, creative works of Ssu-ma Ch'ien have been acclaimed by enlightened Chinese scholars. They have remained an ever fresh spring. Lu Hsün, the outstanding champion of China's modern revolutionary literature, called the *Shih Chi* a "masterpiece of historical writing."

It is not my purpose in this article fully to analyze and evaluate the *Shih Chi*. What I would like to do is to give my personal views on its popular character and the philosophic principles that underlie it.

Ssu-ma Ch'ien was one of the greatest thinkers of old China. His world view was plainly one of naïve materialism. This we may ascribe to his connection with science: He knew something of astronomy (his father had been court astronomer and archivist) and helped in the revision of the Chinese calendar under the emperor Wu Ti. The stanchness of his materialism may be seen from his relentless battle against superstition, particularly the theories of the *yin-yang* (male and female principles) and *wu-hsing* (five elements) that were then rampant. "The astrological books," wrote Ssu-ma Ch'ien, "deal with omens and prognostications; they are therefore heretical." One of his works, the *T'ien Kuan Shu* (*Book on Astronomy*), was written especially to discredit these theories.

From the same critical standpoint, Ssu-ma Ch'ien made a logical analysis of many ancient Chinese classics and legends. "What the *Book of History* says about the nine provinces with their

FROM Hou Wai-lu, "Ssu-ma Ch'ien: Great Ancient Historian," *People's China* (June, 1956), pp. 36–40.

mountains and rivers is fairly reliable," he declared. "But I can put no trust in what the *Yu Pen Chi* and *Shan Hai Ching* say about monsters." Following in the footsteps of Hsun Kuang (a philosopher of the third century b.c.), he ridiculed many yarns which the unscrupulous Han dynasty literati passed off as truth, as well as many legends concerning the remote past. "Scholars have long talked about the Five Emperors," he said, "but the *Book of History* begins only with Emperor Yao. The philosophers all like to talk about Huang Ti (the Yellow Emperor), but their language is too high-flown and a man of cultivated mind will doubt what they say."

Nor did this great thinker believe in any "mystery" of death. "Life dies"—he quoted his astronomer father—"when the spirit is separated from matter. What is separated cannot be reunited and what has died cannot live again." Here, again, we see that he took the standpoint of ancient or naïve materialism in natural science.

Ssu-ma Ch'ien never stated his philosophy of history, but this does not mean that there is no unifying idea in his works. An analysis of the *Shih Chi* shows that this general idea, sometimes veiled but implicit in his presentation of social development and personages of different classes, was again naïve materialism.

It is a fact that those ancients who had a materialist outlook on the world of nature very often fell into the mire of idealism in their view of social phenomena. Ssu-ma Ch'ien himself cannot be isolated from the environment of his time, and his philosophy of history is not free from idealist elements. In the main, however, his social philosophy was popular and predominantly materialist. . . .

As already noted, Ssu-ma Ch'ien saw the peasants, miners, craftsmen, and merchants as contributors to social wealth. These four kinds of men, he said, "are the suppliers of the people's food and clothing." This is why, in writing of ordinary people, he often gave them an exalted position. He put Pai Kuei, a simple merchant, on the same level as great statesmen and commanders.

Enslavement of some men by others, in Ssu-ma Ch'ien's eyes, was a necessary product of the unequal distribution of wealth. "You are an abject inferior to a man who is ten times richer than you," he said. "You are awed by a man who is a hundred times richer; a menial to the man a thousand times richer; a slave to the man ten thousand times richer." This is quite a different view from that of the feudalists, who considered poverty and wealth to have been preordained by divine providence.

The unscrupulous acts of the ruling class were exposed in the

Book of Finance and the *Book of Biographies of Ruthless Officials*. Here financial and ruthless officers were sharply characterized, and the conflict between the rulers and the ruled in feudal
society was brought out with great force. These accounts exemplify the truth pointed out by Engels: that good literature can give
a richer, more varied picture of society than sociological, statistical,
or juridical works.

In the *Book of Finance*, the author shows how the emperor, as
the biggest landlord, confiscated the wealth, land, and slaves of
his subjects. It tells in detail how he ruined hitherto well-to-do
families and how special privileges, conferred on a small number
of despotic aristocrats, plunged the peasants into misery.

In the *Biographies of Ruthless Officials*, the historian points
out that the peasants were driven to revolt by their extortions, that
the revolts were crushed in one place only to break out in others,
and that the officials "concealed the true state of affairs from each
other so as to evade the law."

The "ethics" of rich and powerful men, Ssu-ma Ch'ien declared, are designed to facilitate and justify the seizure of power
and wealth. To make the point, he quoted the following proverbs:

> The common people say: I don't know what virtue is; but whoever
> possesses wealth is virtuous.

> He who steals a sickle is a thief; he who steals a nation is a prince.
> Virtue resides in princely mansions.

Quite different was his estimation of the ethics of the oppressed
and the ruled, which he held in high regard. Among Ssu-ma
Ch'ien's biographies are those of many chivalrous figures of his
time, men who looked upon the despotic landlords as enemies.
Chu Chia, for instance, liked to "aid the unfortunate and give
precedence to the poor." Of the lowly persons whose lives he
recorded, Ssu-ma Ch'ien wrote: "They always keep their word
and never stop in the middle of what they do. . . . They go to
the aid of those in distress, giving no thought to their own safety.
Even when they have saved others from death, they are not proud
but are ashamed to vaunt their merit."

In the biographies, the activities of Chen Sheh, a peasant who
led an uprising against the Ch'in dynasty (221–207 B.C.), are
compared in merit to the writing of the *Ch'ün Ch'iu* (*Spring and
Autumn Annals*) by Confucius, and the founding of the Shang
(sixteenth–eleventh centuries B.C.) and Chou (eleventh century–

403 B.C.) dynasties by the sage kings Tang and Wu. Despite his humble origin, Chen Sheh's biography is placed among those of the "noble families," a very remarkable thing in Chinese historiography. It is interesting to compare the respect shown to Chen Sheh with the acrid contempt for the emperor Kao-tsu, founder of the Han house, who though placed in the "Royal Houses" is called a "swashbuckler."

The amount of attention Ssu-ma Ch'ien gave to the life of the commonalty showed that, to him, the life of the people was the main subject of historical study. This was without precedent.

Finally, Ssu-ma Ch'ien took a scientific approach to the official ideology of his time. The Han emperors had decreed Confucianism to be the only orthodox school of thought for intellectuals. They hoped, by this means, to eliminate all other schools and cement their power over the whole nation. Ssu-ma Ch'ien opposed this trend. In his writings, he placed all schools of philosophy on the same footing with the Confucian "Six Classics." In this, too, he was unique among the scholars of his day.

All these things explain why we hold Ssu-ma Ch'ien in such high regard. In 1955, the Chinese people celebrated the 2,100th anniversary of the birth of this creative genius in the realms of history and literature. Our historians and writers have decided to carry out a comprehensive study of his works, so as to carry forward our great heritage from the past.

ON APPRAISAL OF FIGURES IN HISTORY

WU HAN

On the question of appraising important figures of history, Comrade Mao Tse-tung clearly pointed out 24 years ago:

> Another task in our study is to study our historical legacy and sum it up critically from the Marxist approach. Our nation has a history of several thousand years, a history which has its own characteristics and is full of treasures. But in these matters we are mere schoolboys. The China of today has developed from the China in history; as we are believers in the Marxist approach to history, we must not cut off our whole historical past. We must make a summing-up from

FROM Wu Han, "On Appraisal of Figures in History," *Jen-min Jih-pao* (People's Daily) (March 23, 1962). Translated by American Consulate General (Hong Kong, B.C.C.), *Survey of China Mainland Press*, 2721, pp. 1–3.

Confucius down to Sun Yat-sen and inherit this precious legacy. This will help much in directing the great movement of today.

But this task remains to be fulfilled by us. . . .

Since liberation, our historians have had ample conditions and opportunities to study Marxism-Leninism and Comrade Mao Tse-tung's works and have done much useful work in studying, analyzing, and summing up the important figures of history from the approach of dialectical materialism and historical materialism. Since 1959, in particular, such figures of history as Ts'ao Ts'ao, Wu Tse-t'ien, and K'ang-hsi have been extensively discussed and a gratifying situation of "blooming and contending" has been brought about in historical and literary circles. Misgivings on the part of some people have been dispelled and enthusiasm for penetrating study has been encouraged. Further, a series of questions like nationalities relations, the character of war, the role of peasant wars, etc., have been raised in the discussion of these figures of history. The field is wider and the target is more concrete. This is a good beginning for the academic research from now on.

Needless to say, the achievements are great, but there is still a problem.

The problem still lies in a formalistic approach to the problem. Although it has been more than 40 years since the May Fourth era, and although such absolutism as "absolutely and totally good and absolutely and totally bad" no longer appears in learned discussions, vestiges of formalism still find their market. In certain discussions, figures deserving approval are approved to such an extent that what should not be approved is approved. On the other hand, certain people, not correctly understanding the method of class analysis, carelessly assign class statuses to historical figures, sweepingly disapproving of some figures of the landlord class and not daring to mention or glossing over the good things done by some emperors, generals, and ministers because of their class status. This state of affairs cannot but bring about confusion in many respects.

In the former case, Hegel has said: "We are prone to remold the ancient philosophers by our own mode of thinking. . . . One is very likely to judge ancient people by attributing to the ancient people things familiar to us." Certain well-intentioned historians and men of letters are prone to attribute to ancient people our mode of thinking and things familiar to us and, in doing so, not only remold the ancient people but also modernize them. In some cases, in order to approve a certain figure of history, one may even represent his historical mistakes as a service to the people, thereby confusing the right and the wrong. The figure of history is over-extolled with the result that his merit is exaggerated. Actually, when a man is 60–70 per cent good, and if he is truthfully and scientifically represented as being 60–70 per cent good, the account about him will be convincing; if he is over-extolled and represented as being 100 per cent good or even 120 per cent good, the truth of history is lost and no common conclusions can be drawn.

In the latter case, some people adopt a negative attitude toward most figures of history, except leaders of peasant wars. Or else, even if they are given approval, it is almost always modified by such phrases as "owing to the limitations of the times, they could not have done what was done at later times" in a stereotyped way at the conclusion. Before the general discussion of Ts'ao Ts'ao, some textbooks on history dared not even mention the name of Ts'ao Ts'ao, and this figure of history was expunged altogether from history. Even after the general discussion of Ts'ao Ts'ao, certain textbooks dare to mention only such figures as the First Emperor, Emperor Wu of Han, Ts'ao Ts'ao, and Wu Tse-t'ien, on whom the academic circles have already drawn conclusions, and avoid mention of other figures and, if they have to be mentioned, seldom say something good about them. The result is that fewer and fewer great figures of history are found in our textbooks of history. With concrete historical events divorced from concrete figures, the contents of history, which are actually very rich, are artificially made empty and generalized.

3. HISTORICAL LESSONS FOR THE 1960's:
THE MASSES AND CLASS STRUGGLE

A nationalistic pride in great historical figures and a professional historian's concern that the past not be crudely interpreted in the light of present political values motivated the developments described in the preceding section. However, there were always Party zealots and "redder" young historians who opposed any whitewashing of feudal elements. In this regard, the tradition of peasant rebellions (perennial fighters against China's historical ruling class) could serve as an alternative either to cut-and-dried historical determinism or to rehabilitation of feudal oppressors. Ever since 1949, peasant rebellions have provided a leading theme in Chinese Communist historiography; by the mid-1960's, they had become even more important in reaffirming the importance of "class stand" in the battle against revisionism.

In the following selection, Professor James P. Harrison discusses the importance of peasant rebellions during the recent emphasis on class struggle leading up to and culminating in the Cultural Revolution.

THE COMMUNISTS AND CHINESE
PEASANT REBELLIONS

JAMES P. HARRISON

The Communist treatment of the peasant movements in Chinese history reveals important characteristics of Chinese Communism as well as of contemporary Chinese intellectual life in general. These characteristics are an unprecedented commitment to the doctrine of class struggle, the adaptation of Marxism, and the close relation of ideology to politics. Certain observations on the content and success of the "new history" of the peasant revolts will also be noted.

The increasing emphasis by Chinese Communists on struggle in general and on the class struggle of the peasantry in particular, as observed throughout this study, reflects the passage of Marxism from the established areas of Europe to the more unsettled and more agrarian East. A parallel development in Marxist theory, which represents another side of the evolution to a greater stress on the peasantry, has been the increased weight given to the historical role of "the people" in general. If classical Marxism stressed the economic evolution of history, or the "productive forces," the Chinese Communists stress social revolution and human energy,

FROM James P. Harrison, *The Communists and Chinese Peasant Rebellions: A Study in the Rewriting of Chinese History* (New York: Atheneum, 1969), pp. 265 and 270–76. Copyright © 1968 by James P. Harrison. Reprinted by permission of Atheneum Publishers.

or "productive relations," in history. They do so far more than the Russians, especially in recent years. . . .

In evaluating the successes and failures of the historiography of the peasant revolts, the distinction between the investigation of historical truth and historical propaganda or education must be kept in mind. In the former area, the Chinese Communists have not succeeded. They have made available a great amount of data, and they have raised many important questions concerning Chinese social history in general and the history of the peasant revolts in particular. They have discovered some new materials and called attention to many other documents and references concerning peasant rebels. Yet the millions of words devoted to the subject have not furthered very much the understanding of this phenomenon in Chinese history. Many fundamental questions remain unanswered, including the real composition, goals, and actions of these movements. Even in terms of Marxist theory, many of the most important questions are avoided, especially those relating to periodization, as in the role of the class struggle in the transition from "slavery to feudalism" and from "feudalism to semicolonialism." Most important, the complexity of the historical phenomenon of the Chinese peasant revolts defies simple solution.

Concerning knowledge of history in the "new China," a leading playwright wrote, "the young generation has scanty historical knowledge, being misled by simplified thoughts and made disinterested in history," while a leading historian acknowledged that "some problems [in historical interpretation] will have to wait for our children and grandchildren to solve." Moreover, it is apparent that many young college-educated Chinese are unable to read the classical language with ease. Perhaps most harmful of all, in historical studies as in other areas, is the self-imposed isolation of China, with virtually complete neglect of important advances in non-Communist Sinology.

In terms of the second criterion, however—the popularization of history and of Party policies through the study of history—it can be said that Communist historiography of the peasant wars is a great success. This is undoubtedly the most important goal of Chinese Communist historiography. As one writer put it, "We should not interpret history only objectively. Studying the peasant wars, [we] must look first at the antifeudal nature and goals of the revolutionary peasants and only later at other more objective considerations." In short, the desire to inculcate a belief in class struggle supersedes the desire to "investigate historical truth," though, like their predecessors in imperial China, most mainland historians believe these two goals reinforce each other. In fact, the abundant traditional materials stressing government injustices as a cause of revolt, like the voluminous data on modern imperialism if read uncritically, do seem to support Communist claims of the existence of the class struggle in Chinese history. Although these conflicts obviously pitted the ruled against their rulers and hence were essentially political, there is no doubt that the average reader in Communist China sees them in terms of class struggle, believing that the Chinese peasantry struggled for thousands of years against the abuses of the governing class and that ultimately their "liberation" had to await Communist leadership. Hence, the historiography of the peasant wars has succeeded in its ideological function to the extent that it has made the Communist seizure of power seem both inevitable and justified.

It may be said also that one historiographical tradition has been maintained: the inexhaustible energy with which the Chinese have pursued the writing of history and especially the writing of history in the service of the state. Nor has there yet been the degree of distortion and outright falsification of history that characterized so much of Soviet historical study. There has been selection and emphasis but not much crude cutting and fabrication except in the case of Party history, perhaps as much because Party leaders have not felt this necessary up to now as because of any indigenous respect for history. It is also true, however, that the prodigious efforts to integrate the Chinese revolution with the Chinese tradition are understandable only in terms of a society attempting to come to grips with an immense historical legacy.

In terms of Marxist-Leninist-Maoist theory itself, the religion of contemporary China, there is evidence indicating its deepening roots in mainland historiography. This is especially noteworthy in many of the articles and writings of the younger generation. As popular history, these works are at once more sophisticated and more radical in their interpretations than comparable writings of the early 1950's. They are certainly more Chinese. They are more sophisticated in showing greater skill in handling the complexities of history according to Marxist theory, at least prior to the "Cultural Revolution." They are more radical in their ever greater stress on the class struggle in theory, as if to compensate for its decline in practice. They are more Chinese in their stress on national achievements. Characteristically, these are all combined in the use of most revolutionary and untraditional theories in the interests of Chinese nationalism.

Therefore, almost two decades of intensive ideological education in historical studies have been successful in inculcating a complicated body of historical theory, which has in turn trained new generations of intellectuals in the logic of the dialectic. The converse is not necessarily true: That it has convinced the Chinese historian that the dialectical interpretation of Chinese history is the only logical one. A method can be taught more easily than a belief, but the former inevitably influences the latter. Most important, in terms of content, the "new historiography" has succeeded in presenting the enormous historical legacy of China in terms suitable to the purposes of Communist mass education. Chinese Communist historiography may be termed a political and educational success, given the goals of the Party leaders.

These goals, above all, have been directed to showing that the strivings of mankind were the driving force of history and not deviations from the classical ideals of harmonious social relations. Therefore, the Chinese Communists place maximum emphasis on the history of the peasant wars in order to inculcate a belief in the existence and efficacy of class struggle and the realization that "only through struggle is there a way out." Mainland historians cite ceaselessly the protests of the Chinese peasantry for two millennia against "feudal exploitation" as proof of the "glorious revolutionary tradition of the Chinese people," and they call the historical experience of the peasant wars the "foundation on which the peasants were able to accept the leadership of the proletariat." They stress the "revolutionary struggles" of the Chinese peasantry both "objectively," insofar as the peasant movements "alone formed the real motive force of Chinese historical development," and "subjectively," insofar as the peasantry consciously aspired to replace feudal exploitation with a "peasant utopia." While some historians oppose the latter half of this equation as contrary to fact and to classical Marxist views, and while all obey the injunction that "preproletarian" mass movements inevitably failed, the prevailing Chinese view of the historical peasant rebellions is nevertheless one of enthusiastic approval. This tendency both influenced the form of the "cultural revolution" and was strengthened by it, although eventually a new reaction will inevitably set in.

Compared with Western and earlier Chinese approaches, the

prevailing interpretation of the history of peasant wars is at once more nationalistic and more radical in its class and revolutionary implications. It is more nationalistic in its stress on the peculiarly revolutionary qualities of the Chinese peasantry, and it is more radical in its unprecedented emphasis on class struggle. It therefore reveals both the chauvinism and Marxist fundamentalism of the Chinese Communists. This simultaneous emphasis on Chinese uniqueness and on a revolutionary theory is significant because it shows that the Chinese Communists believe that the best way to advance national interests is by stressing revolutionary heritage and commitment.

4. ARCHAEOLOGY: MATERIAL FOR A
MATERIALIST INTERPRETATION OF HISTORY

As a discipline, archaeology has not had the same ideological buffeting that history has encountered in Communist China. This may be explainable partly in terms of a Marxist fondness for hard material data, partly in terms of a greater removal from ideological issues. In any case, almost all foreign observers have been impressed with the amount of work done in archaeology since 1949, although some are critical of the quality. Professor Cheng Te-k'un of Cambridge University here takes a generally favorable view of Chinese Communist achievements.

ARCHAEOLOGY IN COMMUNIST CHINA
CHENG TE-K'UN

Archaeological work in China is organized on a nationwide scale. Soon after 1949, a set of laws and regulations for the protection of relics and field excavations was promulgated, existing museums were reorganized and thousands of new ones established, and a Bureau of Cultural Relics (Wen-wu Kuan-li Chu) was set

FROM Cheng Te-k'un, "Archaeology in Communist China," *The China Quarterly*, 23 (July–Sept., 1965), 68–69 and 73–77. Reprinted by permission.

up under the Ministry of Cultural Affairs. The Bureau is responsible for planning and conducting antiquarian and archaeological
activities. It has encouraged exhibitions and introduced a wide
variety of research methods and techniques. Its monthly journal,
Wen-wu Chan-k'ao 'Tzu-liao, with a present circulation around
10,000, reviews the work of the Bureau and promotes archaeological work.

In the summer of 1950, an exploration party was organized
under the leadership of P'ei Wen-chung, then head of the museum
section of the Bureau of Cultural Relics. Sixteen scholars and
archaeologists from Peking and Tsinghua universities, the Historical and Palace museums, and other institutions were invited to
take part. All veterans in their respective fields, they were organized into two teams to survey the archaeological and architectural
remains in northern Shansi. In forty days, the party made a general reconnaissance of the region and excavated two Han burials.
The official report, published under the title *Yen-pei Wen-wu
K'an-cha-t'uan Pao-kao* (*Reports of the Yen-pei Exploration
Party*), includes diaries of the teams, eight articles on archaeology,
and four on architecture. This first attempt, modest though it was,
marks a new era in Chinese archaeology, characterized by full
government support, interinstitutional cooperation, organized field
work, group discussion, and prompt publication of the report.

After 1949, China began to build new roads, railways, reservoirs,
canals, and factories in large numbers. These construction projects
brought to light thousands of ancient tombs and cultural relics.
The Bureau of Cultural Relics thus found itself confronted with
an enormous task of salvaging the new finds. The Bureau started
a campaign to educate the people, especially the workers in the
construction projects, to give them some knowledge of the underground relics and basic principles of excavation. Archaeologists
were obliged to keep in close contact with them in the field. In
this way, it was claimed that not a single relic suffered from destruction. By 1954, a total of more than 140,000 objects (not
counting potsherds) had been recorded and preserved. The
Bureau put 3,760 of the finer examples in a special exhibition at
the Peking Historical Museum and catalogued them in two folio
volumes. "The protection of underground relics," concludes
Cheng Chen-to, Director of the Bureau, in his introduction, "is
not only . . . to preserve the cultural heritage of the past. The
function and significance of this work is deeper; it is to develop
the culture and art of today and tomorrow." Archaeology in China

has assumed a new role, to carry out a social as well as a historical mission.

Steps taken by the Bureau of Cultural Relics in the capital are soon followed up by the provincial authorities in every region. Regional Committees on Cultural Relics or similar organizations, usually under the leadership of a few veteran archaeologists and scholars, cooperate closely with the local museums to take stock of all relics and register them. Field teams are organized to work side by side with construction workers. Some of these ordinary laborers, while serving as apprentices in the field, have acquired the trade quite readily and distinguished themselves as worker-archaeologists.

The provincial archaeologists are just as busy preparing exhibitions and reports as they are in the field. The reports are usually produced by group discussion and published under the name of the committee or the museum or both. Provincial workers also publish a large number of monographs by their own efforts. Many of these are of very high quality in scholarship and production. . . .

It is generally accepted that the writing of history is more or less a political act. As a handmaiden of history, archaeology cannot help but be involved in politics. Chinese archaeology occupies a rather privileged position politically, and yet it is still expected to act as a branch of the political movement, now geared to Marxism-Leninism.

In the early years, when the Chinese Government adopted the policy of "leaning to one side" and maintained a close alliance with the U.S.S.R., Chinese archaeologists began to introduce Russian excavating techniques and research methods. Many Russian scholars were invited to China, among them S. V. Kisséley, who gave twenty-three lectures to a total audience of 22,500 people. . . .

The Sino-Russian cultural and archaeological cooperation was seriously impaired, however, when grave ideological and political conflicts began to develop between them around 1959. The curtailment of Russian technical assistance and the recall of Russian engineers in 1960 forced the Chinese Government to adopt the policy of "relying on yourself and working with a will." Almost simultaneously, the Chinese archaeologists stopped translating Russian works and no more articles on Russian archaeology appeared in Chinese journals.

It is interesting to note that the influx of Russian archaeology does not seem to have left much impression on Chinese archaeology. Now that the Russians are using archaeology to support their claims in the border territories, one wonders how long Chinese archaeologists can remain aloof from the border dispute.

Archaeologists have played their part in the even more acrimonious conflict with the United States by denouncing American cultural aggression and criminal activities of American scholars, museum directors, and collectors. Lists of important cultural relics illegally acquired by Americans have been compiled. The United States is held responsible for robbing such famous collections as the relics of the Peking Man and the treasure of the Palace and the Central museums and the National Library of Peking.

Archaeologists in China are also involved in internal political movements. In the first few years after 1949, archaeologists were busy reorganizing their works and salvaging relics which were being unearthed in the construction programs. In 1955, a campaign was launched against spiritualism and capitalist mentality in archaeology and the handling of cultural relics. It specifically accused Hu Shih, Li Chi, and Hu Feng as part of the general anti–United States, anti-Formosa campaign.

The ideological struggle in Chinese archaeology was soon channeled into a more positive movement of learning from Marxism-Leninism. It was claimed that only through such study could Chinese archaeology be redeemed from the traditional capitalistic attitude and practice. In a National Symposium of Archaeological Workers attended by 180 experts from every province, it was resolved that archaeological activities should seek the support of the masses and the work should proceed side by side with the people and for the people.

Archaeologists responded rather slowly to the first proclamation of the Hundred Flowers Movement and their indifference aroused much criticism. But when they were invited to participate in the campaign, more than 100 people spoke at sixteen meetings which were organized for them. Their complaints were more political than professional. It came to light that some archaeologists were bitter about Party leadership in their field. They openly declared that the present system of government was no better than that of the past and the *wei-hang* (raw hands) should not be authorized to lead the *chuan-chia* (experts): "The express trains of archaeology do not need any locomotives." The attack on the ruling Party, however, was not joined by all the archaeologists and the complaints touched off an antirightist demonstration. A number of the more individualistic experts were severely criticized and were obliged to leave their posts for re-education in Marxism-Leninism and self-reform through manual work.

When the Hundred Flowers gave way to the Great Leap Foward, archaeologists and museum workers voted to follow the principle of *hou-chin po-ku* (paying more attention to the present than to the past), to serve the common people, and to heed the antiwaste and anticonservatism slogans. A large number of standard monographs and publications, including the much-used *Foundations of Archaeology*, were criticized and some *pai-chuan* (white experts) denounced or criticized themselves. Students began to criticize university courses in archaeology. Group activities were in vogue, and institutional competitions in specimen preservation and exhibit arrangement, in publicity and attracting visitors, in diligence and industry, and in the production of *hung-chuan* (red experts) were the order of the day.

The slowing down of field excavations after 1960 gave Chinese archaeologists a breathing spell to consolidate their new discoveries. A number of excellent field reports and research articles were published. Serious discussions were held on social evolution in ancient China, and a three-stage sequence of development was formally adopted in the standard summary of *Archaeology in China*, namely, *yuan-shih* (primitive society in prehistoric times), *nu-li* (slave society in Shang and early Chou periods), and *feng-chien* (feudal society in late Chou and subsequent dynasties). The first stage might have developed from a matriarchal into a patriarchal society, but the division of primitive society into two substages is still open to discussion.

In spite of all ideological struggles and political pressures, archaeology in China manages to develop, maintaining smooth continuity with the past in personnel and organization and in training and research. Since 1963, some of the victims of the antirightist campaign have begun to come back to their work and research. The general tendency in the field is one of industry, purposefulness, and progress. There is so much excavation and research going on and so many papers and monographs being published that an individual can hardly keep up with such an explosion of information. Fortunately, summaries of new discoveries and research results have been published at every stage.

IV

Philosophy

1. THE PAST'S INFLUENCE ON THE PRESENT

Western observers, especially the most superficial ones, have been prone to speculate about the continuing influence of Chinese tradition in Chinese Communism. Frequently this has led to nothing more than vague, specious generalizations about despotism, secular humanism, Sinocentrism, and the like. In the next selection, however, David S. Nivison tries to relate certain aspects of the Confucian philosophical heritage specifically to certain strains in Chinese Communism. It should be noted that he is dealing with Communism in the years before and immediately after 1949. The stress on moral self-cultivation he notes has not necessarily disappeared, but, since 1966, Liu Shao-ch'i would certainly not be cited as an authority on cadre training.

The next essay, by Joseph R. Levenson, takes a different tack. He approaches the question of the past's influence on the present by examining shifting Communist attitudes toward China's greatest historical philosopher, Confucius. But Levenson does not interpret fair words about the sage as indicating any Confucian carry-over or revival. Rather, in his museum metaphor, he sees Confucius, Confucianism, and much of the cultural legacy as being so far removed from the present as to pose no threat to the very different values and culture of Chinese Communism. Museums, physical and metaphorical, enshrine a dead past; they do not recommend its wisdom to the present.

COMMUNIST ETHICS AND CHINESE TRADITION

DAVID S. NIVISON

This paper is an analysis of certain aspects of recent Communist thought in China. By "recent" thought is meant that of the last two decades, and in fact this study is concerned essentially with developments from 1937 to 1949. The study is not based on an appraisal of the whole body of Chinese Communist writing in this period, nor even on a representative selection of it, but it does bring together for analysis some very interesting examples of Chinese Communist treatment of problems germane to the Confucian ethical tradition. The analysis, thus, perhaps indicates ways in which the Peking regime in the future may relate its ideology to the great corpus of traditional Chinese thought. My assumption has been that writers of the new regime, at least some of them, show a tendency, in developing the new thought, to incorporate into it, and synthesize with it wherever possible, native Chinese intellectual traditions and doctrines. This traditional intellectual background is often of extraordinary antiquity; but while writers such as Liu Shao-ch'i quote the words of Confucius because this has been the idiom of Chinese philosophy, there has nonetheless been a sophisticated effort to mesh a new Communist ethic with those aspects of Confucian thought which are especially characteristic of the last three or four centuries and to present Communism as in effect the latest stage of this thought. This has been done deliberately and as part of a well-understood worldwide tactic in Communism to strike local roots and to fit Communist "theory" to national situations.

Many factors have entered into the development of recent Communist ethical thought and, although they are generally understood, it will be convenient to review them briefly. (1) There is first the actual political and tactical situation faced by the Party in China in the period under discussion, *viz.*, the period when the Chinese soviet state had established itself at Yenan. (2) Converging upon this situation are intellectual tendencies and factors of past conditioning, both within the Marxist tradition itself and within modern China's struggle to adjust its thought to

FROM David S. Nivison, "Communist Ethics and Chinese Tradition," *Journal of Asian Studies*, 16, 1 (Nov., 1956), 51, 58–61, and 73–74. Published by The Association for Asian Studies. Reprinted by permission.

the modern world. (3) And, back of all, there are the more basic ethical assumptions of Hegelian-Marxist philosophy, on the one hand, and of late Confucianism, i.e., that of Wang Yang-ming (1472–1528) and the more recent Manchu period (1644–1911), on the other. . . .

Liu Shao-ch'i, in his *How to Be a Good Communist*, sees the problem of "goodness" in Communism and Confucianism as so essentially similar that at every step the concepts of the latter may be used to elucidate the former. Fundamental in Liu's ethics is the notion of self-cultivation. The Party's exile is part of his theme. The Long March and the withdrawal to Yenan are a trial of endurance, indicating that the Party's task is now to cultivate itself for future victory. Its position is that of the man who, having been chosen by heaven for greatness (as Mencius had said), is first tested and steeled with suffering.

Self-cultivation is, first of all, *necessary*, as a remedy for inexperience or undesirable class background. It consists of constantly keeping before one's consciousness one's faults and one's ideals, as classical practice illustrates. By such a development of consciousness, freedom is gained from the determining force of history or situation. All members need cultivation, because "our Communist Party did not drop from the Heavens but was born out of Chinese society, and because every member . . . came from this squalid old society of China and [is] still living in this society to-day. Hence, our Party members have more or less brought with them the remnants of the ideology and habits of the old society." In effect, the class struggle, which changes the character of society in history, is, in Liu's notion of "cultivation," to take place within the mind of each individual and is to lead to a corresponding change in individual character. And such renovation through cultivation is actually *possible:* Marx had insisted that man is capable of basic change, and Confucians have held likewise. Marx, Engels, Lenin, and Stalin are personal models for the Communist in cultivating himself and are not mysterious beings. All can acquire the "great qualities" of these "revolutionary geniuses." As Mencius had recognized, perfect virtue is accessible to anyone: "Any man can become a Yao or a Shun." But Liu is merely urging that Marxist "sages" be imitated in the Confucian manner. It was but a step to the idea that Confucian exemplars of virtue can themselves be taken as models for cultivation. A minor writer, four or five years later, urges just this: "Moreover, we ought to recognize that in addition to Communists, we can all find in the actual historical past many men who in their private lives practiced correct concepts and sentiments, and such men also can serve as our models." The principle was specifically applied, as we shall see, to such "models" as the Sung patriot Wen T'ien-hsiang (1236–82).

One side of "cultivation" is the emphasis on *consciousness* as freeing the individual (or the nation as a whole, as in Mao's *New Democracy*) from a blind inability to cope with influences upon him. If this side of the notion as set forth by Chinese writers has perhaps a connection with the Hegelian-Marxist notion of "freedom" as the consciousness of, and deliberate playing out of, a historical role, it has an equally close affinity to the Neo-Confucian notion of self-cultivation as freeing the individual from the tyranny of blind habit and unconscious selfish motivations. Once again, Wang Yang-ming supplies surprisingly close analogies to Communist thought. Wang quoted one of his students as writing: "I continually test my own mind to find out the way in which I am affected by joy, anger, sorrow, and fear. Though I am exceedingly under their influence, nevertheless when my intuitive faculty once realizes it, these passions are stopped and forthwith cease." And elsewhere Wang observed that individuals who had succeeded in an external and internal cultivation of virtue "continually see their own faults and are able to empty themselves and receive instruction from others." But while "self-criticism" is part of Wang's philosophy, the mutual criticism of Communist "struggle" meetings would have been much too much for him (perhaps going too far beyond the limits of face-saving?). He is willing to accept the criticisms of others, he says, but advises against considering "the bringing to light of another's misdoings as frankness."

We notice the role played in Chinese Communist thinking by the stressing of conscious critical awareness—of self, of historical situation—and by the deliberate imitation of "models," the fear (as exhibited by Mao) of being unconsciously influenced; and we notice further that these attitudes not only reflect the endemic Communist fear of being "used" by external forces but are an integral part of Chinese tradition itself. We may therefore be able to raise an old question in a new form: Are Communist ideologues *using* Confucian tradition, or are they *continuing* it? Is Confucian ethics in the new ideology a tactic, exploited with fingers crossed; or are Communist writers developing their genuine beliefs? We can hardly hope for a confident answer to this question, for in

the last analysis we are obliged to judge the content of beliefs by
observing behavior, which means observing tactics. But at least we
may note that a conscious didactic use of Chinese tradition is
something that is itself entailed and called for by an acceptance of
that tradition. If theoreticians are striving to keep their reinterpre-
tations of Confucianism a deliberate tactic rather than an intellectual event, what would the event be like, and how would it
differ from what has happened?

What, positively stated, is the content of the ethics the Party
would realize in itself and its members? What are the qualities
they are to cultivate? This must be inferred from the total of Communist ideological pronouncements—obviously more than we can
appraise here—but in places Liu Shao-ch'i has been quite specific.
"The Communist undertaking," he has said, is nothing less than
"to reform mankind into the completely selfless citizenry of a
Communist society." But the model for mankind, as well as mankind's vanguard in the struggle for the new society, is the Communist Party. Being "good" means for a Communist the utter
subordination of individual interest to that of the party and, ultimately, that of mankind. Since the good individual is utterly selfless, he fears nothing and will happily sacrifice even his life for his
principles, i.e., for the best interest of the Party. If we substitute
"prince" for "Party," Confucian "loyalty" could scarcely be better
formulated.

Liu's description of the sort of individual who exemplifies such
an ethic is studded with classical and traditional moral idioms.
The good Communist is "able to love others and hate others"
(from the *Lun Yü*, or *Confucian Analects*, 4.3), i.e., he never in-
jures comrades for his own benefit but vigorously fights enemies of
the revolution. Toward comrades, his attitude is one of "genuine-
ness and sympathy" (*Analects*, 4.15), of "doing nothing to others
that he would not have done to himself" (*Analects*, 15.24). He
"grieves before all the rest of the world grieves and is happy only
after all the rest of the world is happy" (the Buddhist ideal of the
bodhisattva, taken over into Confucianism by the Sung statesman
Fan Chung-yen (989–1052). By such selflessness, he is morally
liberated from the bonds of material circumstance: "He is able to
have a great firmness and moral integrity which riches cannot corrupt, poverty cannot alter, and terror cannot suppress." Having no
"private-mindedness" he is fearless—"his principles (*li*) being correct, his spirit (material energy, *ch'i*) is strong" (a basic neo-
Confucian dualism), and he will defend these principles to the

death, even when he stands alone ("in glorious isolation") opposed by all. He fears no criticism because he is his own most willing critic, and he is able "courageously and frankly to criticize others" because he desires no favors or flattery. He is "able to stand against the current and defend the truth, never drifting with the waves or flowing with the stream." In his study of revolutionary theory and practice, he can achieve perfect understanding because he "has no individual apprehensions or private desires to obscure and pervert his investigation of things and understanding of true principles" (a thoroughly neo-Confucian conception of knowledge and of this knowledge as depending on purity of mind or "sincerity"), and the good Communist is capable of that most prized of Confucian virtues, the ability to "watch himself when he is alone" (cf. the *Ta-hsüeh*, or *Great Learning*, 6, and the *Chung-yung*, or *Doctrine of the Mean*, 1), i.e., he can be thoroughly trusted to do right even when no Party supervision is present or possible.

It would be a mistake to suppose that Liu takes Confucian ethics whole and unchanged. There is not the slightest talk of loyalty to family or ancestral traditions and only a reflection of the notion of the "gentleman's" superiority to the mass. As to specific action, moreover, Liu states that all questions of principle and of right and wrong are to be examined in the light of the practical needs of the Party. But one wonders if Liu, in stressing this last virtue of "self-watchfulness" and in insisting that the good Communist can defend his principles even in "glorious isolation," is perhaps sneaking into Communist ideology, even unconsciously, an uncalculated implication of the Confucian ethic. Along with the call to selflessness, is there a hint that the Communist who has achieved perfect virtue, like his Confucian forebear, has a moral integrity so transcendent that political authority is not to question his honesty or the sincerity even of his criticisms? . . .

I have been attempting in the foregoing pages to analyze, from limited evidence, a problem which is attracting increasing attention: the problem of the importance, and the character, of the relationship between present Communist ideology and earlier pre-Western Chinese thought. To this end I have tried to indicate (1) the lines of thought within the Marxist "tradition" which could account for what we now observe and (2) other lines of thought within the Confucian ethical tradition of the last several centuries which seem similarly to provide some explanation for the present. An examination of important parts of recent ideology, at those points where Communism in China most obviously takes the form of a new ethics, seems to show a need for both these lines of explanation. On the one hand, the student of international Communism will find little to surprise him in these Chinese developments, for Communist theory does call for the "grafting" of Marxist doctrine and the Communist program onto local roots, and in fact the ethical twist that Marxism receives in China is at least anticipated by Lenin and Stalin. On the other hand, the student of China sees in recent Communist writings and pronouncements the continuation of patterns which he notices not only in recent Chinese history but also in periods considerably earlier. His impression is constantly reinforced that what is happening in China could not, in just its Chinese form, have happened anywhere else.

We need not hesitate to allow both Communism and the Chinese background their place in an explanation of what is now occurring. There is no reason to suppose that historical developments must have single causes. But we should note that this analysis has been dealing almost exclusively with verbal statements. And it is perhaps just in this realm that correspondence between the present and the past ought to be most evident. The Chinese must, after all, continue to use their language and certain habitual expressions and hortatory idioms. In the methods of the ethical life, on the other hand, resemblance between the Communist present and the Confucian past seems still appreciable but less close; and, as to the aims and the place in society of this ethical life, the correspondence is least close. For whereas in the Confucian ideal the cultivation of goodness was man's highest activity and the ultimate expression of his dignity, in Communist practice, on the contrary, this cultivation has value just insofar as it completes the subjection of the individual to the tasks the state requires of him.

We should note also that, while the Chinese have in all ages drawn upon their past both for inspiration and for propaganda, Chinese Communists, because of the jarring changes of the twentieth century, are in a position to borrow with far more critical deliberation. The new society's relation to the past, Mao has suggested, is the same as its relation to foreign cultures. It borrows from both, consciously, and, in the borrowing, what is accepted and what neglected is to be determined by present need. But while the Communists are being, insofar as they are able, consciously traditionalistic rather than unconsciously traditional in their relation to their past, we need not assume that they have ceased to find this past interesting in and for itself. Least of all need we assume that all will presently change. For the Communist need to induce acceptance of authority and uniformity of thought is likely to be a permanent one, and it would seem evident from this study that Confucian ethics, whatever its virtues, can be made to serve this need very persuasively.

THE PLACE OF CONFUCIUS IN COMMUNIST CHINA

JOSEPH R. LEVENSON

A grand old question: Is Confucianism a religion? Certainly the problem of Confucianism is rather different from the problem of Buddhism in the Communist era; there was no organized Confucian body whose state could be statistically assessed. Actually, when there was some sort of effort, before World War I, to conceive of it as a church, Confucianism was at its nadir. As far as Communist policy was concerned, Confucianism as a religion was a dead issue. Other questions claim attention. First, did Confucianism enter into Communism? Second (and more important here), what of Confucius himself, his current reputation and its meaning?

There have been observers, with a taste for paradox, who felt that the new regime was "in spirit," in real content, whatever the surface forms of revolution, the old regime eternally returning. This implied a view of continuity in terms not of process but of reality; past was related to present not by sequence but by essence. From this point of view, it was enough to remark that (give or take a few degrees) both Communist and Confucian China were institutionally bureaucratic and despotic, intellectually dogmatic and canonical, psychologically restrictive and demanding. And for those who balked at forcing Confucianism and Communism to match, there was still the "legalist" label for Mao's China. With this, the principle of "Sinological determinism" might still be defended, a Chinese ideal type still preserved against corrosive historical thinking; and with Mao a Ch'in Shih Huang-ti, Confucianism would still be implicitly there, an alternative or a partner, as

FROM Joseph R. Levenson, *Confucian China and Its Modern Fate*, vol. III, *The Problem of Historical Significance*, (Berkeley: University of California Press, 1965), pp. 62–82. Reprinted by permission of the publisher.

in the days of that legalist "First Emperor" or of later dynastic autocrats.

If, in such a timeless, noumenal version of continuity, China were "always China," the place of Confucius in Communist China would be preordained, and empirical inquiry gratuitous or fussily misleading. Yet, if only out of piety to history (or, less grandly, in defense of his occupation), a historian has to assume the authenticity of change, and, in this instance, contemplate not the ideal of a ghostly Confucius in the minds of men who published under Communist aegis. . . .

In a society where an anticlassical education set the tone, what could the classics be used for? In Communist China, where Confucian scholars were invisible, scholars in Confucianism still found employment. Their principal aim was not to extol antiquity, but to illustrate a theory of process.

Accordingly, classics retained no scriptural authority; far from providing the criteria for historical assessments, they were examined themselves for significance in history. The authority they had was as an object of historical study, not its premise.

There was plenty of historical revisionism, turning villains into heroes. But where the classics were concerned, it was the pattern rather than the praise-and-blame which was markedly revised. True, Kuo Mo-jo could stand an old judgment on its head and rehabilitate Chou Hsin of Yin, whom the *Shu Ching* (*Book of History*) made the classic example of the "bad last emperor." But when Kuo said that the latter was really competent, that he struck blows for the Chinese people's expansion and unification, Kuo was fitting him into the annals of Chinese progress; and it was this orientation to progress, more than the bleaching of a blackened name, which put Kuo in the un-Confucian stream. In Communist use of the classics for making historical points, Marxist process was the governing idea, not, however revalued, a moralistic absolute. . . .

In short, the Marxist approach to the classics was neither necessarily to damn them as feudal (some did), nor to praise them (in the Confucian vein) as timeless. They were subject to scrutiny from a mental world beyond them; they did not govern the mental world (as once they did) themselves. As a Communist Mencius study-group expressed it: *They* (traditional intellectuals) used *Mencius* as a vehicle—Chu Hsi did it to carry his neo-Confucianism, Tai Chen (1724–77) did it to correct Chu Hsi; K'ang Yu-wei did it as a "modern-text" Confucian reformer, all of them summoning up antiquity to sanction innovation. But *we* use the tool of Marxism-Leninism for an analytic critique.

This meant, of course, that a Marxist commentary on Mencius conveyed Marxism. In this it might seem to be doing *mutatis mutandis* just what Chu Hsi, Tai Chen, and K'ang Yu-wei did. Yet, while such Sung and Ch'ing commentators may not, indeed, have been doing what they claimed, expounding Mencius or Confucius "authentically," still they assumed that only if they did so would their own views be valid. However individual their interpretations, however eccentric they seemed to their opponents, these earlier scholars had to establish—for their own satisfaction as much as for anyone else's—that classical Confucian authority was being duly upheld. But Marxists scouted Confucian authority, considering it a specimen to be analyzed (not idolized) and put in its place in history—a place in the flux of the past, not an eternal place of ever present judgment. . . .

Thus, praise of Confucius (e.g., for seeing the true relation between "ideology" and "reality") tended to be patronizing, not a reverent expression of discipleship. Confucius could not guarantee this truth; he simply decorated the discussion. One pointed up a thesis perhaps, by referring to the classics, but legitimacy flowed back from Marx (Lenin, Mao), not forward from Confucius. "Ideology" and "reality," in our example, were *wen* and *tao*, luminous classical terms—but here, metaphorical, used clearly in the expectation that no one would misunderstand. And nothing marks so much the relegation of values to the past, to historical significance, as metaphorical drift, when originally literal statements become rhetorical allusions. . . .

Publicity for a "people's tradition" against a "gentry" (Confucian) tradition was not inconsistent with a restoration of Confucius. Once, during the days of the Paris Commune, the great historian Jakob Burckhardt rushed to believe a rumor of something he rather expected, the burning of the Louvre and all its contents; to Burckhardt, the treasures of art and culture seemed destined for ruin in the dawning age of destruction of authority. What should they do, revolutionaries from the lower depths, but destroy the products of the old high culture, symbols of their own subservience?

But Burckhardt might have remembered the first French revolutionaries' preservation of the Bayeux Tapestry as a national treasure, even though, as a relic of the grandeur of nobles, it had been threatened, like its associates, with destruction. And Burckhardt (in a heroic feat of clairvoyance and broadening of sympathies) might have applied the lesson in envisioning the fate of Confucius: "The people," without abandoning hostility to bearers of the "other culture," could conceive of themselves as capturing it. Like The Hermitage in Leningrad, all over China palaces and temples and varied relics—all things in absolute terms remote from Communist sympathies—were simply appropriated, "relativized," and materially preserved. And like these materially, Confucius morally did not have to be shattered; he could be preserved, embalmed, deprived of life in a glass case instead of in a cultural holocaust. He could be restored, in short, not as an authentically resurgent Confucianism (or an immanently Confucian Communism) might restore him, but as a museum-keeper restores, his loving attention to "period" proclaiming the banishment of his object from any living culture. What could be more aggressive than that (new masses *versus* old *elite*) and yet more soporific? Revolutionaries, in a *metaphorical* way, kissing off into the past instead of blowing up in the present, committed the destruction which Burckhardt half-literally expected. As the Communists claimed to stand for the whole nation, the ancient mentor of a high, once mighty part was quietly taken over and given his quietus. Nobody raises his voice in a National Gallery—on either side of the picture frames.

Under the new dispensation, then, Confucius could have one or another class-association, as long as it was ascribed to him *for his own day only*. Make him "slave" or "feudal," but only for late Chou. He could then belong to the modern nation by being in its history, or (to say the same thing) by being *for now* declassed, that is, out of historical action. Thus, "the feudalist system which set up his name as a symbol has gone for good; but the name of Confucius himself is, and always will be, respected and cherished by the Chinese people." And another writer, in the same business of extricating Confucius from the past for present admiration, consigned him to the past, too, as a matter of practical influence: "I, myself, am not a Confucianist, and I think, to speak frankly, that what he taught belongs now irrevocably to history. . . ."

Confucius, then, redeemed from both the class aberration (feudal) of idolization and the class aberration (bourgeois) of destruction, might be kept as a national monument, unworshipped, yet also unshattered. In effect, the disdain of a modern pro-Western *bourgeoisie* for Confucius canceled out, for the dialecticians, a feudal class's premodern devotion. The Communists, driving history to a classless synthetic fulfillment, retired Confucius honorably into the silence of the museum. In a concrete way, this was evident in the very making of museums in Communist China.

For the Confucian temple at Sian was restored, to house a historical museum. The temple and tomb (and environs) of Confucius at Ch'ü-fu were repainted, regilded, and preserved. In April, 1962, over the traditional "Ch-'ing-ming" spring festival for worshipping at graves, streams of visitors were drawn there, in a market-fair atmosphere, officially contrived, along the route of procession from the "Confucian grove" to the temple. (The *K'ung-lin,* "Confucian grove," had once been proposed as the Mecca and Jerusalem of Confucianism as a religion.) And such acts of piety (consistent with, not confounded by, a "feudal" identification) conveyed the Communists' sense of synthesis in arresting physical ruin. Products of the old society, which might be (and earlier, were) deemed proper objects of iconoclasm, provocative symbols of a social type which Communists ought to attack, nevertheless had suffered neglect and depredation, not loving care, from the society which the Communists succeeded. This neglect, combined with foreign plundering, came to the fore as a cultural crime of the old society, overshadowing the inequities of the even older society which made the relics in the first place. If anything, it was the pre-Communist neglect which consigned these things to history, which stamped them *noncontemporary.* When the Marxist historicism of the current society revitalized its "restored" Confucius to a remote stage of society—and preserved him for the present through the museum's trick of dissociating art from any life at all—it only confirmed the action (or inaction: neglect) of the society just before this one. In a satirical fantasy from that Kuomintang era, the 1930's, the novelist Lao She, ultimately quite acceptable to the Communists, mordantly pictured two things, perceived as a combination: conservative spirit in clinging to a moribund culture and material failure to conserve. For the museum in "Cat City" was empty, its possessions all sold to foreigners.

Any contemporary assault against Confucius, then, while still a sort of ritual exercise for some writers in Communist China, was ideologically superfluous. Sometimes, of course, impatience with mere history before the heady tasks of the present still peeped through. A reporter, praising a cooperative at Ch'ü-fu, declared that in three years, after some 2,000 years of poverty, the people of

Confucius' village were at last improving their economic and cultural life; this showed the superiority of socialism to the Confucian classics. People who thronged to see the Confucian temple and the Confucian grove would do themselves no harm if they went out of their way to take a look at this cooperative.

But the animadversion was mild. One could afford to be merely wry and reserved about Confucius' historical standing—just because it was kept historical. The Communists knew they had living men to assail, non-Communists as modern and post-Confucian as themselves, not the stuffed men from a costume past (whose clothes they were stealing anyway, to display as their "national heritage"). The stake was now title to the prestige of science. Science, as we have suggested, sets up values alien to the Confucian, and a Confucian challenge on this score could hardly be an issue. But antitraditionalism of a non-Communist variety could not be stripped of a claim on that title so easily. An attack on a biologist for basing himself on Darwin instead of Michurin was a more typical accusation of "rightism" than an attack on grounds of Sinocentric narrowness. The Confucian literatus, who might have been narrow in that way, was now so faint a memory that no one got credit in heaven, as a new man, just for being a Western-trained scientist. The latter was now the old man (the Confucianist was the dead man), and the "postbourgeois" scientist, the new.

Scientists came to be less harassed by ideologues in a technologically hungry China, but the demand for "red and expert," the redder the better, had long been heard in the land and could doubtless be heard again. The question has been raised of a possible affinity between this demand and the Confucian preference for the highly indoctrinated universal man over the specialist. If the affinity existed, then the Confucian spirit might well be thought, in a sense, imperishable. Yet, the "red and expert" formula could better be taken, perhaps, to prove the opposite: Scientific expertise, specialized knowledge, far from being inferior to the general, was indispensable. It was because it was indispensable that it was so important to capture; it must not be seen as independent or as anything but derived from the Marxist point of view. The Communists had to own science—or *they* would appear not indispensable.

A Chinese world in which science had to be owned, to be captured, was the very world in which Confucius could only be captured. He could not be free and dominant. Where science was all-pervasive (even seeping into the rhetoric that described the social system), Confucius was under lock and key and glass. It was the curators, not the creators, who looked to Confucius now. Unlike the Confucius of the Confucianists, the Confucius of the Communists had to be entombed to be enshrined. No longer a present incitement to traditionalists, for these had been crushed, Confucius was ready for history.

But not for "the dustbin of history." The museum where they posed Confucius may be a storehouse of value and inspiration. And "museumified" is not "mummified." Still, the "mummified" Confucius does not speak; when he is no longer involved in the handing down of judgments, he is not very much involved in clamorous class struggle. One is neither quartering Botticelli nor taking his as the last word for a contemporary jury when one hangs him on the wall, far from the social context of his patronage. The critics, by and large, call him masterly. They also call him *quattrocento*. Confucius, too, is wise today for many revolutionaries and may grow wiser as his patrons grow deader. But Confucius is also *Chou*.

The first wave of revolution in the twentieth century had virtually destroyed him, and seemed to destroy with him a precious continuity, a historical identity. Many schools have tried to put these together again. The Communists had their own part in the search for time lost and their own intellectual expedient; bring it back, bring him back, by pushing him back in history. It was a long peregrination, from the Confucian *tao*, K'ung's Way, to the past recaptured.

2. THE PRESENT'S SCRUTINY OF THE PAST

With Leninist and Maoist Marxism in command of philosophy, the study of Chinese philosophy has been almost entirely the study of its history. Yet there have been attempts, usually quickly whistled down by the Party, to dress up some traditional philosophical concepts in Marxist clothing. Donald J. Munro refers to some of these in his survey of attitudes toward the great seminal period of Chinese philosophy that produced Confucianism and Taoism.

The second selection presents what may be the final publication by the venerable philosopher and historian of philosophy, Fung Yu-lan. Probably the most famous non-Marxist philosopher in China, Fung has reformed his thought several times to accord with the new principles of philosophy. In each period of relaxation, however, he has come back to defend elements from China's philosophical legacy. The essay translated here is a very guarded defense of that legacy's value for present-day study. But, with the storm clouds of the Cultural Revolution already gathering, it was a brave attempt to prevent complete annihilation of the cultural legacy in philosophy. His justification is put entirely in terms of its usefulness for disseminating Marxism; his examples are drawn entirely from the works of Chairman Mao himself. But written when it was, in the summer of 1965, its intent clearly is to plead for some toleration of China's past culture and thought. Nothing has been heard from Fung Yu-lan since.

CHINESE COMMUNIST TREATMENT OF THE THINKERS OF THE HUNDRED SCHOOLS PERIOD

DONALD J. MUNRO

Although there is no detailed definitive Chinese Communist interpretation of the thinkers of the Hundred Schools period, this does not mean that one cannot isolate certain constants from which deviation is not permitted. The sayings of Marx-Engels and Mao Tse-tung, which are directly relevant to the early thinkers, if not strictly about them, have obviously been the primary guidelines for the scholar in Communist China. Especially in the material produced since 1957, when relatively intensive study of the period began, one becomes aware of more specific trends in interpretation. With the basic tenets of Marx and Engels as tools for interpretation, it is axiomatic that understanding the class struggle of a given time is the key to understanding the thought of

FROM Donald J. Munro, "Chinese Communist Treatment of the Thinkers of the Hundred Schools Period," *The China Quarterly*, 24 (Oct.–Dec., 1965), pp. 119–25 and 132–37. Reprinted by permission.

that time. The "contention" among the Hundred Schools is taken to be a reflection of the intensity of class struggle in the Warring States period. It is also axiomatic that the history of the struggle between progressive and reactionary forces is reflected in the enduring philosophical struggle between materialism and idealism. But the philosophical concepts associated with materialism and idealism are not native to China, nor are their Marxist definitions universally accepted in the history of Western philosophy. Therefore, in interpreting the thought of the Hundred Schools period, scholars most frequently cite Marx-Engels definitions as support for their own interpretations or to criticize those of others. Engels states that all those who take spirit as prior to the existence of the natural world and thus in the last analysis admit a creator (Old Testament variety or the more sophisticated Absolute Spirit of Hegel) belong in the idealist camp. Those who take the natural world as primary belong to the different schools of materialism. A variation on the theme is that those who hold that physical existence determines thought, and hence regard matter as primary, are materialists. Those who hold the reverse, i.e., that reality depends on consciousness to exist, are idealists. A further division is made between "objective idealism" (the view that the true nature of all things is mental, e.g., Reality is one Absolute Mind) and "subjective idealism" (the doctrine that things exist only in minds). The Chinese are accustomed to making this kind of distinction which resembles the neo-Confucian debate over the priority of li "principle" (or tao) and ch'i "ether."

The statements of Mao which are quoted are more relevant to the Confucian thought of the period than to that of other schools. The first concerning human nature (hsing) reads, "Is there any such thing as a theory of human nature? Of course there is. But there is only concrete human nature, namely, human nature with a class background in the class society, and there is no abstract Human Nature transcendent of classes." Secondly, there is no love of others (denoted by jen in the early works) transcending classes. Mao says, "As for the so-called love of humanity, there has never been such a unified love since humanity was divided into classes." A corollary of both of these statements is an affirmation of the relativity of moral values. "The concepts of morality, immorality, good, and evil are not instinctive and cannot be deduced rationally from the so-called eternal truth or from the traits of the supposedly nonchanging Human Nature," says one Communist theoretical work.

Chinese scholars must ask several questions in considering a thinker of the Hundred Schools: Was his thought idealistic or materialistic (or predominantly one or the other)? This question frequently is broken down into subquestions, e.g., concerning the idealistic or materialistic nature of his "world view," epistemology, etc. What class did he represent or the interest of which class was expressed in his thought (feudal lord, sunken slave-owner [*mo-lo nu-li-chu*], rising landlord, craftsman, peasant)? What contribution did he make to history—or was his thought progressive or conservative? Scholars are encouraged to investigate the annotation and dating of texts in order to invalidate the interpretations of later (e.g., Sung) commentators who read into the early works ideas appropriate to a later age and thus to discover the original meaning.

The importance of these constants as charts for interpretation and evaluation is clear to anyone who reads publications on the early thought. More dramatic evidence is available from an examination of targets of criticism. The unfortunate Liu Chieh, of the Department of History, Chungshan University, is a case in point. As a Roman commentator once said of Epicurus, he has "the whole pack of philosophers barking around him." Drawing his inspiration largely from the Ch'eng-Chu school of neo-Confucianism and supplementing it with a dose of Hegel (he is classified as an objective idealist), he has violated many of the above guidelines. He rejects the theory of class struggle as a tool for the study of ancient history, and his key for the study of Chinese thought is not the materialism/idealism struggle but simply the question of the nature of the union between heaven and man. He and many others accept the Mencius definition of human nature as an endowment to all men from heaven and ignore its class character. Unmindful of the relativity of virtues, he treats "human heartedness" (*jen*) as an abstract concept transcending time and class, appropriate to any time and any class. In fact, he treats all four cardinal virtues isolated by Mencius ("human-heartedness," "justice," "ritual," and "knowledge") in this manner. It is pointed out that he clearly is unaware of the fraud in Mencius' belief that such virtues have universal validity for all people in any age. Thus he is guilty of uncritically glorifying the thought of the early Confucian thinkers and failing to see the deception in their claims of universal validity.

Liu is not alone in this error by any means. Fung Yu-lan sees some class content in *jen* (human-heartedness). But, after finding what he believes to be Marxist sanction for his view, he goes on to accept as not entirely fraudulent the claims by members of the new (landlord) class in the eastern Chou (770–221 B.C.) that *jen* has universal validity. His Marxist references state that, in the beginning while a new class formulated its own interests, it has some interests in common with other classes. Fung would include all classes as objects of "human-heartedness" in definitions of the concept of *jen*, such as "It is to love all men" and "not doing to others as you would not have done to yourself." But it is held that Fung's view is clearly erroneous and that he distorted the words of Engels in seeking support for it. Attempts by Liu and Fung to find universal validity in a concept such as *jen*, so that it is applicable today, too, are considered not only erroneous but dangerous. They run against Chairman Mao's instruction never to carry out benevolent government to the enemy.

Those scholars whose studies are not directed by the questions mentioned above but by certain others have been quickly attacked. A common error has been to inquire in what way an early thinker was modern, i.e., of what truths of dialectical materialism was he aware. For example, some scholars have tried to show that the classic work, the *Chou I*, contains the principle that "practice is the source of knowledge." This is considered dangerous because it leads to worship of the ancient. The value of seeing the eternal truths of Marxism in *embryonic* form in the early thinkers is not denied. But it seems that one is approaching dangerous ground when he attributes to the ancients ideas that are too sophisticated (from the Marxist point of view). For example, it would be proper to see embryonic dialectical thought in the *Chou I* but not to find therein the law of conversion from quantity to quality. Another error is to carry out one's own study and then simply add a coating of class terms in order to achieve orthodoxy. It is also erroneous to ask which ancient truths can guide our conduct today.

These, then, are the broad constants guiding the interpretation of the thought of the Hundred Schools period. Coupled with the fact that the contemporary Chinese scholars of the period tend to haggle over a very limited number of the same passages in putting forth their theses, the result is an expected impression of some uniformity. . . .

Why should such studies of the early thought be carried out? There are several immediate uses for these studies. They give practice in using Marxism to analyze the philosophical systems which have emerged in history. They provide the opportunity for

struggle with erroneous doctrines, such as nihilism, the doctrine
that denies any basis for knowledge or truth, sometimes attributed
to the early Taoist thinkers. And they lead to the discovery of the
laws of thought, or the laws of philosophical development, such
as the law derived from the study of Chuang-tzu that any search
for the beginning of things in the world, things which are without
beginning and end, is bound to lead to idealism. They also increase an understanding of the era in which a given thinker lived.
Commentators continually point to the fact that, since subsequent
rulers adopted many of the views of the Hundred Schools thinkers,
their hold remained strong.

But the more fundamental answer is found in Mao's statement
that, as Marxists, the Chinese must not cut themselves off from
their historical past but must "critically sum it up using the
Marxist approach" and then proceed to "inherit this invaluable
legacy." The essence is to be kept, the dross discarded. The fruits
of the studies will then, among other things, become grist for the
education of the youth.

Thus, interpretation of the early thought must be guided by the
obligation to "critically inherit" that philosophical legacy. But
"inheritance" is a vague word, one which must be explained in
Marxist terms. Briefly stated: Due to the dialectical course of
history, present Chinese society contains elements of essence and
dross from the past. These elements dictate the limiting conditions under which Marxism is to be applied to China. Since each
country has its own tradition, Marxism must be adjusted to those
traditions. A knowledge of China's legacy is of great importance
in determining which elements of Marxism must be played up and
which played down in China, i.e., what in present-day Chinese
thought, attitudes, and conduct must be overcome and what
should be preserved and built upon. Within the sphere of philosophy, one must look for essence in even the most erroneous world
views so as to be mindful of what is vital in the heritage. Just as
Marx stood the idealist Hegel on his head, so it is possible for the
Chinese to inherit the positive aspects of their own idealistic
philosophies.

No official evaluation of the philosophical legacy has yet been
issued. But certain conclusions shared by almost all scholars seem
to be emerging. Among these, the most important observation is
that Chinese thought *even in the early period* was rich in materialistic and idealistic philosophies. This gives the thought its
place in the sun and in part may explain the severity of attack on

those (e.g., Liu Chieh) who do not see thought in such terms. . . .

An important aspect of the materialistic world view is atheism, which according to Hou Wai-lu emerged concurrently with materialism toward the end of the late Chou. Tzu-ch'an (sixth-century B.C. statesman) was one of the progenitors. Whether or not Confucius saw heaven as a willful anthropomorphic deity is debated, but his skepticism about spirits and his new focus on man is rarely contested. Lao Tzu may have conceived of *Tao* as absolute spirit, but he denied the existence of anthropomorphic gods. No one could question the atheism in Hsün Tzu's denial of any unity between heaven and man and in his naturalistic conception of heaven. Clearly, too, Han Fei Tzu denied the Heavenly Mandate. Instead he held that the people choose the king, and historical events are determined by nontheistic (e.g., economic) factors.

Another positive legacy from the early period is a rudimentary dialectical theory which developed in the late West Chou. Some see it in the thought of Confucius, e.g., in the dialectical relation between native "substance" (*chih*) and "refinement" (*wen*) in the cultural sphere (a union of both being necessary in the superior man) and in the internal dialectical relations of quality and quantity (as in the proposition that "doing too much is equivalent to doing nothing at all"). It was developed to a high level in Taoist thought, though still with grave shortcomings. . . .

This is the "essence" in the thought of the Hundred Schools period, a rudimentary materialism, an atheism, and a rudimentary dialectics. Probably other matters could be added to the list, such as Confucius' views on education and teaching method, developed to a more sophisticated level by Confucianists of the Warring States period. But this essence is always mixed with dross in the early thought. One may be pleased to find rudimentary dialectical thought in Lao Tzu but then will discover that he was an idealist and that the two are contradictory. Hence the problem of removing the dross is always present.

One of the most important pieces of dross discovered in the thought of the Hundred Schools period by present-day scholars in Communist China is the lack of any appreciation of the value of struggle between opposites. There was, of course, a struggle going on between materialism and idealism, but the thinkers themselves usually were totally unaware of the scientific value of struggle as they were of the incompatibility of opposites, which they often tried to "unite" or "harmonize."

Some contemporary scholars see Confucian virtues as tools to harmonize contradictions between classes or to bring about "compromises" between other contradictory phenomena. Kuan Feng and Lin Yu-shih regard the Confucian *jen* in this light. Loyalty and altruism have the function of harmonizing relations between rich and poor, ruler and minister, etc. The call to "love all men" has the same end. The doctrine of the "mean" was an attempt to justify compromises between mutually contradictory matters, such as belief in heavenly *ming* and reliance on human effort. In addition, Confucian discussions of an abstract "human nature" were meant to cover up class contradictions. Since later representatives of the feudal rulers adopted these doctrines, the evil was long perpetuated in China.

The failure to understand the nature of struggle between opposites is most clearly manifest in the rudimentary dialectical views of the early thinkers. This points to a unique deficiency in the Chinese legacy. In Western thought from the earliest time, there was such an understanding. Heraclitus spoke of *strife* between opposites as essential to the coming into being of things and to ordered change. Such an idea found its way to the idealism of Hegel and thence to Marx.

Kuan Feng and Lin Yu-shih hold that dialectics and idealistic philosophies are basically contradictory, for dialectics means constant development through the clash of opposites, while in an idealism such as that of Lao Tzu all opposition disappears in the Absolute. There is no development and change in *Tao* through the clash of opposites. A host of modern commentators offer variations on the interpretation that Lao Tzu's dialectic seeks to eliminate all struggle between opposites. Chuang Tzu is said to carry the denial of struggle even farther, to the point of seeming to deny the existence of opposites. His dialectics become an attempt to avoid contradictions. He preferred to take a middle position between opposites (e.g., between good and bad, strength and weakness) as an expedient means for preserving life. Or he would make a "head in the sand" escape from conflict by "transcending" it with a flight into "absolute freedom" or "pure experience." . . .

The concern over the negative legacy takes concrete form in the attacks on scholars suspected of perpetuating the dross of the past with an overlay of Marxist terminology. Liu Chieh was one victim, and the contemporary popular philosopher Feng Ting was another. Like his predecessors in the old China, Feng Ting has been interested in studies of "human nature," in discovering what is common to all men. He takes biology as his point of departure and focuses on those environmental factors biologically favorable to the human species and the "instincts" common to all men. His "error" lies in attempting to obliterate class boundaries and reconcile class contradictions by seeking to derive an abstract human nature through biology. The most recent manifestation of concern about the negative legacy is the polemic surrounding Yang Hsien-chen, elderly philosopher at the Higher Party School of the Party Central Committee who has been under attack since the spring of 1964. In discussing dialectics, Yang had talked of "the combination of two into one," a process with roots in early Chinese discussions of the unity of opposites. Yang was accused of opposing dialectical materialism because "emphasizing combining two into one" instead of "dividing one into two" was said to be equivalent to stressing compromise rather than struggle.

Two reasons, one international and one domestic, stand out among the main causes for the focus on struggle today. One is the tendency which the Chinese see in the doctrines and policies of the Soviet and Yugoslav "modern revisionists" to soften the relationship between capitalist and socialist countries (ideas such as "the nature of capitalism has changed," "peaceful road to socialism in imperialist countries," etc.). What is the "peaceful coexistence" of the revisionists but a policy of compromise (with capitalism)? The Chinese see their historic role as opposing a new version of the revisionism that appeared in the doctrines of men like Edward Bernstein during a similar crisis in the Marxist camp at the turn of the century. The other reason is the fear of resurgent capitalism in China (demand for more private markets, for private enterprise, etc.) and other bourgeois tendencies indicating the continued presence of antiregime voices and the consequent need to keep the pressure up.

ON THE PROBLEMS OF INHERITING CHINA'S
PHILOSOPHICAL LEGACY

FUNG YU-LAN

Why do we want to inherit the philosophical legacy? Fundamentally, this question has already been answered—"to make the ancient serve the present." Recently, however, there have been

FROM Fung Yu-lan, "On the Problems of Inheriting China's Philosophical Legacy," *Che-hsüeh Yen-chiu* (*Philosophical Research*), 4 (July, 1965), 63–64. Translated by the editor.

doubts about this answer. Some of the questions raised recently are: Why have the ancient serve the present and how can the ancient serve the present? For example, a person who has studied the history of Chinese philosophy might feel that it is not useful in conducting the Socialist Education Movement. . . .

Why, then, do we want to inherit China's philosophical legacy? And, furthermore, how can we inherit it? The principle of critical inheritance, in concrete application, still is not without difficulties. This short essay intends to answer these two questions about inheriting the philosophical legacy. The first question relates to the goal in inheriting; the second relates to the methodology.

Actually, on the Cultural Revolution front in the last year, these two theoretical questions have already been answered. Taking the reform of Peking Opera as an illustration, originally many people believed that Peking Opera just sang of emperors, generals, talented officials, and feudal heroes. Separate it from these themes, and it would not be Peking Opera. However, after seeing *Red Lantern* or *Sha Chia Pang*, they realized that operas singing of contemporary revolutionary heroes not only still is Peking Opera but is also unfettered, improved Peking Opera. Themes of contemporary revolutionary heroes, cleverly combined with Peking Opera tunes, really are an improvement.

Peking Opera on contemporary themes still is Peking Opera. This is inheritance. The goal of inheritance is to have Peking Opera use national style to display socialist content. The method of inheritance is critically to utilize Peking Opera tunes, to cleverly adapt all good traditions for present use.

Actually, Chairman Mao's poetry already provides the best model for artistic creativity. Chairman Mao's poetry uses national style to display the highest standard of socialism and Communism.

In artistic creation, national style is more than just poetic meter. It also includes the diction, texts, stories, and other good traditions from the Chinese literary legacy. Chairman Mao's poetry is very regular in meter. Even more important, he uses all suitable diction, texts, and stories from China's literary legacy. . . .

Now do we not also need national style in philosophy? Of course we do. Chairman Mao in his "Oppose Party Formalism" called for comrades to read the four essays. Chairman Mao said:

The most recent essay is the report of the Sixth Party plenum on nationalization of propaganda. We said "Marxism separated from the special characteristics of China is just ivory-tower Marxism."

That is to say, we must avoid empty talk about Marxism. Rooted in the life of China, the Communist Party must study Marxism in connection with the realities of the Chinese revolution. . . . Foreign-style essays must cease, ivory-tower theorizing must be minimized, dogmatism must stop. These must be replaced by a fresh lively Chinese flavor and character that is welcomed by the masses. . . .

What we "propagate in a national style" is Marxism. Its propagation requires a national style. That is to say, it must be connected with the realities of the Chinese revolution. In propagating Marxism, we must adopt a Chinese flavor and character. Chinese flavor and character are precisely what "national style" means.

Do we have models for this? Of course we do. The works of Chairman Mao and Chairman Liu are models. We must study these models and see how our leaders do this.

Naturally, the first point is to study Marxism in connection with the specifics of the Chinese situation. This is fundamental, but we will not discuss that here in connection with inheriting the philosophical legacy.

The first thing we want to discuss here is how to adopt a Chinese flavor and character in propagating Marxism. Besides studying the language of the masses, we must study the language of the ancients. . . . In this, examples from Chairman Mao's writings are too numerous to mention. The most prominent is his use of the classical philosophical phrase "base actions on reality." . . .

Our second point is that we must relate to the problems raised in ancient philosophy. Thus, in his essay "On Practice," Chairman Mao uses the classical, philosophical terms "knowledge" and "action" in the subtitle. . . .

Our third point is that we should use stories from ancient philosophy to illustrate modern principles. Chairman Mao took the story of Yü Kung moving the mountain from *Lieh Tzu* to illustrate that the Chinese people definitely could move "the twin mountains of imperialism and feudalism that were crushing them." . . .

Finally, we must assimilate the experience of the ancients and adapt it for our use. . . .

I believe that the main function of inheriting the philosophical legacy is to "propagate in a national style." Artistic creation is propaganda; philosophical discussion also is propaganda. Each aspect of propaganda, if it has a national style, can be even more effective.

There are some people who want to take anything from the philosophical legacy, regardless of whether it is useful for Marxism. There are others who do not want to take anything from the philosophical legacy, who believe we do not have to inherit the philosophical legacy, who even believe there is no need to sort through and study it. Both of these views are one-sided.

V

Religion

1. CHINESE BUDDHISM:
BURIAL WITH SOME HONORS

For most of China's history, religion came far behind philosophy or history in social and intellectual prestige. Its status has not improved in Communist China. According to Holmes Welch's account of what has happened to Chinese Buddhism, the largest and most coherent religion of traditional China is well on its way to elimination as a living religious force. Though not overtly persecuted, its organization is so controlled by the government and its teachings have become so "reformed" that its continued survival as anything but a museum piece seems very problematical. The short article "Buddhism and Chinese Art and Culture" shows a good deal of why Buddhism qualifies for inclusion in the national museum. The third article in this chapter, by Joseph Levenson, discusses Taoism and other folk religions. His conclusion is much the same: burial with some nationalistic honors.

THE REINTERPRETATION OF CHINESE BUDDHISM

HOLMES WELCH

One basic element in the Buddhist tradition is withdrawal from the world in order to seek enlightenment through meditation and other religious exercises. Such exercises are hampered by family responsibilities and the necessity of earning a livelihood—

FROM Holmes Welch, "The Reinterpretation of Chinese Buddhism," *The China Quarterly*, 22 (April–June, 1965), 144–52. Reprinted by permission.

hence the development of monasteries. Withdrawal is never thought of as permanent but as a preparation for returning to the world and teaching others how to reach the same goals, that is, enlightenment or rebirth in the Western Paradise or release from birth and death.

Buddhist leaders in Communist China have reinterpreted these goals and denied that withdrawal from the world is a useful method of reaching them. The new view is best expressed, perhaps, by Reverend Chütsan in an article entitled "A Brief Discussion of the Future of Buddhism," published in Peking, in April, 1952. Reverend Chütsan was then a member of the National Committee of the CPPCC [Chinese People's Political Consultative Conference] and the editor-in-chief of *Modern Buddhism*, in which the article appeared. He became Deputy Secretary-General of the Chinese Buddhist Association when it was founded the next year. Since he was and is one of the two chief spokesmen of the official line on Buddhism in China, his words have special force:

To treat labor as a religious practice—this is something that ordinary Buddhists cannot accept. But let us ask them: What is the real goal of meditation, of reciting Buddha's name, and of other religious practices? If the goal is the purification of deeds, words, and thoughts, then how long does one have to carry on these practices before he can attain purity and when he has attained it, what comes next? Furthermore, if his goal is complete enlightenment, or release from birth and death, or rebirth in the Western Paradise, then what is this complete enlightenment? After he has been released from birth and death, what does he do then? After he has been reborn in the Western Paradise and looked with his own eyes upon Avalokitesvara, Mahastamaprapta, and Amitābha, then what? Unless these questions can be answered, religious practices can be carried on for a hundred thousand *kalpas* and they will be a waste of time. Let me tell you this: Enlightenment and apprehension do not lie somewhere far off. Only if you are willing to die can you be released from birth and death. Rebirth in the Western Paradise is for the sake of reforming this human world in the East. Purification of deeds, words, and thoughts must be pursued in the midst of action, trouble, and worry. It is to be sought here and now. There is no need to look elsewhere. In short, it is pernicious to talk about religious practices in isolation from everything in the concrete side of life, from carrying wood and drawing water, from all our acts and gestures. To talk about religious practices isolated from the masses of living creatures is like catching the wind and grasping at shadows. . . . Thus we can know that absolutely no one becomes a buddha while enjoying leisure in an ivory tower. Becoming a buddha in an ivory tower of leisure and contentment—this is just another pastime and opiate of landlords, bureaucrats, and petit bourgeois when they are surfeited with wine and food. It has nothing at all to do with Buddhism.

What this means when applied has been spelled out in other issues of *Modern Buddhism*. For example, release from the cycle of birth and death is to be sought through collectivization. "According to the Buddha's rule, when people become monks and nuns, they lead a collective life. Not only is there no private property, but there is no thought for oneself. To take thought for oneself is to keep hold of the ego. If this hold is not broken, there will be something to be born and die." A similar thought is that "with the system of private ownership eliminated, the roots of the three poisons—greed, anger, and stupidity, which are centered on personal advantage—are also eliminated."

As to the Western Paradise or Pure Land, in which most Chinese Buddhists hope to be reborn, it is being constructed right here on Earth by the Communist Party. The idea of the Western Paradise on Earth is not a new one. Some Buddhists have long believed that when a person becomes enlightened the drab objects of everyday life are transformed into the glittering jewels described in the Pure Land sutras, simply because his mental outlook has changed. The Communist interpretation is more materialistic:

> From now on, under the leadership of the People's government . . . since all the people will be producers—either directly through physical labor or indirectly through mental labor—food, clothing, housing, and transportation will be no problem. Everyone will cherish peace and treasure freedom. From now on, there will be no wars, no disasters. From now on, all the sufferings of human life will be eliminated forever. Does not this mean transforming our world into a peaceful, happy, free, and beautiful Pure Land? . . . The Vimalakirti-nirdesa Sutra says: "If you want to get the Pure Land, you must make your mind pure. Once the mind is pure, then the land becomes pure of its own accord." This tells us that if we want to turn our land into the Pure Land, the first step is for the masses of the people to purify their minds. The way to purify their minds is through remolding (*kai-tsao*), self-renewal (*tzu-hsin*), and straightening out of thoughts (*kai-t'ung szu-hsiang*). . . . Fellow Buddhists, rise up with your hearts set on the Western Paradise here in the world.

Some Buddhists abroad have expressed the fear that "purifying the mind" might mean "brainwashing." The Chinese have replied with ridicule. Only last year, an eminent Chinese monk told an English Buddhist:

> The Buddha taught us with special emphasis to "purify one's own mind" and to progress with unslackened energy. We do not understand why one who professes to be a follower of the Buddha should be so terrified by the term "remolding" and join in the clamor against it as "brainwashing." In fact, if dirt is found in one's thought (just as it is on one's body), what harm would it do to advise him to have a wash? . . . After all, the question is with regard to what things are to be washed off. . . . The things that we advise people to wash off are: concern for individual interests at the expense of the collective interests, concern for immediate interests at the expense of long term interests—in other words, lack of patriotism, disdainfulness toward the masses, and like thoughts that are concrete manifestations of greed, hatred, and stupidity.

"Disdainfulness toward the masses" means, of course, disdainfulness toward those who embody the will of the masses, that is, the Communist Party "Lack of patriotism" has an even wider meaning. A citizen is only patriotic if he participates in any and all the programs of the People's Government. But then why not participate in programs that will secure the Western Paradise on Earth? As Chao P'u-ch'u, the General Secretary of the Chinese Buddhist Association, said in 1955, "the first Five Year Plan is the initial blueprint for the Western Paradise here on earth," and the president of the same association echoed the thought by saying that when the plan was carried out, the Western Paradise on earth would be virtually realized.

What Buddhists, like other citizens, are expected to contribute to the Five Year Plan is productive labor. Accordingly, productive labor is called "nothing other than carrying out the bodhisattva vows," because "the highest form of bodhisattva conduct is to benefit all living creatures." (Thirty-four vows are formerly taken by monks and laymen who resolve to follow the path of the bodhisattva, that is, of the buddha-to-be. They include the usual prohibitions on killing, alcohol, and so on as well as minor points of etiquette like failing to bow to other Buddhists, but they do not include any vow to engage in productive labor.)

Another textual sanction is Pai-chang's rule for monks: "When you do not work, you shall not eat." The Communists interpret this to mean that, during the T'ang dynasty, monks did a full day's work in the fields like the peasants around them and that, therefore, the government is right in insisting that the monks do the same now. (What Pai-chang actually advocated was not full-time manual labor, but the kind of chores that monks in large monasteries have always done: cleaning and sweeping, helping out in the kitchen, in the vegetable garden, and in the construction of buildings, but seldom, if ever, cultivating staple crops like rice or wheat. The latter were usually left to hired help or tenant farmers. Otherwise, the monks could not have performed the five to fifteen hours a day of meditation and other religious exercises that the monastic rules prescribe.)

A third textual sanction for productive labor is a quotation attributed to the Buddha: "Amass wealth as if it were the dharma." This means, according to a monk from Chekiang, that Buddhists should increase production, practice austerity, and buy National Construction Bonds. Buying National Construction Bonds has also been compared to practicing the four virtues and the six paramitas of bodhisattva and carrying out Samantabhadra's vow to beautify the land and benefit all living creatures. Perhaps the high point in such comparisons came when Chao P'u-ch'u compared a speech of Chou En-lai to passages in the Lotus Sutra and the Avatamsaka Sutra. These sutras, according to Chao, stated that the bodhisattva must always be at the service of living creatures and, by the same token, be dependent on living creatures for his own spiritual development. He quotes a statement from the Avatamsaka Sutra that "no bodhisattva can attain the supreme enlightenment without living creatures." The implication is clearly that enlightenment cannot be won in isolation from the toiling masses. Similarly, in 1958, an editorial pointed out that the Buddhist principle of "doing no evil" was exemplified by wiping out the system of exploitation, the principle of "doing good to others" was exemplified by socialist construction, and the principle of "purifying one's own mind" was exemplified by the suppression of selfish thoughts of private gain.

The greatest difficulty for the Buddhist in China who has wished to participate in the government's programs has been that so many of them—the Korean War, for example—have required that he break the Buddha's first commandment, which forbids taking the life of any sentient creature. To make things easier for the patriotic Buddhist, this commandment, too, has been reinterpreted. Its new meaning is that Buddhists should not avoid killing bad people but only avoid killing good people. Killing bad people—like American imperialists—is good. This has been made clear in statement after statement by Buddhist leaders over the past fourteen years. Here, for example, is the argument used to explain away the doubts of some young monks who were being encouraged to join the militia: "Buddhist compassion is not without guiding principles. One has to be compassionate to good people, but if one is also compassionate to bad people, it will indirectly help evil people to do bad things. Therefore, Buddhism has the ancient precept: 'To kill evil people is a good resolve!' " No textual reference is given for this "ancient precept."

During the campaign to oppose America and aid Korea, a monk told a group of his brethren in Nanchang that:

> We Buddhists must unite as quickly as possible with other religions and completely support the Chinese Volunteer Army and the Korean People's Army. The best thing is to be able to join the army directly and to learn the spirit in which Shakyamuni, as the embodiment of pity and guide to buddhahood, killed robbers to save the people and suffered hardships in behalf of all living beings. To wipe out the American imperialist demons that are breaking world peace is, according to Buddhist doctrine, not only blameless but actually has merit.

Killing counterrevolutionaries is considered no less meritorious than killing imperialists. For example, in 1951, when a so-called bandit sought refuge in a small nunnery, the nuns urged him to surrender himself and at the same time discreetly sent word to the militia. When the militia arrived and surrounded the building, he made a dash for the river in the hope to get across it and escape, but he was shot dead. As *Modern Buddhism* commented approvingly:

> This shows that not only had the nuns firmly taken the people's side and sworn to destroy the enemies of the people but also that they understood the spirit of Buddhist compassion, namely that "to kill a bad person and save many good persons gives rise to great merit" and is the highest compassionate principle.

Compassion is indeed a very tricky business for Buddhists in China today. Not only is it wrong to be compassionate to bad people, but it is also wrong for bad people to be compassionate to anybody at all, because that might make them appear less bad. There was an amusing episode in 1951, before the editors of *Modern Buddhism* had reached a high level of political awareness. In their February issue they printed the suggestion that Buddhist landowners should "with a glad heart take all their land and tools and wholeheartedly give them to the People's Government for distribution to the peasants, thus giving the peasants their wish and gaining great merit." By the end of the year the editors had realized their error and advised readers that the suggestion had been a bad one because it "blurred class consciousness in the class struggle. The essence of land reform is for the peasant class to wage a revolutionary struggle against the class of feudal landowners. It is not a question of the landowners offering charity to the peasants." The Buddha, of course, opposed class distinctions, or distinctions of any kind, and preached charity by all creatures toward all creatures.

The Mahayana Buddhist withdraws from the world not only to avoid involvement in such distinctions but also because he considers that the world is empty or illusory. According to one Mahayana school, nothing is permanent or solid. According to another, everything in it is a mere projection of the mind. If that is the case, why bother to reform it? Such a view challenges materialism at its very foundations, and the Communists have responded sharply. Their response has been all the sharper, perhaps, because the Dharmalaksana School, which holds that the world is a mental projection, has won the largest following among the Chinese intellectuals over the past half century. One of the leaders of this school is Lu Ch'eng, a disciple of Ou-yang Ching-wu. Some people consider him to be the most eminent lay Buddhist scholar in China today. In 1955, a Buddhist journal in Shanghai was being suppressed for spreading counterrevolutionary propaganda. When Lu Ch'eng's turn came to stand up and be counted, he said that the editors of the offending journal had deceived people into:

> taking the path of passivity, pessimism, and escape from reality, in the belief that this was Buddhism. . . . They portrayed the real world as full of suffering, as empty and changeable, as a dream, a play, as if it were nonexistent and worthless, as if worldly things and Buddhism were thousands of miles apart. This is pure nonsense! When was Buddhist doctrine ever like this?

What an extraordinary passage! Lu Ch'eng knew perfectly well that Buddhist doctrine had always been like this, and to pretend that it had not was rewriting the history of Buddhist thought on a scale that leaves one open-mouthed. Of course, no one was taken in by this whistling in the dark, valiant as it was. In 1960, the president of the Chinese Buddhist Association said that most

Buddhists "have discarded their tolerant, transcendental, negative attitude of rejecting the world, *which has been handed down from the past,* and they have been stirred . . . into a 'positive attitude of entering the world' so that they have a completely new mentality."

Since 1958, the non-Marxist minority parties in China have been permitted to exist for one main purpose: to teach their members how to follow the leadership of the Communist Party and to educate them in Marxism. In the case of the Buddhists, there has been a difference: The Marxism in which they have been educated has been presented partly in Buddhist dress. This does not mean that the Chinese Communists find the dress attractive. As one of them recently stated:

We cannot hand the label of Marxist principles under the name of Confucius or any other ancient figure. . . . It is likely to lead people to the road of worshipping the ancients blindly. . . . To moderate the ideologies of the ancients and to say that there is almost no difference between them and Marxism and that they are something which transcends classes and time will result not in inheriting valuable things of ancient times but inevitably in affixing a proletarian label to the thought of the exploiting class.

Chinese, like Russian, Communists are critical of efforts to "polish up" Buddhism as something which is not in contradiction with Communism. "Anything of this nature is doomed to failure." They are unalterably opposed to ideological compromise with Buddhism or any other religion. We read in *Nationalities Unity:* "To think that religious belief and Communism are not contradictory . . . is obviously completely mistaken. . . . The religious world view is reactionary, antiscientific, antisocialist, and anti-Communist. . . . In a socialist society, it is now as before completely contrary to Communist thinking." Generally speaking, they have been content to write the history of ideas "straight," pointing out which ideas were progressive for their time, but being very careful to emphasize that what was progressive then may be reactionary now.

Why then have they allowed Buddhists to find sanction in Buddhist texts for what is stated much more explicitly in the works of Lenin and Mao? Why are Buddhist writers allowed to do what is supposed to be forbidden—that is, "to modernize the ideologies of the ancients" and to "polish up" Buddhism for use in a socialist country—so that the *Sukhavativyuha* has become, so to speak, background reading for the text of the Five Year Plan?

I cannot offer any wholly satisfactory explanation. No other body of traditional doctrine has received this doubtful compliment.

One reason is, I think, that Buddhism is the only traditional doctrine that still appeals to a large number of Chinese. The Republican period saw an impressive revival of Buddhist devotion and practice, whereas the other main Chinese religions, Confucianism and Taoism, lost ground. They had nothing comparable to the burgeoning Buddhist movement, with its newly founded schools, publishing houses, and lay Buddhist societies. The Communists, therefore, considered the Buddhists an important group to mobilize—important enough, at any rate, to give them their own national association, their own journal (*Modern Buddhism*), and a role to play in almost every mass movement. The people put in charge of these efforts were religious progressives who had a sense of identity as Buddhists but whose political and social ideals left them dissatisfied with Buddhism as it was. They wanted to change it as much as might be necessary to make it respectable in the world they lived in, even if this meant changing it to the point where it was no longer Buddhism: No matter, they thought, it could still be *called* Buddhism.

The reinterpretation of Buddhist doctrine, then, was largely voluntary; but it was stimulated by the socialization of China and permitted by the Communist Party (which might, of course, have forbidden it) because the continued existence of Buddhism could be used as evidence of the constitutional guarantee of freedom of religious *belief* (freedom of religious *activity* is not guaranteed). Furthermore, Party leaders were, if anything, more nationalistic than the Nationalists, and Buddhism has contributed to Chinese culture. Finally, and most important of all, Buddhism provides a useful tool for the political penetration of Southeast Asia.

BUDDHISM AND CHINESE ART AND CULTURE
CH'Ü CHUNG

As Buddhism was introduced into China, it came into contact with many elements of ancient Chinese culture such as literature, art, architecture, sculpture, printing, phonology, astronomy, medicine, and philosophy.

In literature, Buddhist translations enriched our language by

FROM Ch'ü Chung, "Buddhism and Chinese Art and Culture," *Kuang-ming Jih-pao* (Peking) (June 12, 1962). Translated by the editor.

introducing many Buddhist terms. China's famous writers since the fourth and fifth centuries have frequently used the elegant words of Buddhist scriptures in their poems, songs, and other writings. These were warmly welcomed by the people. Many kinds of Buddhist stories had a close connection with popular literature. Similarly moving stories from Buddhist scriptures often became subjects for paintings by great artists. . . .

In architecture and sculpture, a large number of the extant pieces of ancient Chinese architecture are Buddhist monuments. The Brick Pagoda of Sungyüeh Temple in Honan, Nanch'an Temple in Shansi, the T'ang dynasty, wooden construction Fu-kuang Temple, and so on are all precious surviving monuments for studying ancient Chinese architecture. . . . There were progressive thinkers, such as Li Cho-wu of the Ming dynasty and T'an Ssu-t'ung of the Ch'ing dynasty, who used the anti-oppression strain in Buddhism to challenge feudal ethics and morality. . . .

In a word, Buddhism has been very closely bound to Chinese culture since its introduction almost 2,000 years ago. Those cultural objects and relics preserved through Buddhism are our country's precious cultural legacy. Therefore we must consolidate this cultural legacy by assimilating the essence and discarding the dross.

2. TAOISM AND OTHER RELIGIONS: ANOTHER FAREWELL

THE COMMUNIST ATTITUDE TOWARD RELIGION

JOSEPH R. LEVENSON

As a Chinese, the Chinese Communist never lets the West forget the Opium War—a sinister name. As a Communist, the Chi-

FROM Joseph R. Levenson, "The Communist Attitude Towards Religion," in Werner Klatt (ed.), *The Chinese Model* (Hong Kong: Hong Kong University Press, 1965), pp. 19–20, 22–25, and 29–30. Reprinted by permission of the publisher.

nese Communist never forgets a sinister metaphor—"opium of the masses": religion. In the last analysis, there is nothing to say in its favor. Religion is idealistic and hence in its view antiscientific; it is a slavery of the mind, a relic of outworn social systems, and will vanish when exploitation ends. But the last analysis is not so easy to reach. There are several steps before the last, before the simple anathema, and the Chinese past—not just the Communist will —affects the Chinese Communist's thinking on the problem of religion.

To begin with, the Chinese literati, whose temper was deeply conservative, were leaders in the old imperial society (*feudal* in the Communist lexicon). And the literati by and large had never been happy about religion. Popular rebellions, which they hated, usually seemed to be fired with Taoist, Buddhist, Muslim, Christian, or syncretic enthusiasm. From a Confucian point of view, religion could be a dangerous stimulant to the masses rather than an opiate. Therefore from a Chinese Communist's point of view as well, its status is ambiguous.

The Communists see themselves at a point of historical synthesis. They are true to the dialectic and true to a modern Chinese need for an antitraditional yet still a Chinese history. "Antifeudal," they mean to relegate Confucian China firmly to the past —"anti-imperialist," they mean to repel that other foe of Confucian China, the West. Accordingly, a "people's tradition" comes in for loving care. Nonliterati and non-Western, it has obvious points in its favor. But premodern and pre-Communist, it can hardly be taken as the last word, or what would the Communists' occupation be? Hence, religion as a popular expression, nonliterati, often antiliterati, wins a kind of indulgence; but it also awaits a final dismissal. That is what Mao implied in 1927, when he declared, "Buddha was erected by the peasants." This had a nice ambiguity. It was an argument for gradualism, for at least a passing respect for a "people's religion." And it was an argument, ultimately, for atheism. . . .

Because Christianity was foreign, it was doomed to be cast off as a "feudal" sacrifice. It served as a parallel to native, outmoded Confucianism. But indigenous religions were affected otherwise by the fate of Confucianism, fate of the high culture (of the highly placed) brought low. On the whole, these religions belonged to the lowly placed and were traditionally disdained as culturally low. Therefore, antitraditionalists had to revise the estimate. Confucianism, when challenged by the West of the "imperialists," had to be defended, if only by a *tu quoque*, the spurning of Christianity. But Confucianism, cherished by the "feudalists," had to be challenged at home. At least, modest respect had to be paid to the creeds of those whom the "feudalists" exploited.

The Communists preferred historically identifiable creeds, which could be retired honorably to "historical significance," praised for their past in the Marxist historical process, but properly beached upstream. Taoism and Buddhism, somewhat artificially abstracted from eclectic religious life, answered this description better than the congeries of popular cultic practices. These, having no known beginnings, looked intractably as though they might have no end, and Communist patience became rather frayed. More as a matter of tactics than of friendly appreciation, Communist political workers, during the war against Japan, were told to respect the religious beliefs of the popular secret societies. After their victory in the civil war, Communist authorities were less benign. People like *yin-yang* experts and fortune-tellers and spirit-mediums were put down; after 1958 especially, the ancestor cult was seriously discouraged. There was still some grain of acceptance for "religion of the masses." But there was a rising note of menace against the "use of religion by the reactionary class."

Religious Taoism, while certainly no smooth-working ecclesiastical machine, had more of a visible structure than the amorphous cults and more of a line of history. Thus, there was something for the regime to see, to organize bureaucratically, and to historicize intellectually.

Earlier in the twentieth century, in Chinese radical circles, popular Taoism was usually written off as an excrescence of the old society. It was taken to be an incubus of ignorance, a backward, antiscientific mystagogy. And there was a tendency to see Taoism, socially, as a refuge for failures in "feudal" society, an escapist corollary to exploitative Confucianism.

But Communist victory over "feudal" society (or "semifeudal, semicolonial") brought the chance, and the need, to soften the tone. Once the grip of the leaders of the old society, at both its higher and lower levels, was broken, the passions of the struggle to break it might be allowed to cool and old ideas be relativized to history. The very moribundity of Taoism made it acceptable for *historical* rehabilitation, now that its dead hand had been shaken off the present. Commentators on Taoism began to find in it not so much depressing quietism but rousing rebellious action, not just superstitious magic but the seeds, and some of the fruits, of science.

There was really something to work on here. The aim of classical, philosophical Taoism was mystic union with eternal Tao, the first principle of all things, eternal, impersonal, immanent in all. But popular Taoism, prominent since Han times, emphasized the physical, and one can see in it a set of physical parallels and parodies of the philosophical concepts. All sorts of dietetic, respiratory, and alchemical practices abounded.

The latter were most important for attracting modern sympathy. There had been a long search for ways to transform elements of matter, in hopes of finding an elixir of life. This included such efforts as to arrive at the *essence* of gold—that is, to separate its immanent *tao* from dross, so as to get a potable form of underlying reality. And there was another sort of alchemy, to the same end: the effort to produce "life-preserving" substances like jade and cinnabar artificially, to release them from the inhibiting "impurities" of their natural state. From here it was not far to secular goals like those of Western alchemy and protochemistry, such as efforts to make gold from baser metals. That is how the affinities of science in China came to be mainly popular-Taoist. It was quite consistent of Confucianism, looking with such fearful scorn on Taoist religious enthusiasm, to be a drag on science as well. And it was quite consistent of Communism also to turn Confucian scorn into Communist indulgence.

Indulgence, however, is something that a superior dispenses. There could be no question of Taoism renewing claims to pre-eminence. For science, the saving title that restored the Taoist reputation, had become an ideal of Communists in a context of antitraditionalism, both anti-Confucian and anti-Taoist. The Communists had to feel, first, that they had succeeded in crushing Taoism, that it was now a thing of the past. Then it could have its place in a gallery of national achievements, its *early* place, with *early* science, while Marxists took over these latter days. When Taoism (and other products of the past) could be smoothed out of life and into a still museum, the Communists would own the living present. Only when Taoism was exorcized from history—that is, from a claim to affect the future—could it be put back in history; and then it was really back, to a place of harmless honor in the people's past.

In short, Marxist relativism makes Taoism at best a progressive force in a historical stage. It must be an anachronism in the present, and the regime suppresses Taoist claims to be accepted now on grounds of absolute value. Communist policy is quite in line with Communist interpretation: Contemporary Taoists have been given the spades to dig their grave in history. A Taoist Association exists. What is it to do? It decided in 1961 to compile the history of the Taoist religion. It took charge of Taoist monuments. And so the Taoist temples, no longer active and therefore no longer nests of "deceivers," have ceased to be "feudal" in the sense of moralistic epithet; they are feudal just in the nomenclature of "scientific history." A temple is not a disgrace but an antique. Communists, instead of exhorting the masses to crush the infamy, urge them to preserve the relics. That is crushing enough. . . .

The Communists mean to save their history by using an idea of history. As ostensibly scientific moderns, postmedieval or post-Confucian, they claim the future for their history at least as much as Europeans do: The latter, indeed, in their eyes, are not as post-medieval or post-Christian as they ought to be. And just as the chances of Christianity in China were affected by the Chinese inner intellectual struggle, so Taoism and Buddhism and the popular cults are affected. In a grudging way, Marxist history en-nobles them. They make an alternative Chinese history (which Christianity could never do) to weigh against the class-tainted Confucian great tradition. But they not only make a history in the new Communist reading. They lie stranded in history, put out of their modern misery by being consigned to the past. As a Communist, the Chinese Communist is ready enough to bid farewell to religion. As a Chinese, for the Chinese specimens, he may stretch to hail and farewell. But still, farewell.

VI

Language and Literature

---

1. REFORM OF THE WRITTEN LANGUAGE

So far, the museum metaphor has stood up fairly well in our description of the motivations behind Communist cultural policy. We now turn, however, to aspects of the cultural legacy for which it seems less appropriate. Language, literature, art, theater —all these belong in the world of the living, not behind museum glass with the relics of the dead. Thus, in these areas it has not been possible to honor while ignoring the cultural legacy. The problem has been how to inherit the legacy of the past critically and fuse it with the culture of the present. Historical relativism— praise for the past, but only in the past, not for present emulation —cannot provide a solution.

The practical present-day problems of the cultural legacy are nowhere more pressing than in the Chinese written language. The ideographic script was both the glory of Confucian culture and the cement that held it together over an area larger than Europe for more than 2,000 years. It is still the chief symbol and essence of what is Chinese, but it is a poor tool for modern mass-scientific culture. Professor C. P. Fitzgerald, an eminent historian of ancient China, discusses the content and significance of Communist language policy. Chou En-lai's authoritative report on language reform follows. In the decade since this was given, no further steps have been taken away from the ideographic script.

FLOOD TIDE IN CHINA
C. P. FITZGERALD

The belief that the Chinese Communists intended to undermine and finally destroy the traditional culture of their country was

FROM C. P. Fitzgerald, *Flood Tide in China* (London: Cresset Press, 1958), pp. 147–53. Copyright © 1958 by Cresset Press. Reprinted by permission of the publisher.

122

supported by alleged evidence that they also intended, as a means to this end, to reform the written language, abolish the use of the Chinese ideographic script, and introduce an alphabetic system, probably the Russian Cyrillic or some new form derived from that prototype. It is certainly true that some such reform was mooted in Communist circles and had its ardent advocates. However, this idea was neither new nor specifically Communist. Ever since the original revolution of 1911 against the monarchy, there have been groups of Chinese intellectuals, usually the foreign-educated, who urged such a reform. Many foreigners, who did not themselves read Chinese, and a few who did, supported the idea. It was argued that no real widespread popular education, and thus no true democracy, was possible if children had to spend years learning how to read and write; no scientific advance could be hoped for if all the literature had to be written in ideographic script which cannot employ foreign, and therefore scientific, terms except in a clumsy and inaccurate transcription into Chinese characters having only a vague correspondence in sound with the foreign words.

These are serious objections, and they were not the only ones. Chinese ideographs are often complicated and hard to both memorize and reproduce in writing. Their use has produced a double language, spoken and written, often very unlike. For the ideographs, standing for ideas and not for sounds, enable a sentence to be written very tersely, whereas speech is more diffuse, and thus written Chinese was widely different from the colloquial language, which in turn was never written as it was spoken. It was argued that only the innate conservatism of the Chinese made them cling to a system which was cumbersome and archaic.

Recent events have cast some doubt on the theory that the Chinese are an inherently conservative people. The objections to the ideographic script also ignored the very strong arguments in its favor. The first of these is that the script, standing for sense and not for sound, is independent of dialect variations in the spoken language. Just as the Arabic numerals, used by all European peoples, convey the meaning but not the sounds of the words which in the various languages denote the numbers, so the Chinese ideograph, on an identical principle, gives the meaning but not the sound of the word. A newspaper article written in Peking can be read with equal ease by those who see it in Canton or Foochow, although if these readers were to speak the words aloud the Peking author of the article would not understand a word of what was said. The unity of the Chinese people, in spite of the very diverse dialects in the southern provinces and minor but important speech variations in other parts of a vast country, has been preserved very largely by the fact that there was but one written language equally intelligible to all who could read, even if utterly closed to all who could not.

Secondly, the written language was also very largely independent of time. The most ancient literature, of the first millennium B.C., may indeed present considerable difficulty to those who have not made a special study of it, but even this archaic literature is more easily read by a Chinese scholar than Chaucer would be by an English student. The Chinese literature of the later ages, from the Han period (200 B.C.) onward is substantially identical in style with the literary language used until modern times. Chinese literature has thus a greater and closer continuity than any other and is more easily accessible to the modern educated person than the old literature of any other culture.

Further, it is not in fact necessary for children to spend many years learning the classical style of writing before they can read at all. If this was so under the empire, it was because the educational system was designed to make reading and writing a difficult and distinguished accomplishment reserved to a scholar class. Since the republic, and long before the Communists came to power, popular education had been modernized and simplified. It was found possible to teach children and illiterates 1,000 or even fewer characters in the first place, make books and newspapers which used this more limited vocabulary, and, having thus started the pupil with a "basic Chinese," enable him to increase his range by progressive exercises, or simply by reading more widely. Educational reform on these lines had already sharply reduced illiteracy, especially in the great cities where it was more fully operative, well before the Japanese invasion. The main handicap to universal literacy was not the ideographic script but the lack of teachers and schools for the peasant millions.

It had long been accepted that the Chinese ideographs were often written in an unnecessarily complicated form, another consequence of the old exclusive attitude to literacy. In common practice, though not in print, people used many abbreviated forms, some of which had been current for centuries. There was no real reason, other than academic conservatism, why these simpler forms should not be made general and used in all script. This might make the reading of old books more difficult, but new editions could be printed in the modern form and in fact in the third century B.C. Chinese script had at least once undergone such a major reform, the older form of script having since that time been reserved for seals and fancy inscriptions, much as Gothic script still lingers in English usage.

The disadvantages of abandoning the ideographic script were thus very formidable. It would mean a serious blow at the cultural unity of the nation. Whole provinces in the South would be divided from the rest of the nation, and from each other, even further among themselves, by new languages, written as well as spoken. It was obvious that such a development might have political as well as cultural consequences. The literature of the past would be lost. Even if, at an immense cost of trouble and work, this literature was transcribed into a romanized or a Cyrillic script, it could not but be transformed in the process, since the old literature, in its terse classical style, was simply not susceptible of transcription into modern Chinese. It would need to be paraphrased as well as transcribed, in a word, rewritten. This made it obvious that no such immense task would ever in fact be accomplished.

The critics and opponents of the Communist regime were acutely aware of this problem; they feared that if the talked-of reform of the script meant the introduction of an alphabet, one of the great attractions of such a change for revolutionary Communists would be precisely the ease with which they could wipe out the literature of the past and only reproduce such small part of it as suited their purposes. Tocsins of alarm sounded across the Strait of Formosa and were echoed in anguish in the universities of Europe and America.

Meanwhile the Communist Party and government were approaching this problem with wary caution. Undoubtedly, they saw all the disadvantages of the ideographic script, and they were also well aware of the uses for propaganda purposes of an alphabet. Equally, they cannot have ignored the dangers of provincial separatism, the threat to national unity—to the ideal of "All China"—in any proposal to abandon the ideographs. How far they felt respect and affection for some part at least of the ancient cultural heritage can be gauged from their subsequent policy. After the capture of Peking and the establishment of the People's Republic, they set up a commission of expert linguists to advise and report on the problem of language reform. The impression prevailed in Chinese academic circles that the commission had instructions to go very thoroughly into the question, to take its time

—if not to waste it—and thus to allow a cooling-off period to elapse while the government took stock of the problem. The commission did not report for six years.

Long before that it was already clear that the main decision in favor of a less drastic reform had already been, in effect, taken. The campaigns against illiteracy, based on the established method of teaching a limited vocabulary, the "Thousand Character Mass Education Movement," which had been initiated soon after World War I, were pressed forward with the far greater resources and superior organization which the People's Republic could command. The movement to simplify the script and use abbreviated characters for all purposes arose first among the civil servants and secretaries of the administration, men pressed for time and working long hours. As a very eminent member of the government put it, "My secretaries began using these abbreviated forms, and although I cannot always easily read them, it is no use protesting, so we thought it better to make them widely known so that they can become the established forms." The movement thus obtained official approval and was launched with all the weight and energy of the system of persuasion behind it. The reform is not so radical as to make the older, elaborate forms of the characters wholly obsolete, although it is certain that the more complicated of these will fall out of ordinary use; future generations who are taught the new forms would find that an old text presented the same kind of difficulty as sixteenth-century spelling does to the modern English reader. Equally, there is nothing to prevent the republication of old texts in the new simplified characters, just as, say, a modern edition of the Paston Letters need not keep the original spelling.

The decision to retain but simplify the ideographic script did not remove the need to find some more practical method of rendering foreign words and names than the clumsy approximations used in the past. A system which could only render the word "Russia" by using characters which are read with the sounds "ou-lo-ssu" has always been a grave handicap in Chinese historical and other literature in which foreign words and names must be mentioned. The practice of interposing the foreign name in Latin script was sometimes employed, but the disadvantage which limited this practice was the fact that Chinese is normally written in vertical columns, from top to bottom, and from right to left on the page. The Latin script word had thus to be printed sideways, and the page turned round to read it: printers greatly disliked the inconvenience of this device.

At an interview given to members of an Australian Cultural Delegation which visited Peking in May, 1956, the Prime Minister, Chou En-lai, explained the policy which had been adopted to deal with this and kindred problems of language reform. It had been decided to use an alphabet as a secondary script for writing foreign names, words such as internationally used scientific terms, and as an aid to teaching illiterates the Chinese ideographs. The question of what alphabet to adopt had been thoroughly discussed, and the decision had been that the Roman or Latin script should be used, "because it is the most widespread in the world today." Some dispute still prevailed as to whether this system of romanization should employ all the twenty-six Latin letters or discard some of them or add a few to their number to meet the peculiarities of Chinese pronunciation. To facilitate the use of the romanized script for these limited purposes, it had been decided that, in future, written Chinese would be printed in horizontal lines, from left to right, following the practice of Western literature, which, the Prime Minister pointed out, had other practical advantages of speed and convenience. The new romanization, when finalized, would also become the official form in which all Chinese names and words would be rendered in foreign languages, maps, and publications.

If any further reform should one day prove advisable, it could safely be left to future generations to decide, for no wholesale change of script was either possible or desirable in the foreseeable future. He pointed out that a prerequisite of further changes would be a unification of the spoken language, which was far from attained at present. It was the policy of the government to promote the use of what is now called *pu-t'ung hua*, standard speech, which he defined as the educated speech of Peking. This speech is, in effect, what was formerly called *kuan hua*, official speech, or, by foreigners, Mandarin. The use of standard speech is spreading fast and under the former name of "National Speech" had already in nationalist times made great headway among the dialect-speaking population of the South and the Overseas Chinese.

Modern means of mass communication, the wireless, and the cinema, which use standard speech, had greatly aided this development, and the fact that the Japanese forbade the teaching of it in the occupied areas of South China and Southeast Asia made the southern Chinese and their overseas relatives all the more enthusiastic pupils. Nevertheless, it will be many years, if ever, before the great southern dialects die out or even before the huge rural population of those provinces become bilingual. The present policy of republishing the classical and historical literature of China in the new format, but with the ideographic script unchanged or slightly simplified, is evidence in itself that there is no expectation of a sudden change to a romanized script or any intention to allow the old literature to perish through neglect.

CURRENT TASKS OF REFORMING
THE WRITTEN LANGUAGE

CHOU EN-LAI

The third task is to draw up and popularize the scheme for a Chinese phonetic alphabet. It should be made clear at the outset that the scheme is to annotate the characters phonetically and to popularize the common speech. It is not to replace the Chinese characters. Its first function is to give the pronunciation of these characters.

The second function of the scheme is to transcribe the common speech, serving as a useful means of teaching and learning the common speech. In learning the common speech, listening and repeating are not enough. One easily forgets. To attain good results, it is necessary to have a set of phonetic symbols which can be used to compile phonetic reading material and pronouncing dictionaries so that learners may refer to them to correct their pronunciation.

The third function of the scheme for a Chinese phonetic alphabet is to serve as a common basis on which the various national minorities may create or reform their written languages. Of the nearly fifty nationalities in China, a large number still have no written language of their own. Some of them have written languages which need improvement. Among those nationalities having written languages, besides the Hans who have Han characters, there are the nationalities who use the Tibetan alphabet, Mongolian alphabet, Arabic alphabet, Korean Unmun alphabet, or other kinds of alphabet. What kind of alphabet should be used as a basis

FROM Chou En-lai, "Current Tasks of Reforming the Written Language" (speech to meeting sponsored by the National Committee of the Chinese People's Political Consultative Conference, January 10, 1958), *Reform of the Chinese Written Language* (Peking: Foreign Languages Press, 1958), pp. 17, 19–22, and 26–28.

when our brother nationalities create or reform their written languages? Can the Han characters be taken as a common basis for the written languages of the various nationalities? Such an attempt was made years ago; it failed, proving that this was impractical. If each of the several tens of nationalities should adopt an alphabet of its own, it will hamper mutual learning and exchange of experience among them. It will also necessitate the making of different sets of printing, typing, and telegraphic equipment which will adversely affect the development of their culture and education. Many nationalities have expressed the hope that they will adopt the same alphabet as the Han people to facilitate cultural exchange, the learning of the Han language, and the adoption of Han terminology and technical terms.

The fourth function of the scheme is to help foreigners to learn Chinese and thus to promote international cultural exchange. As China's position in international affairs is rising with each passing day, more and more people, and primarily the people of our fraternal socialist countries and the friendly Asian and African countries, desire to learn Chinese. The great difficulty they encounter is the characters, and they feel that the task is hopeless. Now we have a scheme for a phonetic alphabet. We can use this alphabet to compile textbooks, dictionaries, and other reading materials for the people of other countries to learn Chinese. This will help them overcome difficulties.

The scheme also has other uses. For example, it can be used to transliterate the names of foreign persons and places and scientific and technological terms and the names of Chinese persons and places in documents, books, and newspapers dealing with other countries and to compile indices, etc.

It is not an exaggeration to say that, considering the uses we have listed, the formulation of the scheme for a Chinese phonetic alphabet is a great event in the cultural life of the Chinese people.

Will the adoption of the Latin alphabet in the scheme for a Chinese phonetic alphabet be inconsistent with the feeling of patriotism of the Chinese people? Can we not devise an alphabet ourselves or continue to use the *chu-yin tse-mu* (phonetic transcript)? Starting in 1952, the Committee for Reforming the Chinese Written Language spent nearly three years in an attempt to create an alphabet—including the revision of the *chu-yin tse-mu*. The attempt had to be given up as no satisfactory result could be obtained. The Latin alphabet was then adopted. At present, more than sixty countries use the Latin alphabet as symbols for writing, including Britain, France, Germany, Italy, Spain, the Netherlands, Denmark, Sweden, Norway, Albania, Hungary, Poland, Czechoslovakia, Romania, Vietnam, Indonesia, and three Union members of the U.S.S.R.—Estonia, Latvia, and Lithuania. In adopting the Latin alphabet, these countries make necessary adjustments and improvements to suit the needs of their own national languages. So, the Latin alphabet has become the alphabet of each nation's own alphabet. In another respect, we can say that the Latin alphabet is a set of symbols of international usage, and no country can claim it as its own. We cannot say that Frenchmen use the English alphabet any more than we can say that Englishmen use the French alphabet. We can say only that Frenchmen use the French alphabet and the Englishmen use the English alphabet. Likewise, when we adopt the Latin alphabet, in which we make necessary adjustments to suit the needs of the Chinese language, it becomes the phonetic alphabet of our language and is no longer the alphabet of ancient Latin, still less the alphabet of any foreign country. An alphabet is a means of transcribing pronunciation. We make it serve us just as we make trains, steamships, automobiles, and airplanes serve us. (And, from the point of origin, all these are imported.) It is also like using Arabic numerals for counting and calculating, the Gregorian calendar and the Christian era for recording the year, kilometers for measuring distance, and kilograms for measuring weight. The adoption of the Latin alphabet will, therefore, not harm the patriotism of our people.

One remaining question with which we are all much concerned is the future of Chinese characters. We all agree that as a written record they have made an immortal contribution to history. As to whether or not they will remain permanently unchanged, whether they will change on the basis of their original forms, or whether they will be replaced by a phonetic language—Latin letters or other phonetic scripts—we need not draw a hasty conclusion. Any language is, however, subject to change, as evidenced by the changes of the characters in the past. There will be changes in the future. We can also say that there will be a day when the languages— written and spoken—of the different peoples of the world will gradually become one and the same. The trend in the development of the languages of mankind is that they gradually approach one another until, at long last, there will be no wide difference. This is a good and not a bad anticipation. As to what scheme will be adopted, it is too early to hazard [a guess]. On the question of the future of the Chinese language, there may be various views. We can bring them out for discussion and debate. I shall not dwell upon it any further since it does not fall within the scope of the task of the language reform.

2. NATIONAL FORM IN LITERATURE

Ever since their days in Yenan, the Chinese Communists have been concerned that their new literature maintain a distinctively Chinese style. This meant retaining or borrowing from many of the forms of traditional literature. The motivation behind this policy has been both practical—in the sense of promoting a literature that the masses can understand—and nationalistic. Cyril Birch traces this policy back to well before 1949 and provides examples from Communist literature.

CHINESE COMMUNIST LITERATURE: THE PERSISTENCE OF TRADITIONAL FORMS

CYRIL BIRCH

What pessimistic observers have lamented as the collapse of Chinese civilization is exactly the necessary undermining and erosion without which there could not have been a regeneration of an old civilization. . . . The product of this rebirth looks suspiciously occidental. But scratch the surface and you will find that the stuff of which it is made is essentially the Chinese bedrock which much weathering and corrosion have only made stand out more clearly— the humanistic and rationalistic China resurrected by the touch of the scientific and democratic civilization of the new world.

If this statement of Hu Shih's is applied specifically to the literary works of the years following 1917, it will be found substantially true. Time and again, we shall recognize the basic concerns, the

FROM Cyril Birch, "Chinese Communist Literature: The Persistence of Traditional Forms," *The China Quarterly*, 13 (Jan.–March, 1963), 74–80, 83–84, and 86–91. Reprinted by permission.

mode of thinking, and even some of the literary techniques of the work we are examining to be essentially Chinese in character. What at first glance seemed to be a thoroughgoing westernization of the entire mentality of a writer turns out in fact to be no more than incidental. He has borrowed a set of devices to help him escape from a literary convention he feels as a stultifying dead weight. But his mind is at grips with the central problems of his own life and society as he sees them, and, as he writes, he appropriates and reconditions even the devices he has borrowed so that they too become assimilated into Chinese literary experience. J. D. Chinnery's study of Lu Hsün's *Madman's Diary* is an acute recognition of this fact. Or we could look at the first sentence of Lu Hsün's *My Native Place* [*Ku-hsiang*]: "Braving the severity of winter, I returned to the native place between myself and which had lain more than 2,000 li of land, more than twenty years of time." Nothing could differ more sharply from the opening to the Chinese short story such as we know it from the past, with its dating, location, and identification of characters deliberately reminding us of the official historiographer. We should have here, we imagine, a first-person narrative in the European introspective vein. Yet, *My Native Place* is in fact hardly a story at all, though perhaps the finest thing written in modern Chinese. "In its gentle lyricism," as C. T. Hsia says, "[it] approaches the reminiscent personal essay." The opening sentence is indeed exactly the kind of personal reference we find so helpful an introduction to many a classical poem.

My own recent attempts to analyze the metrical patterns of the New Verse of the 1920's, particularly those of Hsu Chih-mo, strengthen my inclination to accept Hu Shih's contention that "scratch the surface and you will find that the stuff of which it is made is essentially the Chinese bedrock."

Yet the addiction to foreign modes of expression was precisely what drew the heaviest fire of the Communist critics. The "foreign eight-legged essay" was a tendency to be rooted out and destroyed. "Foreign-slanted pedantry and obscurantism must be abolished, hollow and abstract clichés must be discouraged, and dogmatism must be arrested so that a fresh and vivid Chinese style and manner, of which the Chinese masses are fond, may take their place," as Mao Tse-tung said in a speech in 1938. With every intensification of Party control, these sentiments are echoed and elaborated: Witness Lao She, twenty years later at the time of the Great Leap Forward, on the importance of purity of diction:

Section six (of what I mean by "foreign eight-legged essay"):
speaking in a foreign language. That is, refusing to use language
which is there ready for you but insisting on imitating the Chinese
of a foreigner. In Chinese, "backing" is enough for "carry on the
back"; you don't have to say "carry on the back," because if the
thing rests on your shoulder this is "shouldering," if it's under your
arm this is "clutching," and there's no risk of confusion. I hope our
writers, especially young writers, will go and learn more of the
nature of Chinese. The study of classical works can be of great
help here.

The "Chinese style and manner, of which the Chinese masses
are fond" were embodied in a host of productions which utilized
forms resuscitated from popular, folk, and local literary traditions.
There is no space here even to list the principal new specimens of
these many genres, of "oral tales," "quick patter ballads," "drum
songs," or of the innumerable types of "local dramas." J. Prusek's
Die Literatur des befreiten China und ihre Volkstraditionen
covers a wide sampling of the productions of the 1940's. One
highly acclaimed novelty was the *yangko* play, which incorporated
the Shensi peasants' "rice-planting dance" and various popular
song forms into an otherwise spoken drama: The success of the
White-haired Girl inspired numerous imitations.

The shorter genres, referred to as "literary side-arms," had the
advantage of reflecting topical interests with great speed. Sputnik
I was launched in October, 1957. In November appeared a ballad
of the Szechuan "cart-lamp" type with the intriguing title "The
Artificial Satellite Stirs Up the Palace of Heaven." In my translation of the following passages from this piece, I try to suggest the
homespun quality of the original.

(When Sputnik enters heaven, the Jade Emperor in alarm con-
sults the various spirits, who confess themselves powerless to deal
with the intruder or with the mortals who are responsible for it):

In Magic Mist Hall, commotion over all,
Worthies civil and military consult with each other.
The Jade Emperor summons up the spirits to report:
Should not troops be sent at once to deal with all this bother?
With Father Thunder, Mother Lightning kneels in the Cinnabar
    Court:
"We've lost our trick of scaring them, I and this my brother.
No use laying on a five-peal thunderstorm—
There they are with lightning-rods to keep them safe from harm."
Uncle Wind, Master Rain next made report:

"Mortals now have weather forecasts, fast and accurate,
  and they've planted groves of trees to keep the cloudbursts out."

(Not only can the spirits do little now from their vantage point in heaven; their earthly representatives are themselves having a thin time of it):

The Kitchen God said, "The more I think of it, the more I feel depressed:
In the past the well-to-do gave me a daily feast,
Even poor people, short of clothes to wear and food to eat,
At all the proper seasons paid their respects at least.
But nowadays, with everyone well-fed and properly dressed,
They've no use for a Kitchen God, they've chased me from my nest."

(Hearing this and other descriptions of the new state of affairs in the socialist heaven-on-earth, various former residents of earth plan to return. Each of the Eight Immortals in turn is found a niche in the new society. Li T'ieh-kuai, for instance, whose spirit had to be content with a moldy corpse for a lodging when his own body was inadvertently cremated, will now have his leg reset in the People's Hospital. Then):

Even more delighted was the fairy Ch'ang-o;
The Palace of the Moon had long been too cold for her.
Hearing that the moon would be the first objective in space,
She hung the halls with lanterns, and set out pots of cassia by the gate.

                    .   .   .

But when to the Palace of Nine Splendors came the messageboy,
Yang Kuei-fei, the Honored Consort, nearly died of joy.
Ages ago she'd perfected the score of "Rainbow Jacket and Feathered Skirt,"
Ready to share with connoisseurs of music here on earth.
The fairy Ch'ang-o and Yang Kuei-fei whispered their plan to each other:
Hand-in-hand they would come among mortals, to find each of them a handsome young lover, a handsome young lover.

Obviously, while conveying a suitable propaganda message, a contemporary writer can at the same time get a lot of fun out of elements of the popular tradition of the past. And if we now turn to a writer like Chao Shu-li, who has received as much acclaim as anyone over the last twenty years, it becomes very apparent that he is at his best when he assumes most consciously and consistently the role of the storyteller, in quite the traditional style. It is in accord with this style that he puts himself into direct contact with the reader, soon after the start of the *Ballads of Li Yu-ts'ai:*

> Since the war, there have been a good many changes in the village of Yen-chia-shan, and, as these changes have taken place, Li Yu-t'sai has composed new ballads about them. As a matter of fact, it was because of these ballads that he got himself into trouble. I thought of saying a word or two about these changes and copying down a few of the ballads which accompanied them, to give everybody a bit of amusement, and that was how this little book came about.

The story has medium length, a severely limited number of personages and scope of action, and the comic relief provided by the *k'uai-pan* ballads themselves, these last being witty and successful exercises in a folk form. In direct contrast, *The Changes in the Li Family Village* is a full-length novel, a run-of-the-mill indignant denunciation of landlord villainy. It contains no touch of humor and covers a broad field of action—the whole political history of a district from 1928 to 1946—without achieving the sweep and movement possible in a good panoramic novel. When Chang T'ieh-so, whose troubles have dominated the first half of the book, leaves the scene to reappear only near the end, unity is lost, subplots compete for attention, and dullness settles in like a fog. . . .

Just as favorably as *Li Yu-ts'ai* compares with *Li Family Village,* so we might compare Chao Shu-li's latest story, *Magic Spring Caves,* with *Three-Mile Bend.* This new novel concerns the resistance of Shansi villagers to Japanese and marauding ex Kuomintang troops in the years around 1940–41 and is the most realistic and exciting of the war stories I have read. In telling this story, Chao makes his most extensive and most effective use so far of the technical devices of the old storytellers. By questions and anticipatory remarks to the reader at chapter-ends and elsewhere ("What sort of men were Chang Te-fu and Li T'ieh-hsuan? What cave were they going to and what papers were they after? Did Gold Tiger get the message to them? Did they all get away? I'm going to let you have the whole story right now."), the author generates suspense, keeps a tight grip on plot developments, and deliberately puts the reader right back into the heroic world of the old novels. What we might describe as conventional situations are covered in the old novelists' phrases, e.g., setting off on a journey: "Gold

Tiger set out at dawn, and had reached town by breakfast-time" [and] reunion: "When they saw Gold Tiger had come back, naturally they were both pleased and startled, and he and they alike began to exchange questions on everything that had happened." Again and again, the author captures the perfect concise phrase to sum up a situation: "If Silver Tiger was dead, where was his corpse? If alive, where was he?" A good modern parallelism, reconstructed from old phrases but apt and clear, occurs [later]: "When Little Fatty's mother saw the young couple, she was both pleased and saddened—pleased because the children of her old neighbor were lost and found again, saddened because her own Little Fatty was still somewhere unknown."

It must be emphasized that clichés such as I have listed are not at all a necessary concomitant of any attempt to write narrative in modern Chinese. One would not find them to anything like the same extent in the pre-Communist "modern" writers, even in those who, like Ting Ling or Ai Wu, continued to write in the Communist period. These phrases appear in the work of Chao Shu-li as the result of deliberate choice.

I am not suggesting that *Magic Spring Caves* is a well-wrought novel simply because it is loaded with storyteller phrases. Simple narrative thrills (Gold Tiger's escape from forced labor and his exploration of the caves with Little Orchid) are an important contribution to success. The propaganda message is so general—it was a good thing to resist the Japanese and the marauders—as to be unexceptionable (unless one was a Japanese or a marauder). There are some fine portraits, as of the old shepherd Li Hung with his countryman's simple delight in mystification: "It was only because of the potatoes that we came here." What I do suggest is that this is no pale imitation of the old-style heroic tale (as *Three-Mile Bend* is a pale imitation of a Soviet Russian novel about life under socialism) but a true descendant of the Chinese narrative line, which draws its strength from the peasant life of North China and could have come into existence nowhere else. . . .

Unfortunately, too few other writers have succeeded in incorporating traditional elements into new work in such a natural and organic fashion. For a clear instance of an unnatural straining after the "folksy," it is instructive to look again at *Wang Kuei* and *Li Hsiang-hsiang*, a long narrative poem by Li Chi which was greeted with rapture on its first appearance. This poem consists of some 400 rhymed couplets, with a line of regularly seven syllables, occasionally one or two more, and, with almost absolute regularity, four beats. This constituent couplet was a folk-verse form current in northern Shensi, known as the *shun-t'ien-yu*. A writer under the name of Lin P'ing quotes certain *shun-t'ien-yu* he has transcribed, of which Li Chi has received lines verbatim into his poem, e.g.:

If for three days I don't see your face
I ask each traveler on the road.
If for three days I don't see your face
I draw your likeness on the wall.

and

Think of you till midnight, can't get to sleep,
After midnight think of you and have to light the lamp.

A feature of these *shun-t'ien-yu*, as of much folk verse, is what we might call the "detached simile," stated in the first line of the couplet and seldom related in any explicit way to what follows in the second.

The following couplets describing the two lovers were singled out by the critics for their naturalness:

Flower of the lily blossoming red,
Hsiang-hsiang grew into a lovely girl

and the parallel, a few lines later:

Thickets of willow clustering green,
Wang Kuei was a fine young lad.

Some of the similes incorporate proverbial material in every apt application:

Blind man on dark road, hardship piled on hardship:
What the poor peasant fears is a year of famine.

At other times, though, the poet strains so hard that his effect is artificial or even quite wrong. The following couplet is spoken by the villainous landlord, who is apparently but implausibly referring to himself in the first line:

Smoke from the chimney, soot on the beams,
When I get home that lad will be in trouble.

In the case of the next image, of the leadership of the Communist Party, it is hard to believe that the author actually intended to flatter:

Flock of sheep on the move follows the sheep in front:
In North Shensi has arisen the Communist Party.

T'ien Chien's long ballad *The Carter's Story* was first put out in 1946, the same year as Li Chi's poem. Its length is even greater, some 12,000 characters all told. The narrative framework is quite similar in that it concerns the overthrow by aroused peasants of a vicious landlord and the liberation of a village girl from his clutches; the girl's father though, rather than her lover, supplies T'ien Chien's hero. But although it received less acclaim, *The Carter's Story* is far superior to *Wang Kuei*. T'ien Chien's success is in the integration of elements from an older popular tradition of poetry into his own highly original mode of diction. In the following passage we can hear how rhythms and reduplications typical of certain classical *tz'u* or *ch'u* patterns enrich the music of that "drum beat" verse which yet remains a personal achievement of this poet; we may notice also how he brings a run of lines to a climax by hammering out a proverb into a ringing close:

> Who could guess, who could guess,
> A poor man's cart
> Filled with tears
> Loaded with hate
> As if it were wrapped in fog
> Drenched with driving rain.
> Though Lan-ni climbed on the cart
> She cried
> The cart cried
> The girl and the cart
> Jolting on
> Through the sound of weeping.
> It was so hard to go
> Hard, so hard to go
> Hard, so hard to go.
> Sorrow to go
> Sorrow not to go.
> Truly, a hatred born in a day
> Takes a thousand years to die!

Writing some time ago on the topic of "Fiction of the Yenan Period," I described this body of work as deeply indebted to the popular tradition, "but not so much by direct inheritance as by raiding of the family vaults." What I had in mind then, but lacked the space to elaborate, was a kind of deliberate recall of the well-beloved popular classics, practiced by the new writers to enrich their own offerings, to conform to the presumably more conservative taste of the broadest public, and no doubt also to soften the shock of the propagandistic message. I can best illustrate this process of "raiding" by considering a favorite type of the *hao-chi*, the "clever stratagem," which is always good for suspense and good for a laugh. This is the stratagem of "bride substitution." The *loci classici* we may take as Chapter 5 of *Shui-hu Chuan* and Chapter 18 of *Hsi-yu Chi*. (The former of these old popular novels is favored above all others as a fountainhead for the sustenance of Communist literary men. Although its outstanding quality is in any case beyond question, certain special factors have contributed to its new eminence. One is the official sanction conferred by Mao Tse-tung himself, who refers to it frequently in his writings. Another is that in stories of the War of Resistance to Japan; the Eighth Route Army, when operating in enemy-held territory, find themselves in a position very much akin to that of the outlaws of Liang-shan. The intention of the authors of such stories is similar: to establish the type of the champion of the poor, Robin Hood fashion.)

One of Lu Ta's more chivalrous deeds, it will be recalled, is performed one night *en route* to the eastern capital. He seeks lodging at the farm of an old man, Liu, whose daughter is that very night to be forcibly taken in marriage by a local *tai-wang*, or bandit-chief, Chou T'ung. Lu Ta persuades old Liu to let him try his skill at "expounding the doctrine of karma" to the unwanted bridegroom, when he arrives, in an attempt to soften his heart. It is, of course, rather his head that Lu Ta softens, with his great fists, when the groom creeps at last into the darkened bridal chamber where Lu Ta lies stark naked on the bed in the bride's stead.

The similar episode in *Hsi-yu Chi* relates how Monkey poses as the poor maltreated captive wife of the monster Pigsy. The comic possibilities of the situation are more fully exploited here than in the *Shui-hu* story, but the general principle of rescue is the same.

Now we may look at two (and there are probably more) forced weddings in the fiction of Communist writers. First, a bride substitution in the *New Son and Daughter Heroes*. Hsiao-mei, who is eventually to marry the hero Ta-shui, attracts the attention of the local Japanese commander. Wedding plans are forced on her, but, when the groom enters the bridal chamber to claim his rights, he finds that the veiled figure he "married" is no pretty young girl but Ta-shui's younger brother, a militia leader. This time the unwelcome groom is neither beaten nor enlisted in a pilgrimage after sutras but shot dead.

In the novel *Heroes of Lu-liang,* the forced marriage is planned of Mei-ying, daughter of Second Teacher, a specimen of the enlightened poor gentry, to a sergeant of the puppet forces whose nickname is Snake-in-the-Grass (*ti-t'ou-she,* incidentally a good *Shui-hu*-type name). The rescue of Mei-ying is effected by means other than bride substitution, but I wish to quote at length to illustrate the manner in which the authors re-create the style (if my translation can show this) and narrative technique of the classical models. It may be interesting to note first some closely matching phrases from the *Shui-hu* and *Lu-liang* episodes under consideration:

Shui-hu Chuan	*Heroes of Lu-liang*
gongs and drums came sounding from the hillside	gongs and drums came sounding from the hillside
all the farm people clenched their fists, sweating	couldn't help clenching his fists and sweating
a troop of horses and riders raced up to the farm	a troop of horses and riders in red and green
all bright-gleaming weapons and pennanted spears, red and green silk strips fastened to each	red and green silk streamers tied on their bright-gleaming bayonets
[the bandit chief] rode a great proud-necked curly-haired white horse	Snake-in-the-Grass rode a great proud-necked horse

Here is an abridgment of the *Lu-liang* episode:

Mei-ying was nineteen *sui* [years old] this year, quick and bright by nature, graceful in appearance. Her old parents loved her as they loved life itself. Now that Snake-in-the-Grass demanded her for his wife, what could they be but anxious and grieved? The problem had [militia leader] Wu worried also. Head down, fingering his chin, he paced the floor deep in thought. After a while, he gave a sudden glad cry and said: "What do you think of this way out?" While he spoke, the heads of the four of them stayed together. They all reached agreement, but Second Teacher was still nervous for a while, and his face wore an air of anxiety. Wu thumped his chest and said: "There's no problem, I know some of the men in the engineers' platoon. This is the only way!" And Old Man Chang added: "Don't worry. I can manage the go-between part."

(Old Chang as go-between concludes arrangements for the wedding to take place a few days later):

Around midday, suddenly gongs and drums came sounding from the hillside across. Everyone ran out to look and what they saw was a troop of horses and riders in red and green, who in no time at all had entered the village. It was no one else but Snake-in-the-Grass coming to claim his bride. There in front were half a dozen musicians. "Doo-wah doo-wah" went the blowing and banging and behind came four lantern-bearers and two men with banners, on either side of the bridal sedan-chair. Snake-in-the-Grass rode a great proud-necked horse and wore a gown and riding-jacket, ceremonial head-dress and leather boots. Four policemen, fully armed, red and green silk streamers tied on their bright-gleaming bayonets, martial and majestic, marched up to Second Teacher's door.

Three shots were fired and the sedan-chair was set down. Snake-in-the-Grass dismounted, and people ready-waiting bowed and greeted him and led him in, straight to the main room. Second Teacher himself came to keep him company and smoked and drank tea and chatted with him, deliberately wasting time. He talked of things ancient and modern, the last 500 years and the next 500 years, of things in heaven and things here below. Now Snake-in-the-Grass actually didn't have a single aperture open to admit knowledge, but in order to make a show of status before his father-in-law, all he could do was wiggle his eyebrows in every direction and make some sort of wild reply. It was late afternoon before the wine and the feast were served. Second Master himself offered wine, and relatives and friends all in turn came up with a bowl, then K'ang Shun-feng started offering wine, and although Snake-in-the-Grass had a good capacity, with such nonstop drinking it was like trying to dam the flow of a stream; by the time he'd eaten halfway through the feast, he already showed signs of tipsiness. The four policemen also had someone to look after them and drank wine and guessed fingers and made a continuous yelling. Not till the time to light the lanterns had come did they set out on their way.

Snake-in-the-Grass wore a cross of red silk, and the bride wore her phoenix head-dress and a red gown and was carried into the sedan-chair weeping and wailing as though she couldn't bear to leave. By now the gauze lanterns had been lighted, the musicians struck up, and the sedan-chair was lifted and carried off. The bride's cousin was escorting her and followed behind the sedan-chair. Second Master watched the party leave, and he couldn't help clenching his fists and sweating.

Having drunk so much wine, Snake-in-the-Grass lolled about in his saddle, and the four policemen had drunk themselves dizzy and

staggered unevenly after him. On they went until they were entering a copse of birches, when suddenly with a swoosh from among
the trees a ball of fiery sparks came flying straight at Snake-in-the-
Grass. And there he gave a shrill yelp and fell off his horse, which
reared and pranced in alarm. But who'd have guessed it, when
Snake-in-the-Grass fell off his horse one foot stayed in the stirrup,
and the horse faced off, right back to Han-chia-shan, dragging him
along upside-down behind.

From these examples, which could be multiplied almost indefi-
nitely, it is obvious that a concerted drive has been under way for
twenty years now to restore to Chinese writing a specifically Chinese appearance, albeit this appearance must harmonize with the
popular rather than with the more esoteric tradition of literature.
That this drive is not motivated merely by the need for a readier
mass intelligibility becomes clear as soon as one considers work in
other fields. Historians, anxious to replace the shameful past image
of stagnation by that of a dynamic society, have emphasized the
part played by peasant revolts. And in the last three years or so,
there has been a shift of interest toward the establishment of a
truly heroic past. . . .

Yet with all its glitter and glamor, the ultimate end served by
all this rehabilitation of the "national," the "traditional," is no
more than a matter of justifying and glorifying a revolutionary
government. The great men of letters of the past would have
understood perfectly such a purpose, and each could point out
many a cautious eulogist among his colleagues and acquaintances.
But a Ch'u Yüan, a Tu Fu, a Shih Nai-an, or a Ts'ao Hsüeh-ch'in
would never have felt that the heights of truth were to be scaled
by adulation of the regime in power or by acceptance of the way
the world went.

We end in paradox. The writers of protest of the literary revolution, for all their outlandish garb, were heirs to a noble literary
civilization. Their Communist successors have rejected and over-
thrown the whole concept of what that literature was and means
but are busily engaged in decking themselves out in its outward
forms.

3. POETRY: NEW VOICE OF A NEW AGE

In traditional China, poetry was the highest form of belles lettres. The mandarins who sustained the traditional art are long gone, and in no other genre has form as well as content changed so drastically. The old carefully regulated verse forms have been almost entirely forsaken (with the exception of the verse of the poet featured in the last section) in favor of freer, more popular forms; the elegance and tranquil beauty of the past have given way to a boisterous confidence in the socialist future.

Kai-yu Hsü introduces the poetry of Communist China, translating several short poems in the process. The next selection is taken from the enormous collection of "new folk songs" avidly collected from among the common people and promoted during the Great Leap Forward. They represent a somewhat artificial, hothouse kind of folk poetry and are often extremely crude. Nevertheless, they constitute a significant voice of the new China and, as the last poem says, at their best they do have "the taste of freshness." Moreover, it is worth noting in these poems the frequent references to popular folklore and historical figures—but always now the masses have "outstripped the heroes of old."

Finally, we turn to a poet who is certainly no semiliterate peasant and who writes in the classical shih and tz'u forms of his mandarin predecessors—hence the half-apologetic letter accompanying Mao Tse-tung's first published collection of poetry. His poems are also full of allusions to ancient history and literature, just as a traditional scholar's would be. But the message of these poems is certainly not traditional. Whether he is celebrating the natural beauty of China as in "Snow," reflecting on historic sites as in "Peitaiho" and "Swimming," or commemorating his dead wife in "The Immortals," each poem concludes with a reaffirmation of his faith in the greatness of the revolution, the superiority of the present over the past. The last poem, an exchange with his poetry-writing scholarly friend Kuo Mo-jo, shows no mellowing in old age as he castigates revisionist insects foreign and domestic. The poetic allusions draw from China's rich past (they are understandable only to someone familiar with its history and literature), but the moral is unmistakably for the present: "Seize the day, seize the hour!"

TWENTIETH-CENTURY CHINESE POETRY

KAI-YU HSU

In Yenan, the Communist headquarters in the 1940's, leftist writers gathered together to re-examine the direction in which literature was developing. They agreed that waging war against a foreign enemy was the writers' duty, but that, beyond this, the writers should follow the road to social realism by learning from workers, peasants, and soldiers. Though this notion had first been brought up by the Creation Society's Kuo Mo-jo in the early 1920's, it was in 1942 that the dictum was officially pronounced in Yenan by none other than the Communist leader, Mao Tse-tung (b. 1893), who is himself a skilled writer of classical-style verse. "Social realism" has since become the official Communist policy that has guided the new regime in directing the nation's literary activities, including the few purges in literary circles. Poetry, however, could not be legislated into being, and it was left for the poets to find themselves in a rapidly changing society.

Where could these poets go after 1949, after the end of the open war with the Japanese and the Kuomintang? Soldiers and guerrillas were no longer dying on the front line, but the battle was by no means over. Order had to be born out of chaos and a purpose in life restored to the populace. The sense of urgency had not departed, but a breathless demand to rebuild had been added to the urgency of survival. Activities became ever more feverish in postwar China. The poet had no chance to return to tranquil contemplation. Organized political forces dictated against any such return. The general intellectual atmosphere veered away from all traditional values except one: life, the physical existence of man. To insure this existence in the world of today, man must fight for his group. The poet who has been nurtured in this atmosphere tends to identify his ideal with the interests of his fellow men. He may occasionally allow his imagination to roam on a wider intellectual horizon, but these are rare occasions nowadays. The pressure of the pace of life is ruthless. Probing the deeper meaning of life, of truth and beauty in any form of abstraction, will continue to seem irrelevant in China for a long time to come. Meanwhile,

FROM Kai-yu Hsu (ed.), *Twentieth-Century Chinese Poetry: An Anthology* (New York: Doubleday Anchor Books, 1963), pp. xxxix–xliv. Copyright © 1963 by Kai-yu Hsu. Reprinted by permission of Doubleday & Company, Inc.

who is the hero that deserves the poet's praise? The answer is, of course, he who has changed his sword for a plow or for a pair of wrenches. Listen to the songs of the laborers in a steel plant, at a growing dam, or on a newly communized farm. Only yesterday, many of these same hands were digging the trenches on the battle-field. It is of them that the poets are singing now.

Thus Ho Ch'i-fang, who twenty years ago recorded his feelings upon visiting a friend who was not at home, now hears the majestic singing of dike-workers that overpowers the rumble of the river itself.

I seem to be standing in the river with you,
Completely forgetting cold and danger,
I hook my arm with you
Bracing the dike with our bodies.

And the metaphysical turn of Rilke yields to the romantic ecstasy of Goethe in that diligent student of German poetry, Feng Chih, when he sings of the Anshan Steel Complex near Mukden:

I sing of Anshan steel.
Because of many wishes, I sing of Anshan steel.
When the train reaches the riverside, we wish for a bridge;
When the survey team arrives in wild mountains, it seeks deeper
    ore deposits;
For all these wishes, I sing of Anshan steel.

The younger poet, T'ien Chien, who won acclaim by giving voice to the drumbeat of war a few years before, sees another kind of heroic mobilization aimed at an equally great challenge:

Towering mountains are a brass gong.
Strike it up now! Listen, our motherland is cheering.
At the ringing of the picks in the air
Life advances a step forward.

A new vision looms up in his eyes when men start planting trees on a stretch of desiccated land:

We plant this tree
To crown the desert with a jewel.
Jewels may return to dust, but
The green tree will remain forever jade green.

Just as everything inconsistent with the war effort a decade before was denounced and satirized, the poems written during the early 1950's mirrored the waves of political and social tides that swept away the remnants of the old order—bad as well as good. The Korean War episode revived, for a spell, the wartime themes, but the main trend carried on, beating the drums of reconstruction. The dynamite blasts of the road builders silenced individual voices.

A strange and perhaps terrifying phenomenon is sweeping the literary front in China today. We have been following the development of modern Chinese poetry through the works of a few well-established poets. The post-1949 era has witnessed the rise of a large number of young poets with very diverse backgrounds. The new leaders in China seem determined to see every front "blossom" at the same rate in the same direction; the rate of dam construction and production increase must be made proportionate to the increase in literary output. Consequently, with every drive to increase the production of steel, there has been a comparable effort in the publication of poems. Teams of cultural workers, including inexperienced college students as well as seasoned writers, have been visiting the countryside, the factories, the farms, and the frontier areas. Like their counterparts in technological fields, these cultural workers encourage the farmers and laborers to learn reading and writing and urge them to tell their stories and compose or recite their folk rhymes. The rhymes are then recorded and, after various degrees of polishing, are published. Literally thousands upon thousands of these verses have appeared in recent years. And along with these verses, a new crop of poets has emerged whose names have become familiar in publishing circles and to readers.

The future of Chinese poetry rests in the hands of these younger writers. They are applying themselves to the task with a set of convictions that are extensions of a historical continuum in Chinese literature. The political pressure driving them to go "to the soldiers, farmers, and workers" is by no means the only force guiding their creative energy. As Kuo Mo-jo said with vigor in the early 1920's, many writers of twentieth-century China are genuinely convinced that only by going back to the common people can fresh blood be injected into literature. In a variety of ways, the same theme has been re-emphasized by many literary leaders since Kuo Mo-jo. Tsang K'o-chia, for instance, wrote in 1947, in his preface to *The Zero Degree of Life*, "After fifteen years of polishing my verses, now I realize the beauty of simplicity. Breaking away from my own little circle, I happily face the boundless field of poetry." And he rededicated himself to "expressing the truest hatred and love in the simplest terms—expressing them deeply, forcefully, and beautifully." Clearly there has been a reorientation in the aesthetic sense of the modern Chinese poet, and it is futile to try to surmise how much of it has been a conscious effort or how much of the present result has been sincerely accepted. Without dismissing the political pressure under which Chinese poets are working today, the reorientation must be faced by any student of modern Chinese poetry as a fact.

The poet who goes to the villages to record folk rhymes remembers another age-old tradition in Chinese poetry. Many emperors in Chinese history maintained an official bureau to collect folk songs as a gauge of public reaction to the administration. Many of the folk songs thus collected have lived on in China's poetic heritage. Some of the songs and verses recently collected from the frontier areas, such as the long story-poem *Ashima* of Yunnan origin, have a disarming charm. Even imitations of these folk verses have achieved a good measure of the frontier atmosphere and flavor. Wen Chieh's "Love Song of Turfan" is representative:

> Young lad under the apple tree,
> Please don't, don't sing any more;
> A girl is coming along the creek,
> Her young heart throbs in her bosom.
> Why is her heart throbbing so,
> So violently, even skipping beats?

The effort to preserve genuine local speech and the question of what is the appropriate amount of literary polishing are in conflict—a conflict that has yet to be solved. Until it is, the reader of the latest poems from mainland China may find them disconcertingly crude. Can this be avoided? One wonders. The process of developing an effective new language for Chinese poetry, which started at the beginning of the century, is still continuing, and its destination is still very uncertain. What appears to be quite certain is the momentum which is at present sustained by the overwhelming enthusiasm of a storyteller or a folk singer who has just learned to write a handful of words. There is no doubt about the fertile imagination of the Chinese or about the richness and expressiveness of their spoken language. The unleashing of this rich store of creative energy has just begun. The controlled, written vocabulary that illiterate country people in mainland China are being taught to read and write has been sufficient to generate an ecstasy among the laborers and farmers—now that they too can write poetry! They have been initiated into a new world from which they will never want to retreat. This is the ecstasy we hear in:

Hey, you Three Sacred Mountains and Five Holy Peaks,
Make Way!
Here I come.

Or in the voice of a laborer greeting the first seamless steel pipe:

The old foreman rubbed his eyes,
With his calloused hands
He touched the pipe again and again,
A drop of hot tear fell on it.

Or even in the panegyrics in honor of Mao Tse-tung, to which most readers outside mainland China (and inside mainland China as well, some say) react with nausea. In these poems Mao is com-pared to the sun, the East, hope, salvation, and light. The exalta-tion of his name is comparable to the traditional clichés reserved for the emperor, except that the language is colloquial.

THE SONGS OF THE RED FLAG
KUO MO-JO

No Age Is Better to Live in Than This
Age of Mao Tse-tung

Nothing is higher than the sky or wider than the sea,
No age is better to live in than this Age of Mao Tse-tung;
The Communist Party has opened for us a highway to happiness,
And we shall clothe the countryside with cypresses and pines.

[*Chinghai*]

A Girl Misses Her Mother

I was missing my mother—I'd long been away—
It was only natural to go back to see her.
At midnight I woke up uneasy in mind:
"Tomorrow the co-op will be carrying pond mud."

[*Feihsi, Anhwei*]

FROM Kuo Mo-jo (ed.), *The Songs of the Red Flag* (Peking: Foreign Lan-guages Press, 1959).

Cutting to the Dragon's Palace Gate

Iron mattocks, pounds in weight,
Cut to the Dragon's palace gate,
And the Dragon King is in quite a state!
With a bow he hastens to vow:
   "All right! All right!
   You shall have your water now!"

[Shensi]

I Am a Stevedore

I am a stevedore,
The ten-thousand-li Yangtze bends to my will;
With my left hand I shift Shanghai across,
With my right hand I send Chungking away.

I am a stevedore,
I work with a vigor that bursts through the sky;
I've loaded suns by the hundred thousand,
Unloaded moons by the million.

I am a stevedore,
My production battles are fought on the river;
When I crash the steel down into the hold,
It startles the Dragon King out of his skin.

I am a stevedore,
I go at my work like a fighter in battle;
In order to catch up and overtake Britain,
I load and unload as swift as the wind.

[Ichang, Hupei]

In Praise of the Heroes*

Men and women, old and young, go into battle as one:
The energy of the younger ones is equal to Chao Yün,

---

* The heroes are: Chao Yün, a shrewd and courageous general of the state
of Shu figuring in the famous Chinese historical novel *The Romance of the
Three Kingdoms* by Lo Kuan-chung in the fourteenth century.
   Wu Sung, a courageous, upright hero in a peasant army of uprising, a

The strength of those in the prime of life is equal to Wu Sung,
The youngsters and the children are like Lo Cheng,
The older people's will to work is like Huang Chung,
The planning of the cadres is better than Kung Ming,
The women have even overtaken Mu Kuei-ying,
And every member of the co-op has outstripped the heroes of old.

[*Yingyang, Honan*]

We're Boldly Writing Our Own Poems

After only thirty days at the peasant school
Already we're boldly writing our own poems.
They may be as commonplace as cabbage and beancurd,
Yet at least this humble fare has the taste of freshness.

[*Fengjun, Hopei*]

POEMS

MAO TSE-TUNG

January 12, 1957

Dear Keh-chia and Comrades,

I received your kind letter some time ago and am sorry to be so
late in replying. As you wished, I have now copied out on separate

---

character in the famous Chinese novel *Water Margin* (Shui-hu-chuan) by
Shih Nai-an and Lo Kuan-chung in the fourteenth century.

Lo Cheng, a young hero figuring in the Ming dynasty (1368–1644) novel
Romance of the T'ang Dynasty, of unknown authorship.

Huang Chung, a general of unequalled courage, whose vigor increased with
advancing years, a character in *The Romance of the Three Kingdoms*.

Kung Ming, Chu-ke Liang (181–234), an outstanding ancient Chinese statesman and soldier. He is one of the principal characters in *The Romance of
the Three Kingdoms* and is there described as "very wise and resourceful, a
great strategist and planner."

Mu Kuei-ying a determined and courageous women general in the Ming
dynasty novel *The Yang Family Generals*, of unknown authorship.

FROM Mao Tse-tung, *Nineteen Poems* (Peking: Foreign Languages Press,
1958), pp. 20–22 and 27–31. Although Mao's letter refers to eighteen poems,
a nineteenth seems to have been added to the volume.

sheets all my classical poems that I can remember, and I enclose them. With the eight that you sent to me, they make eighteen altogether. Please let me have your comments and criticism.

Up to now, I have never wanted to make these things known in any formal way, because they are written in the old style. I was afraid this might encourage a wrong trend and exercise a bad influence on young people. Besides, they are not up to much as poetry, and there is nothing outstanding about them. However, if you feel that they should be published and that at the same time misprints can be corrected in some of the versions already in circulation, then publish them by all means.

It is very good that we are to have the magazine *Poetry*. I hope it will grow and flourish exceedingly. Of course, our poetry should be written mainly in the modern form. We may write some verse in classical forms as well, but it would not be advisable to encourage young people to do this, because these forms would restrict their thought, and they are difficult to learn. I merely put forward this opinion for your consideration.

Fraternal greetings!

Mao Tse-tung

Snow, 1945

This is the scene in that northern land;
A hundred leagues are sealed with ice,
A thousand leagues of whirling snow.
On either side of the Great Wall
One vastness is all you see.
From end to end of the great river,
The rushing torrent is frozen and lost.
The mountains dance like silver snakes,
The highlands roll like waxen elephants,
As if they sought to vie with heaven in their height;
    And on a sunny day,
You will see a red dress thrown over the white,
    Enchantingly lovely!

Such great beauty like this in all our landscape
Has caused unnumbered heroes to bow in homage.
But alas these heroes!—Ch'in Shih Huang and Han Wu Ti
Were rather lacking in culture;

Rather lacking in literary talent
Were the emperors T'ang T'ai-tsung and Sung Tai-tsu,
    And Genghis Khan,
Beloved Son of Heaven for a day,
Only knew how to bend his bow at the golden eagle.
    Now they are all past and gone:
To find men truly great and noble-hearted
We must look here in the present.

*Peitaiho**

A rainstorm falls on this northern land,
White breakers leap to the sky.
Of the fishing boats from Chinwangtao,
There is not one to be seen on all the ocean.
    Where have they gone?

More than a thousand years in the past,
The Emperor Wu of Wei† wielded his whip;
"Eastward to Chiehshih," his poem, remains.
"The autumn wind is sighing" still today—
    The world has changed!

Swimming, 1956

I have just drunk the waters of Ch'angsha,
And eaten the fish of Wuchang;
Now I am crossing the thousand-mile-long river,
Looking afar to the open sky of Chu.
I care not that the wind blows and the waves beat;
It is better than idly strolling in a courtyard.
Today I am free!
It was on a river that the Master said:
"Thus is the whole of nature flowing!"‡
Masts move in the swell;

---

* A famous seaside resort west of Chinwangtao in Hopei.
† The famous general Ts'ao Ts'ao, of the Three Kingdoms period (220–80), who founded the kingdom of Wei. He was posthumously entitled Emperor Wu of Wei.
‡ *The Analects of Confucius* records that when the Sage came to the bank of a river he exclaimed: "Thus is the whole of nature flowing ceaselessly day and night!"

Tortoise and Snake are still.*
Great plans are being made;
A bridge will fly to join the North and South,
A deep chasm become a thoroughfare;
Walls of stone will stand upstream to the West
To hold back Wushan's clouds and rain,
And the narrow gorges will rise to a level lake.
The mountain goddess, if she still is there,
Will be startled to find her world so changed.

The Immortals, 1957
[written for Li Shu-yi]

I lost my proud poplar, and you your willow;
Poplar and willow soar to the heaven of heavens;
Wu Kang,† asked what he has to offer,
Present them with cassia wine.

The lonely goddess in the moon spreads her ample sleeves
To dance for these good souls in the endless sky;
Of a sudden comes word of the Tiger's defeat on earth.
And they break into tears of torrential rain.

Reply to Comrade Kuo Mo-jo‡

On this tiny globe
A few flies dash themselves against the wall,
Humming without cease,
Sometimes shrilling,
Sometimes moaning.
Ants on the locust tree assume a great-nation swagger
And mayflies lightly plot to topple the giant tree.
The west wind scatters leaves over Changan,
And the arrows are flying, twanging.

* The Tortoise Hill at Hanyang and the Snake Hill at Wuchang face each other across the Yangtze. The Yangtze Bridge is constructed between these two hills.

† According to an ancient legend, Wu Kang committed some crimes during his search for immortality and was therefore condemned to cut down the cassia tree in the moon. Each time he raises his axe, the tree becomes whole again. Thus he has to go on felling it for ever.

‡ The poem has several references to T'ang literature. *Line 6:* In the short

FROM Mao Tse-tung, "Reply to Comrade Kuo Mo-jo," *Chinese Literature*, No. 5 (May, 1966) pp. 13–14.

So many deeds cry out to be done,
And always urgently;
The world rolls on,
Time presses.
Ten thousand years are too long,
Seize the day, seize the hour!

4. JUSTIFYING PAST LITERATURE BY PRESENT STANDARDS

So much for traditional influences on present literature. What of appreciation for the great store of traditional literature itself? We see in the following selection the efforts to redeem it according to approved Marxist criteria—popular content, realism, class consciousness—plus patriotism. One of the major storms in intellectual circles during the early 1950's was over the greatest novel of traditional China, Hung Lou Meng *(Dream of the Red Chamber). Although the campaign was tied in with the criticism of bourgeois ideological influences, for our purposes we are concerned with how this mystically tinged autobiographical account of eighteenth-century aristocratic life is redeemed in terms of socialist realism. The second selection is an attempt by two traditional scholars to justify study and appreciation of China's long tradition of lyric poetry. Last, we see, in the appraisal of Tu Fu, one of the greatest names in Chinese poetry, how by the early 1960's critical appreciation was accepted for at least some of the classical poetic tradition—although Tu Fu might not have recognized himself when described as a "people's patriotic poet."*

---

story *Prefect of the Southern Branch* by Li Kung-tso of the T'ang dynasty, a man dozing under a locust tree dreamed that he married the princess of the Great Locust Kingdom and was made prefect of the Southern Branch. When he awoke, he found that the kingdom was an ant hill under the tree. *Line 7:* In one of his poems, Han Yu (768–824), a distinguished writer of the T'ang dynasty, sarcastically compared people overreaching themselves to "mayflies which attempt to shake the giant tree." *Line 8:* An allusion to the famous lines of Chia Tao (779?–843), a T'ang poet: "The west wind sweeps over the waters of Wei/And everywhere leaves are falling in Changan."

THE COMMUNIST CRITIQUE OF HUNG LOU MENG

JEROME B. GRIEDER

The Communist interpretation of *Hung Lou Meng* follows quite naturally from the Marxist premise which defines literature as a mirror of existing society, and particularly, at least in a pre-Communist society, as an exposition of the antagonisms inherent in its structure. Thus the Communists' fundamental contention is that Ts'ao Hsüeh-ch'in's description of the decline of the house of Chia is, "in reality," a description of the inner collapse of Chinese feudal society. The literature on this point is voluminous, but the following may serve as a typical example:

> [*Hung Lou Meng*] reflected the fate of the feudal ruling class and its society, its inescapable decline and collapse. *Hung Lou Meng* describes the affairs of the Chia household for a span of only eight years, during which time it falls from its original prosperity to its final ruin, and in this are involved many other decadent households. . . . Can we say that the whole of *Hung Lou Meng* thus demonstrated the inevitable collapse of a group of the nobility? I think we can; but in this we must not consider their collapse to be merely the collapse of several families, and we must understand it to be the collapse of the whole feudal nobility and the entire feudal order. The fundamental significance of *Hung Lou Meng* lies in this.

From this it follows that Pao-yü's revolt against the classical discipline is a conscious revolt against the dying traditional system:

> In Chia Pao-yü, Ts'ao Hsüeh-ch'in has drawn a figure of symbolic significance. Through this figure he opposes the feudal social system of that time. . . . He opposes the examination system, the system of ranks, the marriage system; he opposes the inequality of the sexes.

Or again:

> Chia Pao-yü's unique spirit wants to sunder the fetters of feudalism, to seek the liberation of individuality. . . . He hated his own surroundings bitterly; he was dissatisfied with that rich life; he opposed his father, who represented the feudal order and the feudal morality; he scorned his dissipated, domineering, vulgar, and cruel elders.

FROM Jerome B. Grieder, "The Communist Critique of *Hung Lou Meng*," *Harvard Papers on China*, 10 (1956), 153–56. Reprinted by permission of the publishers.

Another writer concludes that the reason Pao-yü spends so much time in the company of his girl cousins is that, although these young ladies are of noble birth and "naturally possess the characteristics of their own class," nevertheless, "in the organization of the feudal household, before they are married they have had comparatively few opportunities fully to display their class characteristics, and therefore, from Pao-yü's point of view, they seem cleaner than his male associates." This line of argument is pushed to its logical conclusion by still another commentator, who states that Lin Tai-yü shares Pao-yü's hatred of the older generation and that "Everything which Pao-yü opposes in the feudal tradition Tai-yü opposes also. Therefore the fundamental characteristic of their love is its antifeudal content."

Even Pao-yü's final action, his entrance into the Buddhist priesthood, is explained in terms of his revolt against feudalism:

> Because the society of that time could not give antifeudal rebels a way out, the contradiction between Pao-yü's rebellious spirit and the existing society explains his tragic end. Chia Pao-yü's action in entering the priesthood was really dictated by the irreconcilable antagonism between him and society. Pao-yü's entry into the priesthood was certainly not an escape arranged by the author but an act of opposition to the feudal society.

This, say the Communists, is the story which Ts'ao Hsüeh-ch'in set out to tell. If their interpretation is to have the necessary ring of authenticity, they must insist that the class consciousness which they find in the novel was put there by its author, and this they do. "In any society, a great writer always loyally reflects his own attitude toward the existing social order. Ts'ao Hsüeh-ch'in and the people he described all, consciously or unconsciously, took part in the social struggle of their time, and therefore the author himself must indicate in his work where his sympathies lay and what he opposed." The conclusion seems to be that Ts'ao, through the experiences of his own lifetime, came into contact with the universal and eternal law of class conflict, and, although he may not have recognized it as such, he used his book as a vehicle for its expression. Despite this revelation, however, he remained a man of his time, "limited by historical conditions and his class origins," and this fact enables the Communist critic to offer an explanation for the mystical element which runs through this supposedly realistic masterpiece and for such things as Pao-yü's final rejection of the world.

The Communists, then, claim to have discovered the true and intended meaning of *Hung Lou Meng*, and, in thus publicizing their discovery, they contend that they are only rectifying an ancient wrong and paying a great work of protosocialist realism its just due. There are indications, however, that it was the established greatness of *Hung Lou Meng*, rather than any hidden Marxist elements which it contained, which, at least in part, prompted the Chinese Communists to reread the novel. Two quotations from an article by Li Hsi-fan and Lan Ling will demonstrate this inverted logic. The article begins with an exposition of the factors necessary to the survival of a literary creation:

> No matter how great a talent a writer may have, if he puts his pen at the service of an already failing social force his works, in the end, cannot survive. This is to say that the key to a writer's immortality lies not in talent, but in the direction which this talent takes. This is our fundamental point of departure in analyzing and criticizing an author and a work. To put the matter concretely, in the criticism of realistic literature, this is simply the question of literature's popular spirit.

"Popular spirit" and "realism," then, are the coordinate desiderata without which a piece of literature cannot endure. One page later the authors continue thus:

> Lenin has indicated that genuine people's literature must truly and profoundly proclaim the fundamental characteristic of social phenomena—the essential antagonisms and struggle of the class society. *Hung Lou Meng* is a great masterpiece, and its abundant popular spirit must therefore first of all be manifest in its profound spirit of realism.

It appears from this that Li Hsi-fan and Lan Ling have themselves supplied *Hung Lou Meng* with the characteristics necessary to its survival in a Marxist world, on the basis of its intrinsic value as a piece of literature. The question, then, is not whether *Hung Lou Meng* will survive under the new regime but rather why the Communists consider its survival necessary to their purposes. This is a crucial question, and the answer, at least insofar as I understand it, is significant.

In the first place, *Hung Lou Meng* must survive because it is a vital part of the Chinese literary heritage. It is good literature and will remain so even if read through Marxist glasses. In destroying it, the Communists would work an unnecessary hardship on the Chinese people—unnecessary since, with a little carefully guided re-

reading, it is possible to discover in *Hung Lou Meng* elements which render it quite acceptable, and even profitable, material for a Marxist audience. We must concede that, in its new interpretation, the novel provides an excellent vehicle for some aspects of the Communist message. Especially prominent in this respect is the appeal to youth which is now made through its pages. *Hung Lou Meng* is traditionally a work to be read and wept over when young, and the Chinese Communists take advantage of this fact to remind the young people of China that the Party has saved them from the fate of Chia Pao-yü and Lin Tai-yü. "[*Hung Lou Meng*] gives birth to the social demands of the new life. Therefore, in its essential aspect, *Hung Lou Meng* is strong, healthy, and militant. It excites us to advance. It cries to us: I belong to the People! I belong to Youth!"

ON ANCIENT LYRIC POETRY

CH'ENG CH'IEN-TAN AND SHEN TSE-FAN

From antiquity our industrious, courageous, and intelligent ancestors lived and worked on the beautiful soil of the motherland. With a respectful attitude toward reality and yet also a beautiful vision of the future, over many years they created a great ancient culture—one which in brilliance need not take a back seat to that of any other advanced nation.

Literature, as one of the important components of this ancient culture, many centuries ago had shone forth in eternal glory. The abundant and profound literature accumulated in the folk songs of the "Book of Songs,"* the passionate poems of Ch'ü Yüan,† and the writings of pre-Ch'in (221–6 B.C.). Historians and philosophers formed a literary tradition for the motherland which possessed a popular nature in content combined with realism in creative method as its basic feature.

Because our ancestors so loved the motherland, so loved life,

FROM Ch'eng Ch'ien-tan and Shen Tse-fan, Preface to *Collected Essays on Ancient Lyric Poetry* (Shanghai, 1954), pp. 3–7, 22–23, and 28–29.

* One of the six Confucian classics. A large collection of poetry—court, ceremonial, and some originally of popular origins—coming from the early Chou period (1122–255 B.C.).

† A neglected courtier of the southern state of Ch'u in the sixth century B.C., he became the first poet to emerge as a distinct personality. The *Ch'u Tz'u* (*Songs of Ch'u*) is attributed to him.

and so boldly innovated in life, work, study, and struggle, they not only gave us a literature incomparably rich in content but also created many styles and genres suitable for expressing this content—an inexhaustible store of artistic forms. Rich in life, complex in forms, spurring ancient writers on to the very best of their abilities—a great literary legacy was accumulated for us. One important part of this ancient literature was poetry. . . .

Naturally, in ancient poetry (as in other ancient literary genres), the limitations of historical conditions means that not every poet or every poem has value by today's standards. Among them are many that served the feudal ruling class and belong to the dregs of feudalism, but this is definitely not the mainstream in the motherland's poetic or literary history. On the contrary, that is found in those who tenaciously upheld the tradition started with "The Book of Songs" and "Elegies of Ch'u" of combining popular content with creative realism. Moreover, enriched through their own struggles, progressive writers developed this tradition, raised its glories, and opened the road for the literature of the motherland. On this road they erected innumerable monuments truthfully reflecting the joys and sorrows of the people. On these monuments they engraved the people's feelings and also engraved their own achievements, making clear the value of their ancient literary works. . . .

All literary works are the reflection of a certain society's life in a human mind. Life shapes the content of these works, but to manifest this content they rely on form. Therefore in all literary works content and form are closely united. Individual writers all evaluate life according to their own impressions and class standpoint in creating works. Thus, in the creative process, content is prior to form. But when the work is completed, the content is made concrete in the form. If a reader wants to appreciate and understand the life reflected by a writer, or go beyond that to comprehend his creative ideas and the theme of the work and evaluate its ideological and artistic worth, then first he runs up against form, not content. Only after getting through form can he understand content. . . .

In the whole world there are no literatures which do not possess a national form and yet are considered great. Literature is a language art; language is the basic material for literature. Millions of people using a common language for hundreds and thousands of years is the most obvious and most fundamental characteristic of national form. Therefore, if we want to study the form of the motherland's ancient poetry, we must start with studying the language used. In the study of language, Stalin's brilliant *Problems of Marxism and Linguistics* gives us an entirely new Marxist viewpoint, wiping out the fallacy that language is part of a class superstructure and pointing out the basic law that language belongs to an entire people and its development. This possesses incomparable importance for the study of our ancient literature. Before the appearance of this book, many people regarded the classical language used in most of our ancient literary works as expressing the class character of the historical ruling class and wanted to do away with it. This kind of harmful viewpoint must necessarily lead to other incorrect judgments, namely that most of China's literature which had come down from antiquity to the twentieth century was simply a record in the service of the ruling class. This depreciates the value of ancient writings and also reduces our enthusiasm for receiving this excellent legacy. In reality, the classical language was produced from the spoken language of the ancients and, later, when it became the literary language of books, it also possessed a popular character. . . .

As mentioned above, the main purpose of studying poetic forms is to study content better. A writer studies life and thus has his subject; he evaluates life and thus has his theme. Subject and theme, these are the expression of content. Each individual poem can have its special subject and theme (that is, its special content) but a poet's entire work, since it is the result of that poet's study and evaluation of life, necessarily discloses that poet's own life. That life, regardless of whether it is what he directly or indirectly experienced, always is that which concerns him and that to which he pays attention. . . .

Chairman Mao teaches that "Every person living in a class society bears the imprint of his class origins. Therefore, studying a work's content (that is the writer's life, thought, and feelings) must start with his class background. It is not just the content of a work that has a class character. Its form also has the same character, because form is determined by content. Although individual components like language, pattern, etc., do not have a class character, style and esthetics both do. . . . Therefore, an ancient Chinese poet in his works reflects his own feudal thought. There is nothing strange about that. If there was not any feudal thought, then it would be strange, then it would be incomprehensible. Judging them from today, although they possess some feudal thought, still because under certain historical conditions they were able to learn something from real life, these poets were somewhat separated from their original class and rebelled against it. Thus, in subjective feelings, they represented the aspirations of the people and were in accordance with the interests of the people. . . .

Our present-day study of ancient lyric poetry is one part of our learning from and receiving the cultural legacy. This must be carried out according to the teachings of Chairman Mao. Chairman Mao teaches that

> The use of Marxist methods to critically sum up our historical legacy is another responsibility in our studies. This nation of ours has a several-thousand-year history with its special features and its many precious objects. Before this, we are still beginning students. Today's China is the product of historical China. We are Marxist historicists. We should not cut off history.

According to these instructions, in studying ancient poetry, what things should we take as democratic essence and pass on as examples to new poetry and literature? Generally speaking, this is the popular character in content and realism in creative method.

TU FU

FENG CHIH

The T'ang dynasty (618–907 A.D.) is the most glorious period in the annals of Chinese literature and art, and Tu Fu was its greatest poet. His surviving poems number around 1,400, many others have been lost in the intervening years. His love for his land and people and his high artistic technique combine to make his poems a vivid reflection of the life and thought of his time. They are a model of classical Chinese poetry. Millions of people have recited his poems, which shine down through the centuries with an unfading luster.

Tu Fu has not only influenced Chinese letters. He has also gained the regard and respect of many lovers of poetry throughout the world, for his poems are truly a precious heritage of universal culture. . . .

During the time of Tu Fu, T'ang feudal society underwent a great change. The turning point was the An-Shih Rebellion which lasted more than seven years. The greatest period of the T'ang dynasty never recovered. Economic conditions continually de-

FROM Feng Chih, Preface to *Tu Fu: Selected Poems* (Peking: Foreign Languages Press, 1962), pp. i and iii–v.

teriorated. There were constant aggressive wars caused by intruders into the empire. Governor-generals became arrogant warlords defying central authority. The imperial court lost its hold over the land, but the oppressing classes maintained an ever tightening grip over the people, increasing their exactions year after year. Killing people became a small matter. All these changes combined to bring untold misery to the common folk.

A sufferer from poverty, Tu Fu had ample opportunities of contacting other poor people and knowing their misfortunes. He came to understand the contradictions in society and the dangers confronting the land. In his poems he graphically describes those days of insecurity, depicts the people's sufferings, and voices their expectations. Because of this, his works have been called "history in verse."

Since its beginnings, that is from the *Book of Songs* and Ch'u Yüan onward, Chinese poetry has had a glorious tradition, reflecting the times from which it has emerged as well as the thought of the people. Tu Fu carried on this tradition and developed it. With him, Chinese poetry extended over a wider range of subjects than ever before. He gave an accurate and vivid portrayal of the varied social phenomena of his day—from important political, military, and economic developments down to the hard life of the working people in the countryside. He sang praises of the people's honesty and fortitude, while exposing and condemning the ruling class for their dissipation and extravagance. Among the poems included in this book which have been widely acclaimed as representing Tu Fu's best, we may mention: "Ballad of the War Chariots," "Ballad of the Beautiful Ladies," "Beyond the Frontier," "Frontier Stories," "Song of the Road," "The Road North," "On Washing Weapons," "Lament of the New Wife," "The Old Couple Part," "The Homeless," and the three poems on conscripting officers. Though charged with emotion, these poems show his faculty for keen observation, which enabled the poet to reach right into the heart of the problems of his day. They also served as a vehicle for his political viewpoint, one that is positive and progressive and stands for the interest of his land and his people.

Tu Fu did not hesitate to tell of his own troubles as well as his deep concern for his land and folk. In his middle age, he wrote "in grief for the people, burnt up with the agony of it all." When becoming old, he said this: "Still I worry about war, knowing I have no way to set the world aright." He wrote the famous poem about his small thatched hut, which was broken by the autumn wind so that he was unable to sleep. He said that if only there were a great mansion with thousands of rooms to house the poor and homeless, he would not mind being frozen to death himself. This reveals his lofty ideal. In his soul-stirring poems "Moonlight Night," "Written for the Scholar Wei," "Dreaming of Li Po," "Thinking of My Brothers on a Moonlight Night," and "The Unhappy Farewell," the poet expresses his deep affection for his wife, children, brothers, and friends.

In his writings, he brings to life the scenery, birds, flowers, and trees he saw during his many journeys about the land. Unlike some ancient poets who wrote escapist poetry about nature, Tu Fu always bore in mind the sufferings of the people of his day. His poems are deeply emotional and charged with meaning as is seen from "Spring—the Long View," "On Going Up a Tower," "Autumn Feelings," and "On Lo-yang Tower."

Concerned with his land and people as he was, Tu Fu devoted a lifetime to his literary career. No matter how adverse the living conditions, he never allowed his political consciousness and creative ardor to decline.

5. TRULY POPULAR LITERATURE: THE CULTURAL LEGACY IN COMIC BOOKS

The People's government has found in comic books (or in, more accurately, their own term "picture story books") an excellent form for reaching children and the semiliterate masses. An enormous number of these have been produced, many of them portraying traditional stories. Moreover, although the picture story books themselves may be new, the illustrations in them of ancient tales are strongly influenced by traditional styles. They have become a major channel for transmitting classical literature and history to a new generation. The selection from Worker's Daily *indicates, however, that, by the mid-1960's, doubts about the influence of the past were being felt here too.*

CHINESE PICTURE STORY BOOKS

CHIANG WEI-PU

In the libraries of Chinese factories and schools and in the reading rooms of people's communes, the number of which is increasing daily, picture story books are one of the most popular types of reading. In the bookstalls and bookshops scattered through big cities and small towns, picture story books attract thousands of customers every day. During the last few years, picture story books have been taken up, too, by the national minorities. Picture story books are not only favorites with children and adults who can only read a little, but even well-educated readers skim through the best of them when they have leisure.

These books usually have a progressive message or deal with familiar stories, and their form makes them readily acceptable. They tell stories through a series of illustrations with a short explanatory text. The drawings vary in style; the main thing is that they should be expressive, logically connected, and dramatic. The length of the commentary varies also, and sometimes it is in verse, but the pictures are the most important thing. The explanations should be concise, lively, and well coordinated with the pictures to help the readers to understand the contents. If well written, they bring out the value of the illustrations and convey ideas which the latter cannot express.

This form of literature has existed for some time in China. The stories of the Sung (960–1279) and Yüan (1279–1368) dynasties often had illustrations at the top of each page. The popular romances and novels of the Ming (1368–1644) and Ch'ing (1644–1911) dynasties frequently had portraits of the characters at the beginning of the book, and sometimes there were additional pictures at the start of each chapter. These may be considered the forerunners of picture story books. The New Year paintings so popular throughout the country are also sometimes in serial form, for they used to be mounted on screens with sixteen, twenty-four, or thirty-two pictures to one set. Thus they have something in common with picture story books. Then there are serial wall-paintings, like the 112 illustrating the life of Confucius in the Confucian Temple at Ch'ü-fu, Shantung, a monumental work of the picture-story genre.

FROM Chiang Wei-pu, "Chinese Picture Story Books," *Chinese Literature*, No. 3 (March, 1959), pp. 144–47.

Not until after the May Fourth Movement of 1919, however, did the picture story book become widespread as a form of popular literature. While the new comprador capitalists, following the economic and cultural invasion of China by the imperialists, made use of this form for the propaganda of capitalist and semi-colonial ideas, the revolutionaries and progressives wanted it for revolutionary education of the people.

During the War of Resistance Against Japanese Aggression and the War of Liberation, magazines published in the anti-Japanese bases and liberated areas often carried picture stories, usually moving tales true to life, which served to encourage and educate the people. At the same time, the imperialist aggressors and the Kuomintang authorities carried out propaganda against the revolution by selling huge quantities of serial stories based on American thrillers, sex-ridden Hollywood films, and other decadent comics. These reactionary, vulgar, and pornographic picture story books poisoned the minds of many of our people, and had a particularly pernicious influence on children.

Today the situation is entirely different. Picture story books are written for the interests of the people. Tremendous improvement has been made both in quality and quantity. The number of picture story books printed has increased enormously in the last few years, from just over 21 million in 1952 to 52 million in 1955 and well over 100 million in 1956—nearly five times the 1952 figure. Whereas in 1952 there were about 670 titles, in 1957 there were more than 2,300. The Great Leap Forward on the production front in 1958 was followed by tremendous developments in the cultural life of the people. In the first six months of the year, more than 1,600 titles were printed, including 700 new titles.

A large proportion of the new picture story books deal with the revolutionary struggle and socialist construction. Examples of these are stories about the anti-Japanese war, like *The Shepherd's Message*, and tales of the Liberation war, like *Reconnaissance Across the River* and *Defend Yenan!* the story of the 25,000 li Long March *Across Mountains and Rivers*, and *Volunteer Heroes*, depicting the struggle to resist U.S. aggression and aid Korea. Picture story books have also been published about heroic men and women of modern China who are worthy models for the younger generation—Tung Tsun-jui, Huang Chi-kuang, Lo Sheng-chiao, Liu Hu-lan, and others.

Another large percentage of these books is devoted to stories of historical figures, revolutionary struggles, patriots of the past, and pioneers in the search for freedom and truth. Such picture story books as *Water Margin* and *Romance of the Three Kingdoms* in many volumes are extremely popular. Other favorites are those based on old legends, dramas, fables, or folk tales, like *School-Master Tungkuo, The White Snake, Mistress Clever, The Love-lorn Peacock Flies Southeast, The Western Chamber,* and *The Angel Maid and the Mortal.*

A number of picture story books are designed especially for younger children. These usually have shorter texts and the main themes are folklore and legend, children's life at home and at school, scientific subjects, or tales about great men and women. Such books help to mold the children's moral character and increase their general knowledge. Some of the illustrations are in color, and these are particularly liked by children.

A READER'S COMPLAINT

ANONYMOUS

Comrade Editor,

One day as I came home to rest, I found my children together with several small friends of the same alleyway deeply engrossed in drawing pictures. What they drew was not bad. But a close look showed that their drawings were all unhealthy in content, involving emperors, generals, prime ministers, scholars, beauties, and the like. I asked myself what had put such things into the minds of these small friends. Involved here was quite a big problem. Later, I had a talk with my oldest child. I asked, "Who told you to draw such things?"

"I drew them just for fun!"

"Did you work all this out from imagination?"

"No, I read serial pictures and copied them."

Afterward, I took a look at the serial picture books they had borrowed. Some of them even dealt with stories from such old novels as *Cases of Shih Kung, Cases of P'eng Kung,* and *Living Buddha Chi Kung.*

Small friends take a great interest in serial pictures. At present, available for hire on bookstalls are many good serial pictures reflecting life in the struggle of socialist construction and revolution.

FROM "Do Not Let Serial Pictures Poison the Minds of Children," *Worker's Daily* (Peking) (May 18, 1965).

They are of great educational significance as reading matter for children. However, available at the same time are some hackneyed serial picture books with pictures of emperors, generals, prime ministers, scholars, or beauties. They can do much harm in the education of children and would even leave some bad influence on them. Therefore, I suggest that the leadership departments concerned should check and purge according to plan all the serial picture books to be published, issued, or offered for hire. The unwholesome serial picture books should not be allowed to poison the minds of our youths and children.

P'an Yu-ch'un,
Chinshan *hsien*, Shanghai Municipality

VII

Chinese Opera

1. THE STRUGGLE OVER CHINESE OPERA: TWO VIEWS

"Opera" is a poor translation for the word for traditional Chinese theater, but it does suggest something like the combination of instrumentation, singing, and acting that comprises this unique theatrical form. Although not the oldest element in the cultural legacy—it took essentially its present form about 700 years ago— it has been one of the most important for reaching all levels of society. The plots are largely historical, being either derived from actual historical episodes or adapted from famous works of fiction, which themselves are often historical. Opera has thus been the illiterate common man's history book for the last seven centuries, bringing to him the nation's long, colorful past and helping to account for the deep popular historical consciousness in China.

The Communists, as we see in the following two summaries of their theatrical policy, have shown the deep ambivalence to Chinese opera that is characteristic of their whole attitude toward the cultural legacy. In fact, the stage has been a central battleground for the conflicting attitudes of the Communists' national pride and their suspicion of the past's feudal ideology. The shifts of Party policy on traditional theater, Peking Opera in particular, have served as a barometer of policy toward the cultural legacy in general. Writing before the latest reform of Chinese opera, Travert and Scott outline these shifts and present rather different conclusions on the prospects for Chinese opera's survival as a distinctive theatrical form.

THE ATTITUDE OF THE COMMUNIST PARTY
TOWARD CHINA'S CULTURAL LEGACY

ANDRÉ TRAVERT

In no other field has the Chinese people's attachment to its cultural traditions shown greater vitality than in the classical theater, and the Party's efforts to amend the popular taste failed most conspicuously here.

While some of the present Chinese leaders, like Chou En-lai, have never disavowed their deep liking for what is called *ku-chü* (old theater) or *kuo-chü* (national theater) in contrast to the Western-inspired *hua-chü* (spoken theater), a strong feeling has always existed against it among China's progressive intelligentsia, a feeling which can be traced back to the May Fourth Movement and even to Lu Hsün, whose contempt for the old theater expresses itself in many passages. "Reform of the old theater" was in the air decades before the Communists took power in China.

This hostile trend reflected itself in the very first years of Peking's regime. As early as the beginning of 1950, the Association of Chinese Theater Workers . . . and other Party-controlled organizations undertook to draw up a list of the *Ching-hsi* (Peking opera) and *ti-fang-hsi* (local operas) traditional dramas considered detrimental to the ideological progress of the masses. An article published in 1951, in the *Jen-min Jih-pao*, perfectly reflects the views of these censors: Historically, the theater is the product of Chinese feudal culture and is deeply impregnated with Confucian and Taoist philosophies; it bears the indelible stigmas of its origin. Its plays have spread the feudal concepts of hero, filial piety, loyalty to master and family above loyalty to the country, as well as a fundamentally fatalistic conception of life. With the establishment of the New Democracy, such ideas must be totally rejected as incompatible with the new social conditions.

So, in 1951–52, many traditional dramas were banned from the stage by the Ministry of Culture under various counts of indictment: superstition, feudal mentality, lewdness, contempt for national minorities, etc. . . . Among them were some very popular

FROM André Travert, "The Attitude of the Communist Party Toward China's Cultural Legacy," in E. F. Szczepanik (ed.), *Symposium on Economic and Social Problems of the Far East* (Hong Kong: Hong Kong University Press, 1962), pp. 365–68. Reprinted by permission of the publisher.

plays like Ssu-lang T'an Mu (The Fourth Son Visits His Mother), Ch'i Yuan-pao (The Strange Revenge), T'an Yin-shan (A Visit to Hades), Hu't'ieh Meng (The Butterfly Dream), to cite but a few; while others like Chieh Tung Feng (Chu-ke Liang Borrows the East Wind) were cleansed of their so-called noxious aspects to the point of being deprived of all originality and interest. At the same time, cultural authorities were eager to attract the public toward modern hua-chü plays dealing with the political and social movements then in progress.

It was soon apparent the former had misjudged the "objective conditions" and underestimated the fondness of the masses for the old repertory. Consequently, in 1953, the Theatre Reform Committee reduced to sixty the number of forbidden plays. The Hundred Flowers slogan—which actually appeared in the theatrical sphere long before being expanded to the whole cultural field —helped to cover a retreat whose climax occurred in May, 1957, when the Minister of Culture lifted his ban on twenty-six ching-hsi and ti-fang-hsi dramas which had remained ostracized, considering that their detrimental influence had been considerably reduced by the "ideological advancement" of the masses.

At the same time, the general policy of rediscovery and revalorization of the folklore expressed itself in the theatrical field by the revival, on government initiative, of many varieties of local operas (ti-fang-hsi, spoken and sung in dialects and with distinctive technical characteristics) which were at their last gasp at the time of the "Liberation" or had even disappeared from the stage years before 1949. Although this unearthing of long-forgotten local operas was meant to serve propaganda purposes, it must be placed to the Peking government's credit.

Nevertheless, Chou Yang at the Third Congress, when dealing at length with theater, remarked that "notable innovations," both in the script and in the performance, had been made in many traditional dramas. "With our new wisdom and technique," said he, "we have further enriched the fine achievements of our forefathers. What we mean is not merely to edit our old heritage but to create something new." Chou Yang also stressed the "successful experience" acquired in using traditional dramatic forms to express modern themes. To what extent this experience can be called "successful" can be judged by seeing, or merely reading, the "new" ching-hsi masterpieces like Daughter of the Party or, still better, Red Sputnik Storms the Heavenly Palace, an up-to-date adaptation of the old play relating the feats of Sun Wu-k'ung (King of the Monkeys), a well-known figure of Chinese mythology.

Encouraging as might appear the May, 1957, removal of the interdictions decreed by the government, the theater was soon again restricted in the following months by the impact of the antirightist campaign in the theatrical world. Examples had to be made, in this sphere as well as in others, and quite a few eminent actors, like Li Wan-ch'un, were branded as rightists, while their fellow actors were invited to castigate such "bad elements." As for the repertory, the authorities could hardly contradict themselves by restoring the interdictions just removed; the late Mei Lan-fang at their head, they "spontaneously" took a pledge: (1) to continue under Party leadership to improve the ideological and artistic level of the drama and to influence audiences in socialist and patriotic ways, (2) to stage more plays of rich educational and technical value and to reform dramas that, although meaningless, possess a technical interest, and (3) not to stage any more plays that are "ugly, indecent, and harmful to the physical and mental health of the people." When the famous actress T'ung Chia-ling, for instance, pledged herself never again to perform plays like *The Butterfly Dream*, which were her forte and her stock in trade, it simply meant that "bad plays" were still on the unofficial blacklist.

No fundamental evolution or change of atmosphere has been observed in the theatrical field since 1957. The work of reviving vanished local operas has been steadily pursued, with commendable results. T'ien Han indicated in September, 1960, that 470 varieties of operas were then performed in China, as against 120 in 1952. Correlatively, the writing and performing of "new operas on current themes" has been pursued no less systematically, special interest being shown in new plays on historical themes, made to measure in conformity with the re-evaluation of historical figures on which historians are concurrently working.

A festival of new operas on modern themes, held in Peking in April, 1960, was praised by the Chinese press as "a most encouraging attempt to reflect contemporary life in various styles of traditional opera." The most eulogized of the plays then inaugurated, *Song of Life*, was about people taking part in the Great Leap Forward and in the urban commune movement; in April, 1961, a *Hsinhua* feature entitled "Peking Opera Enriched by New Developments" reported with satisfaction the application of modern stage techniques to traditional plays, which it also depicted as benefiting from "better plot development, clearer characterization and interpretation." Even the most fervent supporters of *ku-chü* do not venture to uphold that its interest and value rest in the subtle and sophisticated psychology of its characters; so they may wonder to what extent of oversimplification and ingenuity it can be carried by "clearer characterization"!

In spite of all these innovations and "improvements," the Chinese public still gives its preference to the old plays of repertory, as a mere glance at the program published in the press will show. This vitality of the traditional drama, which stubbornly clings to life in spite of the Party's frown, is well worthy of notice. And yet its fate is sealed; for, while it still shows signs of prosperity and even revival in some of its branches, Chinese traditional drama will have to make continual concessions to the prevailing ethics and ideology, and, therefore, it is bound sooner or later to lose all that remains of its distinctive character and flavor—a sad conclusion for so great an art.

LITERATURE AND THE ARTS IN TWENTIETH-CENTURY CHINA

A. C. SCOTT

Since 1949, the theater has passed through many political phases, but Communists have not been slow to realize the value of a well-run subsidized theater. When they arrived in Peking in 1949, they immediately put a temporary ban on fifty-five plays belonging to the old theater repertoire. The reasons given were that they encouraged superstitious beliefs, were licentious, or depicted the defamation of the Chinese race at the hands of foreign invaders. Among the latter was the famous and exceedingly popular play *Ssu-lang* [*Fourth Son*] *Visits His Mother*, an old favorite of amateur actors. It was finally restored to favor again in May, 1956, with a performance, seen by the writer, in the Chung Shan Park in Peking before an audience of more than 3,000.

From 1949 to 1953, the traditional forms of Chinese art were generally played down in high political quarters, and it was not

FROM A. C. Scott, *Literature and the Arts in Twentieth-Century China* (New York: Doubleday Anchor Books, 1963), pp. 47–52. Copyright © 1963 by A. C. Scott. Reprinted by permission of Doubleday and Company, Inc., and George Allen and Unwin, Ltd.

until the Second National Congress of Chinese Literary and Art Workers in October, 1953, that Kuo Mo-jo pronounced an official blessing which heralded their return to grace. Some months before this, the Institute of Dramatic Research in Peking issued an official breakdown of the position of the traditional theater repertoire. Sixty-three plays were listed as rearranged, fifteen as being new or drastically revised, while more than 200 continued to be staged as before, which says something for the resilience of the old theater during some of its most difficult days.

The banning or changing of old plays has been a favorite weapon of attack on Communist cultural policy from the outside. Without in any way condoning doctrinaire reforms, it might be pointed out that the banning of plays for political purposes is not a Communist prerogative. Although the technique is practiced on a larger scale now, it was also common in Ch'ing and Republican days. Apart from this, many Chinese plays have no rigid version and have been subject to the individual actor's revisions in the past. And since scores of traditional plays take as their theme the struggles of ordinary people against corrupt officials and despotic authority, it has not been necessary for the Communists to change what was already on the stage but only to slant it.

In spite of the fact that the Marxists have constantly poked their fingers into the theater pie during the last ten years, a considerable part of the old repertoire flourishes as vigorously as ever. Among the Chinese it is said that Chou En-lai has been the savior of the old theater, which he admires. He was a talented amateur in his youth and played women's roles; he was also friendly with Mei Lan-fang and visited the great actor in the hospital before he died. Whatever the real facts about Chou's reputed championship of the old drama, no one can deny that it is very much alive today.

State control of the Chinese theater is heavily criticized in some outside circles today, although it is difficult to see how any other measure could have rescued the stage from the bankrupt state it was in before 1949. The Chinese theater as an entity has been saved by state intervention, and the general standards of training and technical resources have been improved. State subsidy allows traditional troupes to be run as permanent working units, and this is important in a theater whose personnel requirements resemble those of Western ballet companies.

There is a much higher general level of technical proficiency among the rank and file of traditional troupes today, while the ill-disciplined audiences and badly kept auditoriums of pre-1949 days have gone, and no one with any love for the theater can regret the fact.

Within recent years, there has been an active trend to revive local dramatic forms throughout the country. Implicit in this is a political motive, because these forms are regarded as unsophisticated versions of theater art, true "people's entertainment." Be that as it may, a wealth of interesting stage material has been rediscovered in the process. A typical example of what is being done is provided by the Soochow drama, *The Fifteen Strings of Cash,* an old favorite of last century, revived in 1956. It is true that the new version has been revised, but merely in the sense that in its old form it would have been tediously long for contemporary audiences, who are not the dedicated connoisseurs their forefathers were. The revisions have been made in the cause of practical working theater and nothing more sinister than that.

When the writer first saw the play in 1956, it was creating a furor, and a good deal of Party ink was being spilled one way and the other because the play was hailed as a successful example of official cultural policy to "weed through the old and let the new emerge." The fact remains it was an excellent piece of dramatic entertainment, which retained the true spirit of Chinese theater. The story is about a young couple wrongly condemned to death by a stupid magistrate on the charge of murdering the girl's stepfather, a drunken old pork butcher, and eloping with his cash. A more perceptive junior magistrate, by a smart piece of detective work, pins the crime on the real culprit, Lou the Rat, gambler, rogue philosopher, and murderer through circumstance, a role played by a comic actor who is more than a mere *farceur.* The mime and expression of the old-style actor who played the part in 1956 constituted one of the great performances of the Chinese stage, reminiscent of Marcel Marceau in the West.

There have been considerable technical changes in staging, lighting, and production within the limits of the proscenium style which is now universal in China. Even the old drama, which at the beginning of the century still had its audience seated on three sides of a square platform stage, today uses the Western proscenium form with a main curtain plus two more, enabling the stage to be partitioned for scene changes. This may seem a little ironical at a time when the Western theater is eagerly exploring the dramatic possibilities of the open stage, but Chinese ingenuity in using methods new to China cannot be denied. The orchestra and the property men are no longer visible to the audience as in the past. The myriad sightseers who used to crowd the stage wings of the old Chinese theater, to the detriment of good play viewing, have been sent back where they belong—to the auditorium—and the efficiency and dignity of the performance are the better for it. . . .

The Chinese theater in general is still in a process of transition. It is a mixture of old and new forms which have not yet reached a harmonious meeting. From an international point of view, it is in the fields of less realistic stage art, mimetic techniques, and dance drama that the Chinese are better equipped to make a contribution to stage art beyond their own boundaries. And the Communists are very sensibly ensuring that the traditional genre is preserved as a necessary basis for a national theater. Although the right creative synthesis for a contemporary theater has not yet been discovered, there can be no doubt of the tremendous potentialities being engendered.

2. REVIVAL ON THE CHINESE STAGE

The three selections following tell of the revival of traditional opera in the middle and late 1950's. In his speech to the Second National Conference of Writers and Artists in 1953, Chou Yang gave guarded approval to the staging of more old plays while continuing to warn against "the ideology of the feudal ruling class." During the Hundred Flowers period, these warnings were in abeyance as many of the old favorites staged a triumphal re-entry. The exuberance of the second article, and its jabs at "modern philistines," testifies to a very different intellectual climate. The weather changed soon after, but traditional opera endured the chill of the antirightist drive and Great Leap Forward in 1957 and 1958. With state support, such as the Peking Opera School described below, it not only survived but by the end of the decade was more vigorous than it had been for more than fifty years.

THE PEOPLE'S NEW LITERATURE AND ART
CHOU YANG

To develop the people's new literature and art, it is necessary to eliminate not only the reactionary literature and art which served the interests of imperialism, feudalism, and bureaucratic capitalism; we must also put an end to their influence on the people's literature and art. Also, we must take appropriate steps to reform the traditional literature and art still in circulation among the people, so as to meet the new requirements of the people. Old opera is an important heritage of China's national art; it has close links with the masses and is very popular among them. At the same time, as a product of the feudal period, it contained much poisonous feudal ideology and was, over a long period, used by the feudal ruling class as a tool to deceive and drug the toiling masses. Therefore, the reform of old opera is a very important task and one that involves a complex ideological struggle. We have adopted the method of reforming old opera gradually, first in content and then in form. We are opposed to regarding it simply as a means of recreation, promoting it uncritically for its artistic form while ignoring the harmful parts of its content. We are also opposed to the viewpoint and method of those who regard the whole of old opera as feudalistic and, therefore, assume the attitude of completely discrediting it and even ban it by administrative fiat. This of course would be wrong. The fact that the masses like old opera shows its popular character. That the people like it is a question of ideology, and any question concerning the ideology of the masses can never and should not be solved by way of administrative orders. We should realize that, as the political consciousness of the masses rises, they will naturally become critical toward the feudalistic and retrogressive traits of old opera and discard them. In the reform of opera, we must start from actual conditions. First of all, the old operas should be judged from the standpoint of whether or not they conform to the people's interest. We must restrict the scope for those operas which are detrimental to the interests of the people, exposing their reactionary content so that drama troupes will voluntarily refuse to perform them, and the

FROM Chou Yang, *The People's New Literature and Art* (Peking: Foreign Languages Press, 1954), pp. 72–75 and 84–85.

masses will not want to see them. Operas beneficial to the people, expressing opposition to feudal oppression and corrupt officials, or lauding the fiber and undaunted spirit of the nation and lauding public spirit, are the kind of cultural heritage that should be accepted and encouraged. Old opera popularizes the history of China, but, to a certain extent, it is a history steeped in the ideology of the feudal ruling class—a distorted, perverted kind of history. Our duty is to present historical truth without any distortion and to create a historical opera according to the concepts of historical materialism, an opera that will give the masses a new and scientific interpretation of history. During the past few years, we have created such operas, for instance, *Escape to Liang Mountain* and *The Storming of Chu Village*. Their chief value lies in that they indicate that Peking opera is developing into new historical opera.

Of course, after revision, the old opera, especially the different kinds of opera flourishing in various parts of our country, can also depict modern life. All old operas should be made to develop in this direction. The new Shensi opera, the new Shaohsing opera, and the new *Ping Chü* have all manifested this possibility with marked success. . . .

If we are to reform old opera, we must rally together and reform the opera actors and singers. Under the people's new government, the position of performing artists is much higher in society than ever before. Most of them are willing to reform and to adopt new concepts and methods to raise their ideological and artistic levels. Guided by Mao Tse-tung's principles on literature and art, writers and artists of both the new and old types have not only formed a united front but they are also gradually eliminating the differences that separate them.

Opera still occupies an important place in the cultural life of the masses, both in the cities and in the countryside. This is a fact which cannot be ignored in our popularization work. The reform of old opera must be carried out systematically, in a planned way. Experience proves that the masses welcome the reformed Peking and local operas with their new content and that actors are willing to rehearse these new operas and are actually doing so. The present problem is that there are not enough new scripts. Thus, the reform of opera hinges on an adequate supply of scripts. We must, therefore, organize the actors, together with the new writers and artists, to create new scripts or revise the old ones. The People's government and departments concerned with guiding our literature and art will give them the necessary assistance and leadership.

We must not be impatient in reforming old opera. On the other hand, we must oppose the erroneous conservative approach which puts inordinate emphasis on the artistic "uniqueness" of old opera and thus lacks the courage to tackle old opera and break with the old forms.

Under a correct policy, mobilization of and reliance on the unified efforts of the actors will certainly bring new and greater results in the reform of old opera.

OLD OPERAS COME INTO THEIR OWN

ANONYMOUS

Many old Peking operas, long denied a chance of performance, are now playing to packed houses. Some were bowdlerized by reactionaries in the past; some were disapproved of by modern philistines.

Hou Hsi-jui, now nearly seventy and famous for his warrior roles, has revived one of his best characterizations: that of the hero in *Lien Huan Tao Mountain*. This opera fell out of favor with some modern critics because the hero, Tou Erh-tung, a brave rebel outlaw, is made to submit to a rebel turncoat. Huang Tien-pa, a "reformed" outlaw in the imperial service, was ordered to recover the emperor's horse stolen by Tou Erh-tung, a sort of Robin Hood outlaw. Knowing well that he is no match for Tou, Huang challenges him to a duel and at the same time cunningly contrives to steal Tou's favorite swords. Tou, losing confidence, surrenders the horse and throws himself on the emperor's mercy.

This opera, with its many opportunities for heroic stage gestures, was once a great popular favorite. But immediately after liberation, like other operas paying tribute to "lackeys of the emperor," it came in for a certain amount of criticism because it seemed to let evil triumph over right. Today when the people's regime is firmly established, public opinion is more tolerant and understanding of the demands of artistic truth.

FROM "Old Operas Come into Their Own," *People's China*, vol. I (Jan., 1957), 40–41.

Monuments great and small: Marchers pass the Gate of Heavenly Peace on National Day in Peking, and students visit Tu Fu's "thatched hut" near Chengtu.

Mei Lan-fang plays Yang Kuei-fei in a Peking Opera performance of *The Drunken Beauty.*

An aged boatman ferries his charming passenger across a stormy but entirely imaginary river in the Peking Opera version of *Autumn River.*

"The Chinese stage has too long been dominated by scholars, generals, prime ministers, and famous beauties," Chiang Ch'ing asserted in July, 1964. This is a scene from a traditional Cantonese opera.

Chou En-lai congratulates Chou Hsin-fang on his sixtieth year on the stage. This veteran Peking Opera star was later denounced for his opposition to Chiang Ch'ing's reforms of that institution.

Yang Tzu-jung is the disguised hero of the Peking Opera's version of the revolutionary *Taking the Bandit's Stronghold*.

Three generations of a heroic revolutionary
family defy their captors in the Peking Opera
The Red Lantern.

Story-teller puts on lute performance of *The Pearl Pagoda.*

A traditional Chinese orchestra plays a new composition, "Gongs and Drums on the Sea."

The transfer of old arts to new media is illustrated by this juxtaposition of traditional shadow puppets and a scene from the animated movie *Monkey*.

Peking Opera has produced more than 1,000 operas in its hundred years of development. Not all of them by any standard are worth preserving but it is no easy matter to sift the wheat from the chaff. This is work that requires extensive knowledge, breadth of vision, and infinite patience. There is no place here for snap judgments. But not a few influential critics took it upon themselves to judge the traditional opera strictly according to current standards of political or social fitness. A general and laudable criticism of superstition, for instance, was made into a virtual ban on any play featuring ghosts or gods. The idea of loyalty to the people was taken to preclude plays singing the praises of honest officials of the feudal rulers. Many pieces including parts for clowns were not performed because it seemed that their buffoonery made fun of the working people. This mechanical application of perfectly sound general principles induced many actors and actresses to discard considerable parts of their repertoire. This heavy-handed treatment of our dramatic heritage was not to be tolerated, hence the present wave of revivals. It will be left to the theatrical world, to the veterans of the profession, to restore and survey the traditional repertoire. Then it will be up to an informed public opinion to assess that repertoire at actual performances.

Some lively discussions have already seethed around some recent revivals such as *How Ssu-lang Visited His Mother*, for instance. Yang Yen-hui, a son of the Sung-dynasty General Yang, has been captured by raiding troops from the Liao Queen who, delighted by his handsome person and bearing, gives him her beautiful daughter in marriage. Several years later the two countries are again at war. The Sung forces are commanded by Yang Yen-hui's younger brother who is helped by his widowed mother. Aided by his wife, Yang Yen-hui steals a pass and crosses the battle lines to see his mother and brother. The dramatic reunion of the family and the return of the young man to rejoin his wife in Liao is the climax of the opera.

Critical opinion is sharply divided. One school holds that the whole performance makes clear the playwright's critical attitude to Yang Yen-hui—a confused, turncoat patriot. Others, while admitting the merits of the piece as it stands, point out that folklore, literature, and historical fact alike present the Yang family primarily as patriots, while in this Peking Opera this outstanding trait of the Yangs has been submerged by sentimentality. Yen-hui's mother and brother have no word of reproach for him. This reduces their stature as patriots. An old version of the story has a different ending. After a battle won by the Sung forces, Mother Yang discovers that Yen-hui, who it was thought had died a hero's death on the battlefield, is actually living honored among the enemy. She herself demands that he be handed over and sent to the emperor for punishment as a traitor. This version is actually used in the Shantung opera version, another of the local varieties of Chinese opera. It appears, therefore, that under the influence of the ruling Ch'ing dynasty, which exerted a dominant influence over the art of the capital, the Peking Opera was obliged to cover up the conflict with the Liao by stressing the domestic tragedy of family reunion and separation. It is still a moot question which version should be preferred.

One of the difficulties of this search through the old repertoires is that many Peking operas were never committed to writing. Veteran actors are now recording all they can remember, and several little gems have already emerged from threatened oblivion. A *Bolt of Cloth*, a satirical comedy, is one that has recently been restaged with the help of Hsiao Tsui-hua, a famous *tan* (female character) actor, who is now nearly sixty, and Ma Fu-lu, a veteran state clown.

The work of discovering and sifting traditional operas is going ahead with a swing not only in Peking but in other local opera circles as well. We can expect a rich treasure trove and a great broadening of the relatively limited repertoire of Peking Opera today.

NEW TALENT FOR PEKING OPERA

WANG LEH

The first group of graduates of the Peking Opera School gave their graduation performance in the latter part of last month before a critical and also warmly appreciative audience that included most of the veterans of the Peking Opera stage. The sixty-five students who acted had completed seven years of rigorous training under expert guidance in acting, singing, acrobatics, and dancing. Now they were on the eve of starting an even more searching school on the public stage. They have all been assigned to the three leading Peking Opera companies led respectively by Mei

FROM Wang Leh, "New Talent for Peking Opera," *Peking Review*, 2, 31 (Aug. 4, 1959), 20.

Lan-fang, Hsun Hui-sheng, and Shang Hsiao-yun, the three foremost actors in *tan* (female) roles today. They will continue to
learn while taking part in performances. For all of them, this seeing the foremost actors of the day at close range, and enjoying
their daily help, will be a unique opportunity to improve their art.
Mei, Hsun, and the others were all in the graduation audience,
watching them with their instinctive little appreciative nods or
frowns, and it was clear that nothing that went on on the stage
escaped their attention.

Seven years ago, most of these youngsters were barely ten years
old. Today they have completed a high-school education and have
learned to perform about sixty operas. Not a few have mastered
as many as ninety. When they started, their school, founded in
1952, was housed in an old temple where Peking Opera actors
were wont to gather for a chat and to do their daily training. All
the equipment it had then was a couple of dozen bamboo sticks
to use as "weapons" and various props; six faded, tasseled whips,
their symbolic "horses," and a mattress for tumbling. Today new
buildings have been built beside that temple. With the help of the
People's government, the school has been turned into a modern,
well-equipped establishment, beautifully surrounded by green
shrubbery and flowers. Ho Shou-chen, who in his day was a celebrated actor in the role of "painted face" heroes, has been its able
principal, and many other veteran artists have been teaching there.

In the old days, the would-be actor faced a tough road to the
Peking Opera stage. As often as not, indenture contracts contained
clauses which put the apprentice actor completely in the power
of his master. With luck, he might come through those long years
of ordeal and rise to stardom; if not, he would have to be content
with some grossly underpaid job backstage or in the crowd. In
those days, the patronage of some well-known "master" or stage
entrepreneur was considered essential to success. Those ordeals
are ended. Li Yu-fu, one of the sixty-five new graduates, has had
all her wants looked after by the state ever since she entered the
school; some of the best masters of the theater have been her
teachers, and now she has been assigned to a first-class troupe. Her
older brother, by contrast, after years of study, was forced to quit
the theater before liberation because he failed to find a suitable
patron. With families connected in one way or another with the
theater, most of the graduates are able to compare yesterday with
today. That undoubtedly is one of the ingredients of their high
esprit de corps, their keenness at their studies (they finished their
courses six months ahead of schedule), and their determination

to maintain and develop the splendid traditions of Peking Opera that each of their new teachers represents.

The Mei, Hsun, and Shang companies are among the finest in Peking Opera today. In singing and acting, in make-up and costuming, each has its distinctive features. Each also has a number of operas for which it is particularly famous. Mei Lan-fang has created a great tradition of artistry in *tan* roles; the name of Mei is almost a synonym today for operatic excellence. His performances in *Beauty Defies Tyranny* and *The Drunken Beauty* are remembered as flawless by connoisseurs of the art. Now Li Yu-fu, who has a good voice and has already learned a number of operas that are well known in the Mei troupe's repertoire, will join that troupe. Shang Hsiao-yun is noted in his troupe for another type of *tan* role—the courageous type of woman which requires dexterous acrobatic body movements, vigor in acting and dancing, as well as good singing. Another young graduate, Sung Ching-yuan, has been assigned to his care precisely because she shows talent in these respects. Two other graduates, Li Ya-lan and Sun Yu-min, with particularly clear voices and great delicacy of movement, have been assigned to the Hsun Hui-sheng troupe that makes a specialty of such romantic operas as *The Western Chamber*, with its heroines like the clever, vivacious Hung Niang.

If the youngsters are overjoyed at the opportunities that now open out for them in their chosen art, so are Mei, Hsun, and Shang at getting this access of fresh new talent to whom they can pass on their art. Shortly after liberation, in his *Forty Years of Stage Life*, Mei Lan-fang described the private Peking Opera "school" of the old days as a "little boat drifting on the open seas. In a storm it easily capsized." Today the People's government has put theatrical training on a solid foundation. Students and the art of Peking Opera have an assured future.

3. RENEWED EMPHASIS ON REFORM
OF CHINESE OPERA

During the early 1960's, even as Peking and regional operas prospered, there were more and more voices raised against some of their unsocialist features. The calls to clean up the old theater were evidently strongly resisted in academic and theatrical circles, with support from some persons high in the Party. We see some of the objections in Li Jen's article, which mainly stresses "reforming" (that is, editing) the content of old plays to eliminate harmful influences.

Much more drastic is the production of operas on contemporary themes. This goes back to the Yenan period with the new Peking opera White haired Girl, *the prototype of plays in the old style showing modern-day class struggles. A number of such plays were produced after 1949, especially during the Great Leap Forward, but it was only in 1964 that a really determined drive was launched to replace the traditional repertoire with new plays depicting modern socialist reality. The main event launching this was a festival of contemporary Peking Opera in June and July, 1964. Subsequently, Mao's wife, Chiang Ch'ing (a one-time movie actress), has been given major credit for the new operas and her speech has become a major document in the Cultural Revolution. The message is clear: Traditional opera as it existed in 1964 (and the reference to more than 2,800 companies shows how it dominated the Chinese stage) was not properly serving socialism and the laboring masses. It could do this only by directly portraying modern socialist themes, a complete change in content on the stage. Emperors, princes, generals, ministers, scholars, and beauties —the very stuff of Chinese history and theater—must be replaced by workers, peasants, and soldiers. The style, or form, ostensibly should remain Chinese, but, as Chiang Ch'ing herself recognized, the new content necessitates stylistic innovations. A description of the much-acclaimed Korean War play* Raid on the White Tiger Regiment *may provide some basis for judging whether this is still Peking Opera.*

DEVELOPING THE NEW OUT OF THE OLD

LI JEN

As early as the Yenan period, Chairman Mao set forth the policy of "developing the new out of the old," a correct instruc-

FROM Li Jen, "Developing the New out of the Old and the Correct Treatment of Our Theatrical Legacy," *Hsi-chü Pao* (*Drama News*), 7 (April 15, 1960). Translated by the editor.

tion based on the general law of factual development and on the special features of Chinese opera. Like every other social aspect, the art of Chinese opera must develop along with the development of society and must meet the needs of the new society. During the long history of feudal society, the Chinese people created and accumulated an abundance of excellent traditional plays and theater arts. This rich legacy still remains a spiritual treasure of the people today, a source of artistic enjoyment and healthful spiritual influence. Though produced in feudal times and reflecting feudal social life, traditional Chinese opera was created by the people and, because of its long association with the people in expressing their struggles and reflecting their progressive antifeudal sentiments, it has a democratic aspect. This aspect is the essence of Chinese opera, the part that people of today can accept and develop for their service.

As the product of a feudal period, however, Chinese opera cannot be free from various feudal distortions and feudal ideology. Thus it also has a feudal aspect, which constitutes the dross of Chinese opera and should be discarded as being harmful to people today. Therefore, "developing the new out of the old" means cleaning up and reforming the legacy. Reform is necessary, because, in theater, unlike in literature and painting, we influence people's thoughts and feelings through the stage, where it is impossible to explain explicitly our views on the content of each play. . . .

Hence, "to develop the new out of the old" primarily means inheriting the achievements of traditional opera in order to develop new theater and to create new socialist plays that will portray the masses' age of socialism and serve socialist politics and economy. . . . Similarly, the theatrical legacy should be cleaned up and reformed along Marxist historical and aesthetic lines so that its ideological and artistic standards will be raised and so it can better serve today's politics while providing healthful artistic enjoyment for the people. As for representing the life of ancient people, there must be qualitative improvement as well as quantitative development. Formerly, due to the dominance of the ruling class, few plays correctly portrayed the ancient laboring people and the unity among China's nationalities. The laboring people, the real creators of history, had not been correctly portrayed, and we must therefore give first attention to this in developing historical plays.

In brief, "developing the new out of the old" is both inheriting and developing theatrical arts. On the one hand, we must use the good part of the legacy in creating and developing new plays; on the other hand, we must scientifically clean up, reform, and elevate the traditional plays for present use. Either a rude or a conservative attitude toward the legacy is contrary to dialectical materialism, is contrary to the people's interests, and hinders development. Since 1949, our theatrical affairs have developed by constantly overcoming both leftist dogmatism and rightist conservatism. The former, as we see in the present situation, has been sharply criticized and basically suppressed. But the latter, though somewhat criticized, is still quite influential. It is mainly expressed in overestimating the progressive nature and present-day educational function of traditional plays. It overestimates past achievements as being insurmountable. It cherishes broken and worn-out things while resisting the many necessary changes in traditional operas. It praises the ancient and slanders the present, being content to inherit the legacy while despising or even opposing development. Some of this thought is connected with revisionism. Hence, it is essential today to criticize this thought thoroughly and eliminate its influence. . . .

Our consistent policy is to create and develop new socialist and Communist plays. They will not exclude the theatrical legacy or separate from it, but they must inherit only the excellent and beneficial parts. The socialist stage will not ban the traditional opera repertoire, but the choice of plays to be performed is based on their benefit for people today. We should renovate, clean up, and promote the traditional plays on a scientific basis; we should not "praise the old and ridicule the new" or leave old plays intact because they were good in their own time or, least of all, use them in place of creating new socialist plays. We must gradually bring opera to reflect our great age and the masses' struggles in building socialism and Communism. We must cause it to educate the people in the Communist spirit, while constantly meeting the masses' growing artistic needs.

ON THE REVOLUTION OF PEKING OPERA
CHIANG CH'ING

We must have unshakable confidence in the staging of Peking Opera on revolutionary contemporary themes. It is inconceivable that, in our socialist country led by the Communist Party, the dominant position on the stage is not occupied by the workers, peasants, and soldiers, who are the real creators of history and the true masters of our country. We should create literature and art which protect our socialist economic base. When we are not clear about our orientation, we should try our best to become so. Here I would like to give two groups of figures for your reference. These figures strike me as shocking.

Here is the first group: According to a rough estimate, there are 3,000 theatrical companies in the country (not including amateur troupes and unlicensed companies). Of these, around 90 are professional modern drama companies, 80 odd are cultural troupes, and the rest, more than 2,800, are companies staging various kinds of operas and balladry. Our operatic stage is occupied by emperors, princes, generals, ministers, scholars, and beauties, and, on top of these, ghosts and monsters. As for those 90 modern drama companies, they do not necessarily all depict the workers, peasants, and soldiers either. They, too, lay stress on staging full-length plays, foreign plays, and plays on ancient themes. So we can say that the modern drama stage is also occupied by ancient Chinese and foreign figures. Theaters are places in which to educate the people, but, at present, the stage is dominated by emperors, princes, generals, ministers, scholars, and beauties—by feudal and bourgeois stuff. This state of affairs cannot serve to protect but will undermine our economic base.

And here is the second group of figures: There are well over 600 million workers, peasants, and soldiers in our country, whereas there is only a handful of landlords, rich peasants, counterrevolutionaries, bad elements, rightists, and bourgeois elements. Shall we serve this handful, or the 600 million? This question calls for consideration not only by Communists but also by all those literary

FROM Chiang Ch'ing, "On the Revolution of Peking Opera" (speech in July, 1964, at Forum of Theatrical Workers Participating in the Festival of Peking Operas on Contemporary Themes), *On the Revolution of Peking Opera* (Peking: Foreign Languages Press, 1968), pp. 1–6.

and art workers who love their country. The grain we eat is grown by the peasants, the clothes we wear and the houses we live in are all made by the workers, and the People's Liberation Army stand guard at the fronts of national defense for us, and yet we do not portray them on the stage. May I ask which class stand you artists do take? And where is the artists' "conscience" you always talk about?

For Peking Opera to present revolutionary contemporary themes will not be all plain sailing. There will be reverses, but if you consider carefully the two groups of figures I have mentioned above, there may be no reverses, or at least fewer of them. Even if there are reverses, it will not matter. History always goes forward on a zigzag course, but its wheels can never be turned backward. We stress operas on revolutionary contemporary themes which reflect real life in the fifteen years since the founding of the Chinese People's Republic and which create images of contemporary revolutionary heroes on our operatic stage. This is our foremost task. Not that we do not want historical operas. Revolutionary historical operas have formed no small proportion of the programs of the present festival. Historical operas portraying the life and struggles of the people before our Party came into being are also needed. Moreover, we need to foster some pacesetters, to produce some historical operas which are really written from the standpoint of historical materialism and which can make the past serve the present. Of course, we should take up historical operas only on the condition that the carrying out of the main task (that of portraying contemporary life and creating images of workers, peasants, and soldiers) is not impeded. Not that we do not want any traditional operas either. Except for those about ghosts and those extolling capitulation and betrayal, all good traditional operas can be staged. But these traditional operas will have no audience worth mentioning unless they are carefully re-edited and revised. I have made systematic visits to theaters for more than two years and my observation of both actors and audiences led me to this conclusion. In the future, the re-editing and revising of traditional operas is necessary, but this work must not replace our foremost task.

In the last few years, the writing of new plays has lagged far behind real life. This is even more true in the case of Peking Opera. Playwrights are few, and they lack experience of life. So it is only natural that no good plays are being created. The key to tackling the problem of creative writing is the formation of a three-way combination of the leadership, the playwrights, and the masses. Recently, I studied the way in which the play *Great Wall Along the Southern Sea* was created, and I found that they did it exactly like this. First the leadership set the theme. Then the playwrights went three times to acquire experience of life, even taking part in a military operation to round up enemy spies. When the play was written, many leading members of the Canton military command took part in discussions on it, and, after it had been rehearsed, opinions were widely canvassed and revisions made. In this way, as a result of constantly asking for opinions and constantly making revisions, they succeeded in turning out in a fairly short time a good topical play reflecting a real-life struggle.

Theatrical items for adaptation must be carefully chosen. First we must see whether or not they are good politically and, second, whether or not they suit the conditions of the company concerned. Serious analysis of the original must be made when adapting it; its good points must be affirmed and kept intact, while its weak points must be remedied. In adapting for Peking Opera, attention must be paid to two aspects: On the one hand, the adaptations must be in keeping with the characteristics of Peking Opera, having singing and acrobatics, and words must fit the melodies in Peking Opera singing. The language used must be that of Peking Opera. Otherwise the performers will not be able to sing. On the other hand, excessive compromises should not be made with the performers. An opera must have a clear-cut theme with a tightly knit structure and striking characters. In no case should the whole opera be allowed to become diffuse and flat in order to provide a few principal performers with star parts.

Peking Opera uses artistic exaggeration. At the same time, it has always depicted ancient times and people belonging to those times. Therefore, it is comparatively easy for Peking Opera to portray negative characters, and this is what some people like about it so much. On the other hand, it is very difficult to create positive characters, and yet we must build up characters of advanced revolutionary heroes. In the original version of the opera *Taking the Bandits' Stronghold*, produced by Shanghai, the negative characters appeared to be overpowering, while the positive characters looked quite wizened. Since the leadership gave direct guidance, this opera has been positively improved. Now, the scene about the Taoist Ting Ho has been cut, whereas the part of Eagle—nickname of the bandit leader—has been only slightly altered (the actor who plays the part acts very well). But since the roles of the People's Liberation Army men Yang Tzu-jung and Shao Chien-po have been made more prominent, the images of those negative characters have paled by comparison. It has been said that there are different views on this opera. Debates can be held on this subject. You must consider which side you stand on. Should you stand on the side of the positive characters or on the side of the negative characters? It has been said that there are still people who oppose writing about positive characters. This is wrong. Good people are always the great majority. This is true not only in our socialist countries but even in imperialist countries, where the overwhelming majority are laboring people. In revisionist countries, the revisionists are only a minority. We should place the emphasis on creating artistic images of advanced revolutionaries so as to educate and inspire the people and lead them forward.

RAID ON THE WHITE TIGER REGIMENT

ANONYMOUS

Peking operas with contemporary revolutionary themes which rose to national popularity with last summer's festival have re mained there. One show in the capital for which there are never enough tickets is *Raid on the White Tiger Regiment*, one of the best examples of the "fighting" or acrobatic type of Peking opera.

This type of Peking opera has some unique features. Its conventions have their roots in the martial arts of the past. They include tumbling and aerial somersaults, "flying kicks," "splits," and other acrobatic movements which are difficult to perform but graceful and exciting to watch.

Some were worried that such traditional conventions would find no place in operas on modern and contemporary themes; the hand weapons of modern war, for instance, are rifles, grenades, and submachine guns. The success of *Raid on the White Tiger Regiment* and other new Peking operas of the fighting type has proved these worries groundless. Not only are the acrobatics still used, but, by being adapted to and integrated with modern life to create images of present-day people, they are brought closer to modern audiences.

FROM "Raid on the White Tiger Regiment," *Peking Review*, 3 (Jan. 15, 1965), 30–31.

This particular opera is based on the exploits of a reconnaissance platoon of the Chinese People's Volunteers during the war to resist U.S. aggression and aid Korea. In the story, a CPV commander and liaison man of the Korean People's Army together lead a squad of Volunteer scouts on a reconnaissance mission deep behind the enemy lines. Disguised as puppet troops of Syngman Rhee, they cleverly slip through enemy posts and, aided by Korean villagers, reach and raid the headquarters of the crack "Tiger Regiment." This completely upsets the enemy's plan of attack and helps the main forces of the CPV and the KPA to win a resounding victory.

The courage and resourcefulness of the Chinese Volunteers, and the friendship of the Korean and Chinese people fighting shoulder to shoulder against the U.S. imperialist invaders and their puppets, is an inspiring theme, and the production is packed with dramatic action and suspense. Characteristics of Peking opera are well used.

The scouts start off on their mission on a stormy night. The road is muddy and tortuous, and the enemy soldiers are not asleep at the posts. The actors take full advantage of this for a display of acrobatic prowess.

Heads are bent against the imaginary gusts of wind and rain, an occasional movement to wipe the water off their faces, a sudden slip as the line advances, and half a dozen helping hands offer assistance—a tense picture of the march is conjured up without benefit of stage props or change of scene. With nimble, staccato Peking Opera steps, they circle the stage several times—showing their spirit on the march. Abruptly and noiselessly they drop to the ground—enemy searchlights flit over them. They come up against a barbed-wire fence. With four agile tumbles they get on the run and then leap across the fence with a somersault. They make flying leaps down a high precipice, with an extra somersault in the air. When they alight, an additional "small tumble" is thrown in, indicating that they are trying to steady themselves on their feet.

The climax of the action takes place in the headquarters of the Tiger Regiment. As the scouts pour in, a U.S. "advisor" puts the light out with a shot, and pandemonium ensues. But it is an artfully contrived, perfectly coordinated pandemonium. An enemy soldier makes a headlong dive out of the window; a scout doing a "tiger leap" gains the top of a table and tumbles out the window after him. Scouts and puppet soldiers "dive" at each other in a crisscrossing pattern of flying figures in the air, while the drums thunder and the cymbals crash.

Throughout the play, the acrobatic and the fighting conventions reflect and are woven out of the real life of the scouts. They are closely linked with the dramatic development and are relevant to the story.

In acting, dancing, singing, and music, too—the other important elements of Peking Opera besides the acrobatics—*Raid on the White Tiger Regiment* has introduced new elements. In the opening scene, for instance, the platoon is shown spending a short leave in a Korean village where they had stayed a year before. The re-union between a young platoon leader and a village elder, Grandma Li, is movingly acted. Instead of using the traditional convention in such cases of a respectful but impersonal greeting, they look at each other, pause for a split second, then warmly embrace like mother and son. This is all done in dance movements, rhythmic and graceful. A lyrical passage of singing here by the platoon leader expresses the deep bonds of kinship between the two peoples and adds to the drama of the moment.

When the platoon leader briefs his men on the situation and exposes the hypocrisy of the U.S. imperialists who are holding "peace talks" with Korea and China while actively preparing further attacks on them, he sings: "Although we are holding peace talks, we must maintain our vigilance and be ever ready to give the greedy American wolves blow for blow!" The last half of the sentence is taken from the famous *March of the Chinese People's Volunteers*, as is the melody, but both are well integrated with the traditional melodies of Peking Opera.

VIII

The Performing Arts

---

1. TRADITIONAL ENTERTAINMENTS

Opera has been the main channel for the transmission of the cultural legacy on stage but by no means the only one. There are other types of theatrical performances in traditional style, notably puppet plays and various forms of balladry and story-telling. The Communists have been firm supporters of these popular arts, trying to give them socialist content (as shown in the description "New Story-Tellers") but also rehabilitating many from the serious decay into which they had fallen. The puppet theater is a good case in point.

THE CHINESE PUPPET THEATER

WU WEI-YUN

Puppet shows are common sights in China, whether in city streets or in small villages. This is one of the folk arts enjoyed by everyone, grown-ups—especially villagers—as well as children. The Chinese puppet theater has a very long history and ancient traditions. In early times, puppets were called *kuei lei*, or "strong men." This was probably because wooden puppets were used to portray the heroes who tried to do away with evil and champion the people. According to old legends, as early as the tenth century B.C., a man called Yen Shih made puppets that could sing and dance. . . .

FROM Wu Wei-yun, "The Chinese Puppet Theater," *Chinese Literature*, 2 (March–April, 1958), 122–26.

There are different types of puppets in China. According to accounts written early in the twelfth century, most of the types we know today already existed then. And the names of famous performers in various puppet theaters were recorded, testifying to the popularity and high degree of development of this art in China at that time. The regional variations in our modern puppet shows follow the traditions of the mid-seventeenth century or date back in some cases to the T'ang and Sung dynasties.

Nearly all kinds of local operas are performed as puppet-shows, and so is Peking Opera. There are also shows without a singing accompaniment, like *The Fight Between Lion and Tiger* and *The Dragon Plays with the Pearl*. Chinese puppets are of three main types: glove puppets, marionettes, and rod puppets. In most districts all three types can be found.

Chinese puppetry originated earlier than Chinese drama, but it is closely linked with the Chinese classical theater. Puppet plays imitate the conventions of the local operas. They reproduce beautiful dancing movements and other gestures with uncanny skill and sometimes create effects that cannot be achieved by the living theater. Their repertoire of historical drama is a rich one. In fact, some of the newly rediscovered traditional operas were found in the puppet theater, where the words, tunes, and music have been preserved, as well as descriptions of different scenes and gestures.

One-man puppet shows are still very popular in China. The performer carries his property box from village to village. When he reaches a suitable spot, he takes out his cloth curtains and bamboo poles and sets up his stage. He sounds a gong, a crowd gathers, and the show begins. The stage is less than one square yard, about one and a half yards from the ground, and surrounded by cloth screens. The performer stays behind the screens, where he manipulates the puppets with his hands, sounds the gong and drum with his feet, and sings. In this way he can produce a lively classical drama. Performances like this are given frequently in the countryside, even in remote hilly regions, and as the plots and characters of these local operas are known to every one, they receive an enthusiastic welcome from old and young.

The puppet theater can stage certain episodes that are beyond the power of opera companies. For instance, the latter cannot show a blazing fire burning the enemy forces, nor can Monkey leap up to heaven or down to the bottom of the sea with one somersault, as in the traditional romance. But in puppet shows these scenes can easily be performed and a realistic representation given of beautiful folk stories.

Puppet-making is a sculptural art, and Chinese puppets have distinctly oriental features. A famous contemporary puppet-maker, Chiang Chia-tsou, has devoted the whole of his life to the craft. His young heroes and heroines are strikingly handsome, and the women have elaborate coiffures, reminiscent of T'ang-dynasty paintings. To make a puppet's head, a dozen processes are involved, from carving the wood to applying paint and varnish. The facial expressions show the puppet's age and temperament, and the costumes fit the different parts.

Chinese rod puppets are of three sizes. The small rod puppets in Szechuan are about 18 inches high, the medium size about 28 inches, the largest about the size of human beings. At the end of the Ch'ing dynasty, there were shows with large puppets and real children. The children stood on the shoulders of the manipulators and played the leading parts, while the puppets played minor parts.

The rod puppets of certain districts can move their eyes and are very clever with their hands, able to put on and take off clothes and to button and unbutton them. Some characters, like Pigsy in the romance of the Monkey King, even have movable lips, ears, and noses. And skillful manipulators can make them open doors, fan themselves, shoot arrows, play the flute, light candles, hold umbrellas, or even strum the lute.

The celebrated rod-puppet performer of Shansi, Wang Shao-yu, started learning this art when he was six and, by thirteen, was already famous. He makes his puppets go through all the fine dancing movements of Shansi opera. During rehearsals, he manipulates his puppets in front of a mirror, to ensure that the singing and dialogue are closely coordinated with the puppets' movements. For example, when a man in *The Sacrificed Son* hears that his two sons have accidentally killed the only child of a powerful official, he suddenly stands up and seizes their hands to question them. The expressions of the puppets are so lifelike that spectators say he has brought them to life.

In recent years, performers have shown great enthusiasm and ingenuity and further improved their technique. The rod puppets can now leap on to a horse, smoke a cigarette, sweat, or spit. They move more easily than other puppets and can range freely about the stage.

Glove puppets are also most popular in China. The performer's index finger controls their head movements, his thumb and middle finger their two hands. A skilled performer can manipulate two puppets with entirely different characters and emotions at the same time. Glove puppets are particularly suited to acrobatic and fighting scenes.

Yang Sheng and Ch'en Nan-tien are veteran puppet artists from Fukien with more than thirty years' experience. In the east China drama festival held in 1951, they won the prize for virtuosity. During the last two years, they have performed abroad and won high praise from connoisseurs of the general public. They present a scene from *The Romance of the Three Kingdoms* in which Ts'ao Ts'ao of the Kingdom of Wei sends his officer, Chiang Kan, to a banquet given by the chief marshal of the kingdom of Wu, Chou Yu, and Chiang Kan deliberately steals a letter left in a book by Chou Yu. The audience sees Chou Yu pretending to be drunk, and Chiang Kan trying to look calm but wiping the sweat from his forehead. Their expressions are vividly portrayed to present this battle of wits realistically. In another fighting scene, a hero uses his staff to throw his enemy's corpse into the air and pants with fatigue as if really breathing hard.

Chinese marionettes are attached by strings to a rectangular control-board slightly smaller than a ping-pong bat. One puppet has usually at least eight or nine strings, sometimes as many as twenty-eight. The performer holds the control-board with his left hand, and pulls the strings with his right. He can make a marionette ride on horseback, soar on clouds, row boats, fan himself, wipe his tears, pour out wine, write, undress, and so on. Very great skill and experience are required. The artists usually start their training at about ten and have to practice in a small repertory and study under an expert for three years before they become real artists.

The Experimental Puppet Theatre of Chuanchow, which performed in the film *Puppet Shows of Southern Fukien*, is famous throughout China. One episode from the story of the White Snake is particularly well known. In this, the monk, Fa Hai, beckons angels from the sky, and the sea monsters under the command of White Snake emerge from the water: the crab, the lobster, the conch, the oyster, all true to life. The characters' natures are revealed through their actions—the monk's cruel stubbornness, Green Snake's courage, and White Snake's gentleness. There is an acolyte in this scene guarding the gate for the monk. When Green Snake and White Snake first reach the gate, the young acolyte puts on airs, but the moment Green Snake unsheathes her sword, he is frightened out of his wits.

In the old days, the performers in puppet shows had a very low social status. Oppressed by the reactionary ruling class, they were unable to develop their art. In April, 1955, the first all-China puppet-show festival was held, and though only the artists of certain provinces and municipalities took part, this was something unprecedented in Chinese history. The puppet theaters of different places have distinctive characteristics and styles. In this festival, the artists were able to exchange experiences and received a great incentive to improve and develop Chinese puppet shows.

As pointed out already, most Chinese puppet plays are performances of classical dramas. In recent years, however, puppet players have produced new programs for young people and children and modern dramas. This is a new departure in the Chinese puppet theater and a sign of its healthy growth. A triumphant future may be predicted for this time-honored yet perennially vigorous folk art.

NEW STORY-TELLERS

ANONYMOUS

From time immemorial, China's peasants have listened with rapt attention to the village story-tellers. They brought them legends, homely wisdom, and ideals, knowledge of their history, tales of folk heroes who fought for the people against their oppressors. But this art, like all others, was the arena of a complex class struggle. Interwoven with the healthy strands were others twisted in by the feudal ruling-class culture of the past, with its elements of superstition and enervating idealism and inculcating ideas of humble subjection to the forces of tyranny, exploitation, and reaction.

Since liberation, much has been done to free the good from the dross. As a result, the fine stories of the past are better than ever today. But even more encouraging is that now entirely new stories are being told—tales of the revolution and of contemporary life or episodes from modern novels.

The villages in the rural counties of Shanghai municipality

FROM "New Story-Tellers," *Peking Review*, 47 (Nov. 18, 1965), 23.

give an outstanding example of this new trend in China's popular art. Three years ago, the Shanghai Cultural Bureau and the Shanghai Communist League Committee jointly organized the first class to train new amateur rural story-tellers. A year later, there were 1,000 of them. Last spring, their numbers had soared to more than 10,000. They are all just ordinary commune members but typical of that new generation of peasants who are good at both mental and manual labor. Needing no stage props, they are always ready to enliven a work break, a rest at a tea-house, a wait at a station, or a social occasion at home or at the club.

The Shanghai peasants like the new stories because of their revolutionary realism, revolutionary optimism, and militant spirit. They like the way they fit in with life today.

The new stories have a clear-cut orientation. They propagate the Party's policies, direct attention to new people and new things, spread socialist ideas, and so serve the revolution. In the current Socialist Education Movement, stories of class exploitation and the real-life histories of local families are being widely told in the villages. They remind the old people of the bitter days of the past; they give them a better understanding of the meaning of the happiness of today, they also tell the younger generation of that recent past which they never knew and teach them to be true to the revolutionary tradition.

The story of the *Paupers' Co-op* will not be forgotten by the members of the Hsin-chuang commune. It is about a group of poor peasants whose only property when they set up a co-op farm was their tiny plot of land and a three-quarter share in a donkey. Yet they made their co-op succeed. Discussing the story after they heard it, the Hsin-chuang farmers took heart: "That *Paupers' Co-op* began with only three legs of a donkey; we have half an ox. They succeeded; why can't we?" And today their commune is a big success.

In 1965, in response to the Party's call for an upsurge in agricultural production, the story-tellers of Shanghai's countryside stressed the production angle. They made *Story of Tachai*—about a self-reliant commune—a big favorite. When the Party secretary of the Gold Star Brigade Shou-cheng commune, Chingpu County, cited Tachai at a meeting, everyone knew what he referred to. The brigade was expanding its acreage of double-cropped rice, and its members were discussing the question of asking the state for extra fertilizer. But, with Tachai as an example, in a self-help move they rallied to the initiative of their Party secretary, organized a team to collect silk plants to make compost, and saved money and material for the state. . . .

The direct encouragement of the Communist Party's Shanghai City Committee has been a key factor in the success of the new stories. In the spring of 1965, when it called a meeting of first secretaries of local county Party committees, it devoted one session to a telling of *Story of Tachai* as an introduction to the importance of new tales.

2. NEW PLAYS AND MOVIES

Traditional theater arts have obviously not been neglected, but what about the new forms and media introduced from the West? Modern, or "spoken," drama was largely confined to modern themes when introduced to the Chinese stage early in the twentieth century. In Communist China, however, it has frequently turned to historical subjects for new plays. Phillip Bonosky's description of Kuo Mo-jo's historical drama Tsai Wen-chi *is an excellent example. It is worth noting that the playwright has adopted many techniques from traditional Chinese opera. It is also worth noting that this play and others like it were deeply involved in the controversy over evaluation of historical figures.*

Finally, what of the cinema? Have traditional art forms—opera, music, dancing—been adapted to this new medium? Has it been used to carry Chinese history to the masses after the fashion of traditional theater? The answer to all these questions is yes, but not too successfully. Communist movies have usually been concerned more with modern than with historical subjects, as being more directly useful for propaganda and education. The historical films that the Communists have made carry an obvious message. Hsiung Deh-ta, employed in the British film industry, discusses one of the most celebrated of their historical films, Lin Tse-hsü. *Although in general not much impressed with the People's Republic's film-making, he does have a few kind words for a documentary on Peking Opera training. The selection following Hsiung Deh-ta's describes one of the most ambitious attempts to translate Peking Opera to the screen. This film, too, is a documentary but one that features entire operatic scenes played by the famous Mei Lan-fang and other Peking Opera stars.*

Finally, there are cartoon films that draw from the wealth of ancient tales and folklore and use Chinese art forms. The potential for a distinctively national style, at least in this branch of film-making, seems very high.

DRAGON PINK ON OLD WHITE (I)

PHILLIP BONOSKY

It was something of a triumph getting tickets, for all Peking—perhaps all China—had been talking of nothing else but Kuo Mo-jo's new historical drama, *Tsai Wen-chi*. We were at the theater (where we would also hear Beethoven's *Ninth*) at seven, making our way through crowds of students buttonholing us —for once forgetting their Chinese reserve with Westerners— hoping for an extra ticket. But we sat for a good hour in the auditorium before the curtain went up, because one of the actors was ill.

But when the curtain finally did go up, from that moment on, I ceased to remember or to care who I was or where I was. I had never seen anything like the play that unfolded before me. I was transported, by some incredible magic, to a world of vision and emotion so exotic, on the one hand, and yet so real, on the other, that the combination left me helpless to define just what had taken place. For me the play was not just a play; it was a climax.

It is the tale told of the daughter of Tsai Yung, a scholar of the Han dynasty (206 B.C.—220 A.D.), Tsai Wen-chi, beautiful and talented, who after an early tragic life finally fell captive to the Hsiungnu and married one of the princes of the Eastern Region, with whom she had two children. She is implored by Ts'ao Ts'ao, Prime Minister of the Han, to return to her native home and there help complete her scholar father's work, *The Sequel to the Han-Dynasty History*. The prince of the Eastern Region, her husband, agreed, after some moving moments, to let her go, persuaded that her return would help cement relations between the

FROM Phillip Bonosky, *Dragon Pink on Old White* (New York: Marzani and Munsell, 1963), pp. 28–32. Reprinted by permission of the publisher.

two nationalities; and Wen-chi did go, leaving her two children behind. This leave-taking from her children is probably one of the most heart-rending I have ever witnessed on the stage.

Sunk in the mood of the play, and transported into a new dimension, in which the unknown Chinese words of the speakers was an integral part of the mood, suddenly I was startled, as though struck by a blow, when the boy-child, torn from its mother, cried in piercing English words: "Mama! Mama!"

For a moment, it seemed to me that the power of the grief was so profound that its cry broke through the conventional barrier of language into what seemed English to me—as though for this tragic moment the cry was universal, and for it history knew only one word: "Mama! Mama!" But it was Chinese I heard.

My eyes filled with tears, and I could not hide them from Chen, though the reason for them was more than I could understand then. Perhaps that cry was a climax, too, to my own feelings— my own profound and muffled feelings about all of oppressed, backward, and suffering China, to which I felt so close and so united, and so guilty. Perhaps, too, it was my own child and wife I missed now with a pang . . .

Meanwhile, on the stage, Tung Szu, Tsai Wen-chi's cousin, who comes to take her back home, persuades her to return with him, though it meant parting from her children for many years, by proving to her that her country needed her and that her work on her father's book would be a great contribution to her country's welfare. Placing her duty to her country above her own feelings for her family, Wen-chi embarks upon the long journey home, but only after several nights of agony in which her fears are dramatized on the stage in marvelously evocative and hypnotic episodes, where the images of her terrors take on demoniacal shape, as the visions of her nightmarish dreams. Jealous conspirators almost destroy the mission altogether by charging her with illicit relations with her cousin, Tung Szu. But, in the denouement, she is reunited with her children, now almost grown, and marries Tung Szu after the death of her husband.

The beautiful and remarkably talented Chu Lin plays the title role with absolute authority. This is a tale in which a Chinese woman is shown to display genius and courage in a period when women were still chattel to men. Tsai Wen-chi was a poetess and her famous "Song of the Reed-pipe" is played by a flutist off-stage as antiphonal commentary to her thoughts and emotions. The director of the play, Chiao Chu-pin, writes that he was confronted with a very difficult problem in mounting the play. After wrestling with various schemes for satisfying the mood and action, he finally settled, with Kuo Mo-jo's cooperation, on a style patterned after traditional Chinese opera. The result was remarkably fitting. The decision to violate naturalistic forms and conventional styles of speaking succeeded in producing on the stage something entirely new, something with an esthetic dimension unknown to other drama. With a chorus in the wings and Tsai Wen-chi's music and song commenting on the action, the all-enveloping impression is profoundly moving, almost completely so.

And yet, for all my admiration of the play, I have said "almost." For the fact is, marvelous as are the early scenes of torment and anguish projected as dream visions, the scenes of domestic life, of Tsai Wen-chi's relations with her children, her nobility, her understanding of state affairs—the later scenes seem too hurried and end on a note far more "positive" than seems credible or, at least, credible from an artistic point of view. . . .

THE CHINESE CINEMA TODAY

HSIUNG DEH-TA

"As the motion picture is one of the most popular arts and one of the Party's most effective weapons of propaganda and education, in our film undertakings we must necessarily put political ideological work and the question of creative thinking in the leading position [and] strengthen the Party's leadership over the cinema. . . ." Thus declared Hsia Yen, Deputy Minister of Culture. But the problem is, how much artistic independence must be sacrificed in order to strengthen the Party's leadership over the cinema? The answer seems to be clear after viewing the dozen or so films from China shown recently at the National Film Theatre in London. . . .

The Opium War of 1840 is an important chapter of Chinese history, though it is not an episode in which British historians can take pride. Lin Tse-hsü was the Chinese hero of this war and the film, using his name as its title, is not merely a historical or biographical story. It conveys the sense of real people, real problems, and real relationships. It shows the evil of the opium trade

FROM Hsiung Deh-ta, "The Chinese Cinema Today," *The China Quarterly*, 4 (Oct.–Dec., 1960), 82 and 85–87.

which was imposed on China, the corruption and helplessness of the Ch'ing government, and the struggle of the people against it.

The film opens in 1838 when the emperor, Tao Kuang, dismayed by the way the importation of opium is draining the country of its silver reserves and turning thousands of people into addicts, sends Lin Tse-hsü as high commissioner to the port of Canton to enforce the decree prohibiting the trade. He compels the foreign, i.e. British, merchants to surrender their opium stocks, which he burns at the waterfront. However, he is removed and exiled as a result of the intrigues at court and the work of Lin Tse-hsü thus comes to a tragic end. The story, however, does not end with Lin's defeat but with the awakening of the masses. In the final scene, Lin witnesses how the peasants and fishermen around Canton, organized into *ping-ying tuan* ("put-down-the-British" corps), take up their resistance to the foreign troops penetrating the countryside.

It may be argued here that the film could arouse more sympathy and indignation from its audience if it were to end at the point of Lin's defeat and with China's destiny at stake. Aesthetically, it might be more satisfactory, but, in terms of socialist realism, this would not do, for one is not supposed to have a too pessimistic view concerning any historic event, particularly an event of national importance. Though it was a national defeat, it had to be a defeat of a corrupt government, not of the people.

The most disappointing item in this season was *The Magic Lotus Lantern,* which was described as a Chinese National Dance Film in color but which turned out to be a film of semi-Western ballet in Chinese costume accompanied by pseudo-Western music. The story is an old legend, a love affair between a mortal and a goddess, and how, with the help of their child and the Magic Lotus Lantern, they overcome the powerful god, Erh Lang, the goddess's brother who represents orthodoxy. It is obvious that the influence of Tchaikovsky is strong, but the music here is too monotonous and without any theme. Some of the dances are embarrassingly long and boring. Though the spirit of this experimental venture should be highly praised, it fails in many respects. Let us hope that some more successful attempt will be made in the near future.

An unexpected delight was the film *Five Golden Flowers,* a sort of musical about the young people of the Pai nationality in the province of Yunnan in Southwest China.

Basically it is a love story, but one can see its political significance from characters with names like Deputy Commune Director Golden Flower, Iron-Smelter Golden Flower, Tractor-Driver Golden Flower, Cattle-Breeder Golden Flower, and Fertilizer-Collector Golden Flower. It has some of the wistful charm of Chinese verse, and its poetic regard for the countryside and people amply compensate for some rough edges in the script. Again, it is a little too long. Toward the end, the whole business almost becomes unintentionally funny. One point worth noting is in this film; the Chinese, admittedly two intellectuals, are shown quite helpless and weak compared with the Pai people.

Among the documentaries, the most interesting one was *Training Players for the Chinese Classical Theater*, a detailed and fascinating account of the training of young children for the stage, ending with some impressive demonstrations of technique by senior students and the staff. Others like *Underground Palace* and *Along the Lhasa River* are worth consideration for their seriousness and craftsmanship, though they lack the passion necessary to create a national school.

Judging from these films, the most common theme is how, with the Communist takeover, people's lives changed from hardship and oppression to happiness and prosperity. This seems to fit the quotation at the beginning of this article that the Party's leadership must be strengthened over the cinema. True, most of these films have important themes (human relations, social problems), but from a purely aesthetic point of view, how important is the content of the film in relation to the form? Claude Chabrol, one of the forerunners of the *nouvelle vague* in France, stated that the important or "big" subject is worth no more than the unimportant one and that the smaller the subject is, the more it can be treated greatly. In other words, the more noble a film's subject, the more suspiciously it is regarded.

This view, that form is paramount over content, can be easily dismissed by the socialist realists as decadent. But the Chinese film-makers all seem to make the same fundamental mistake: They disregard the real, human truth of their material. Instead, they adopt some key figures and dramatized incidents to serve political arguments, and the result is films that look like shadows of their own intentions.

With such a long cultural history, China should be capable of producing films that make a genuine contribution to the development of this medium, just as India and Japan have done. It is difficult to be certain whether we can expect any surprises from

China. All the productions so far still have, by Western standards, a slightly dated look. China has yet to produce anything to compare, visually even, with the Polish *Kanal* or the Hungarian *The Merry-Go-Round* or even the Russian *The Cranes are Flying*.

THE STAGECRAFT OF MEI LAN-FANG

WU TSU-KUANG

Admirers of classical Chinese opera have long looked forward to a film record of Mei Lan-fang's art. But this proved beyond the powers of film-workers in old China. The people have always loved the opera, but, in preliberation times, the powers that be were still infected by the old mandarin officials' scorn for it as a not very respectable profession. This was no small addition to the many other difficulties involved in getting together the necessary financial and technical means needed to make a film of Peking Opera.

New ideas, new conditions, reign in People's China. In 1953, the Peking Film Studio put *The Stage Art of Mei Lan-fang* on its production plan. The filming of this, the first full-length film treatment of classical Peking Opera as performed on the stage, was not a job to be lightly undertaken. Peking Opera, with its more than a hundred years of history, is a highly developed synthesis of singing, dancing, and dramatic art. Mei Lan-fang, a consummate artist, has carried on its finest traditions and himself introduced many innovations and refinements that have brought it to an unrivaled peak of perfection. Officials of the government department of cinematography, Mei Lan-fang himself, film technicians, various specialists in Peking Opera, artists, and myself (I had been entrusted with production of the film) held frequent consultations. We found ourselves confronted with a task that bristled with difficulties. Almost two years were spent in preparatory work before actual filming began.

As completed, *The Stage Art of Mei Lan-fang* includes five of his most popular productions. They are *The Meeting at the Broken Bridge* (*Tuan Chiao*), *Sword of the Universe* (*Yu Chou Feng*), *The King Parts with His Beloved* (*Pa Wang Pieh Chi*),

FROM Wu Tsu-kuang, "The Stagecraft of Mei Lan-fang," *People's China*, 6 (March, 1956), 28–29 and 31.

The Drunken Beauty (*Kuei Fei Ts'ui Chiu*), and *The Nymph of the River Lo* (*Lo Shen*). The leading characters played by Mei Lan-fang have long been popular favorites. He shows an astounding versatility in characterizations that differ widely from each other.

The stories of these operas are all taken from Chinese history or folklore. *The Meeting at the Broken Bridge* is an excerpt from *The Tale of the White Snake*, an old folk-tale. A white snake, so the story goes, having observed the austerities of a mystic discipline for a thousand years, finally succeeds in assuming the shape of a woman. Walking with her maid by the shores of West Lake, she meets a young man called Hsu Hsien. They fall in love at first sight and get married. But Fa Hai, a bigoted monk, opposes the union. He denounces the White Lady as an evil spirit and turns Hsu Hsien against her. The episode we have filmed shows the first meeting of the White Lady and Hsu Hsien after their estrangement. The White Lady, loving, lovable, courageous in her misfortune, has come to symbolize the bitter fate of women in feudal China. Mei Lan-fang gives a moving performance in his role. He shows the charm of the White Lady at this meeting with Hsu Hsien, her cold anger in her struggle with Fa Hai, her wavering between love and contempt when she meets Hsu Hsien again. His every movement strikes a chord of sympathy in the hearts of the audience. . . .

This film proved to be a gathering of talents. Collaborating with Mei Lan-fang in the operas filmed were Chiang Liao-hsiang and Yu Chen-fei, two of China's finest actors in the roles of *hsiao shen* (young male characters), Liu Lien-jung, who is well known for his performances in *chin* (painted-face, usually military) roles, and Hsiao Chang-hua, a master of clowning. With the exception of young Mei Pao-chiu, a son of Mei Lan-fang who also specializes in *tan* roles, all the other leading actors in the film are veterans of the Peking operatic stage.

We had many discussions on questions of décor and costuming. Traditional Peking Opera is lavishly costumed but is usually performed on a stage bare except for an embroidered curtain backdrop. Almost the sole props are a table and two chairs. However, we felt it necessary to relax this austerity somewhat and introduce a certain amount of scenery where this would not adversely affect the actors' performance. This provides a background for the play and throws the characters on the screen into sharper relief. We experimented with several ideas and found that traditional Chinese paintings go very well with the performance and costumes of Peking Opera. We have also used a number of folk designs for background decoration. We used fully developed three-dimensional scenery and other theatrical effects only in *The Nymph of the River Lo*. All the other operas are produced much as they are seen on the Chinese stage today. . . .

The film itself is divided into two parts. Part one deals with the life of Mei Lan-fang and incorporates the two operas *The Meeting at the Broken Bridge* and *Sword of the Universe*. Part two presents *The King Parts with His Beloved* and *The Drunken Beauty*. *The Nymph of the River Lo* is being made into a separate film. Part one was released shortly after the spring festival this year. We wait eagerly for public comment. This will help to guide us in completing another film we have begun work on, dealing with Peking Opera. So this record of the art of China's greatest actor is at most only a tribute to him and a beginning of a succession of films which will carry on the great tradition of classical drama in another medium. We have an arduous and responsible task on hand, and we hope to live up to the high expectations of our audiences.

THE NEW CARTOON FILMS

HUA CHUN-WU

I would like to say a word about the national flavor of Chinese cartoons. All those who have seen them realize that these cartoons, puppet films, and scissor-cut films are distinctively Chinese in style. The cartoon film came to China from the West; before liberation, American cartoons were shown in all big Chinese cities, so that for decades our children's minds were filled with Mickey Mouse and the Big Bad Wolf. Though Wan Lai-ming and his brother struggled for years to create Chinese cartoons, they could do nothing at that time. But, now that the working class are in power, our cartoons have grown apace from small beginnings.

When we speak of the national style of our cartoons, we are concerned primarily with content. Many of these children's films are based on folk tales and legends with an educational value. The

FROM Hua Chun-wu, "The New Cartoon Films," *Chinese Literature*, 6 (June, 1960), 71–74.

early puppet film *The Magic Brush* described how a folk artist, Ma Liang, was aided by heaven so that all he painted came to life and he used his brush to help the working people combat the forces of evil. This is a very popular folk tale. Another puppet film, *Master Tung-kuo*, drawn from an ancient fable, tells how an unworldly scholar who wants to protect a hungry wolf from a hunter is nearly eaten by the ungrateful wolf. This film teaches children to differentiate between good and evil. *The Proud General* is a cartoon based on a revised folk tale and describes a general who grows so proud after a victory that finally he is captured by the enemy. The puppet film *Flaming Mountain* takes as its theme an episode from the well-known classical novel *Pilgrimage to the West*, in which Monkey fights with a monster. The cartoon *A Piece of Chuang Brocade* is based on a national minority folk legend. It presents a mother and son of the Chuang nationality who are hard-working and brave. The mother weaves a beautiful tapestry, which is blown away by a great gust of wind, but after many perils the son recovers it from fairyland and the scenery on the tapestry becomes real. A recent scissor-cut film, *Fisherboy*, is drawn from a folk legend about the Boxer uprising and shows how the Chinese people opposed the imperialists who were robbing China. These romantic tales are widely popular with all age groups. And themes such as these help to make our cartoon films distinctively Chinese in style.

Some people have the notion that a national flavor can only be produced by using some national or folk legend and portraying characters in ancient costumes. Of course, this oversimplified view is wrong. Our cartoons not only inherit what is essentially Chinese in those legends and develop it further but also produce films with a national flavor on new themes. During the Big Leap of 1959, our cartoonists carried out certain experiments along these lines. *Mural on a Commune Yard Wall* is a cartoon about our people's fight against nature and their revolutionary enthusiasm. This film shows men and women in real life against a legendary background. The peasants' wall-painting represents their fighting spirit and overwhelming confidence through simple but exaggerated images. Cartoons with new content like this reflect our present-day life and are also unmistakably Chinese. This is one of the encouraging features in our recent film production.

A cartoon is a film and at the same time a work of art. We can therefore also find something uniquely Chinese in the sets and people presented. Many of our cartoons, which employ the techniques of traditional Chinese painting, have colors reminiscent of Chinese landscape painting. Even the flowers and birds in these cartoons owe much to our traditional art. This is evident from *A Piece of Chuang Brocade*, with its enchanting background of green, tranquil hills which blend with changeful clouds, thunder, and lightning into one harmonious whole, appropriate to the development of the story. In the scissor-cut film *Pigsy and the Watermelon*, Pigsy, with his big belly and flowing coat, is familiar to all from the novel *Pilgrimage to the West*. The boy in *Fisherboy* is based on the "twin gods of harmony" in the traditional New Year pictures, and his movements are based on the stylized gestures of Chinese opera. In the cartoon *A Small Carp Jumps Over the Dragon Gate*, Grandmother Carp wears spectacles and carries a stick like that of the old artist Ch'i Pai-chih. All these characters, as well as many of the small animals, are essentially Chinese. Their movements and gestures are based on prototypes familiar and dear to our people.

Scissor-cuts, shadow plays, and paper window-decorations are forms of Chinese folk art. Our shadow plays, evolved in the eleventh century, absorbed certain decorative features of classical and folk art and reached a very high artistic level. The scissor-cuts, which have much in common with the shadow plays, are even more widely popular in the Chinese countryside. And today these different elements of folk art have been used to make new cartoons and a new genre of cartoon—the scissor-cut film. Since folk art comes from the people, these new scissor-cut films have a strong national flavor. They adapt the artistic exaggeration of shadow plays and scissor-cuts to present characters, fully exploit the two-dimensional nature of this art, and use strong color contrasts, instead of limiting themselves to natural colors, in order to convey a world of legend and fantasy. This type of film became widely popular as soon as it appeared. This unique, new Chinese film form, the scissor-cut film, is an important contribution to the socialist film world. Indeed, thanks to the guidance of the Party, Mao Tse-tung's thought in literature and art, and their own hard work and skill, our film artists have produced a new flower for the pleasure of film-goers in every land. . . .

3. MUSIC

Confucius considered proper music an essential part of the political order. Mao Tse-tung and his followers would heartily agree, but their kind of political order and their kind of music are worlds apart from that of Confucius' time. The appreciation of music's emotive power in rousing revolutionary enthusiasm has led to a strong emphasis on popular native tunes and rhythms, "well-known and beloved by the Chinese masses." Many new songs, like the folk ballads discussed in the sixth chapter, put a new revolutionary political message into the old forms. Thus, even in periods of greatest ideological pressure, such as the Great Leap Forward and the Cultural Revolution, the music of China has continued to sound Chinese but with a strongly folksy flavor.

This is not all there has been to music in the People's Republic, however. Apart from popular music, there has also been in times of political relaxation an avid interest both in listening to Western classical music and in exploring China's own classical music heritage. The painstaking work by the Institute for Research into Traditional Chinese Music (founded in 1954) in reviving the almost lost art of playing that most beloved instrument of the traditional scholar, the seven-stringed lute or chin, has been one result of this. In our first selection, the venerable chin master Ch'a Fu-hsi describes this. Other ancient instruments, such as the two-stringed fiddle erh-hu and the guitar-like p'ip'a, enjoyed similar attention.

In fact, in music, as in theater and painting, distinct Chinese and Western styles survived with entirely separate "Chinese music" orchestras playing entirely native instruments. Ho Lu-t'ing, one of modern China's leading musicians, discusses the whole question of national music and a possible synthesis of Chinese and Western styles. While paying due respect to folk music, his major emphasis is on the academy where he expects modern professional musicians to create "a modern national music." Developments since 1963 have not been favorable to this expectation. With revolutionary music for the masses in demand, not only has Western bourgeois music like that of Beethoven and Tchaikovsky been eclipsed, but so has classical Chinese music. As the last selection *indicates, revolutionary airs now must have the "smell of gun-powder."*

THE CHINESE LUTE
CH'A FU-HSI

The *chin* or Chinese lute is one of the oldest stringed instruments in China. Twenty-five centuries ago it was used by the nobility in sacrifices and other ceremonies as well as to cultivate virtue. It was not so much music for enjoyment as a part of the self-cultivation and moral training of the upper class. Confucius, speaking of the self-cultivation of the superior man, said he should first study the *Book of Songs*, then the *Book of Rites*, and attain accomplishment through music. Such was always the view of the old Chinese literati. Thus the Sung-dynasty writer Ou-yang Hsiu said: "Though we strum the *chin* with our fingers, it is the mind that directs the sound, and we hear the *chin* not with our ears but our hearts." In other words, the lute-player should be pure of heart, and his hearers should appreciate the moral message. This is an indication of the importance attached to the *chin* by scholars of past ages. . . .

In every generation, lute-players complained that few could appreciate their art, indicating that there were never too many expert exponents of the *chin* and that there were many different schools with different styles. Nevertheless, for centuries the Chinese people have loved this music. Already 1,700 years ago, the instrument had a fixed form. It is about 1.2 meters long, 0.17 meters wide at one end and 0.13 at the other, about 0.2 meters across at the broadest part—the shoulder—and between 0.03 and 0.07 meters thick. The sound box is convex above and flat below; the strings are stretched from the broad to the narrow end and attached to the pedals underneath. The most ancient *chin*, dating from more than 1,700 years ago, were a little shorter and broader, like the stone *chin* in Chu-ke Liang's temple in Mienyang, Szechwan.

Considerable skill is required to make a *chin*. It was not usually made for sale, and few folk artists could fashion one. But men of

FROM Ch'a Fu-hsi, "The Chinese Lute," *Chinese Literature*, 3 (March, 1960), 128–35.

the Han dynasty still possessed quite a few ancient lutes handed down from Chou-dynasty nobles, and these were of such good quality that, during the four hundred years of the Han dynasty, no new *chin* were made until Tsai Yung at the end of the dynasty revived the art. The great Ch'in-dynasty painter Ku Kai-chih depicted a man making a *chin*, while Hsieh Chuang in the fifth century and other T'ang-dynasty men of letters left sketches and notes on the construction of this instrument. During the T'ang dynasty, there were nine famous *chin*-makers in the Lei family in Szechwan, while the Yangtze Valley had such famous craftsmen as Shen Liao and Chang Yuch. In the Sung dynasty, large numbers of *chin* were made in official and private workshops. Chu Chih-yuan of the Yüan dynasty was a celebrated *chin*-maker, as were Chu Kung-wang and Chang Chin-hsiu of the Ming dynasty. Many well-to-do lute players followed the tradition of leaving good instruments for posterity, which accounts for the thousands of fine *chin* passed down from one hand to another through these centuries. So, although the ancient *chin* was not manufactured as a commodity, the old instrument has come down to us through twenty centuries. . . .

In the past 2,000 years, *chin* music has developed very slowly. The instrument was never produced in large quantities, and the music was seldom performed by more than two or three musicians together. Though scores were written for nearly twenty centuries, no single player could read those dating from more than three centuries before him, for the methods of notation and scoring kept changing. After the fall of the Ch'ing dynasty in 1911, attempts were made to revive the ancient music, but those doing this fell into the mistake of trying to preserve the *chin* as an ancient relic. Hence this did not lead to any real revival. In fact, after the War of Resistance Against Japanese Aggression, many old lute-players died or gave up playing, and most of the old *chin* clubs were disbanded. When the last maker of *chin* strings died, the art appeared to be extinct.

After liberation, however, following economic rehabilitation, in 1953 the Communist Party and the government called a conference of artists and writers and put forward the appeal to let a hundred flowers bloom, to weed through the old and let the new emerge. This directive gave timely encouragement to art and literature and brought about a revival of *chin* music, too.

Amateur lute-players have been organized throughout the country to take part in performances and to teach pupils, while professional lute-players have joined the conservatories of music or research institutes. Many ancient tunes are now broadcast or made into gramophone records. Today, lute-players frequently perform in concerts to thousands of listeners and receive an enthusiastic response. Some of our new historical plays and ballets include *chin* performances; film orchestras sometimes also use the old *chin* music in historical films. The conservatories of music in Peking, Shanghai, Chengtu, and Shenyang now offer special courses in the *chin*; the *chin* clubs and other musical organizations in different parts of the country are searching for lost tunes, composing new tunes, and teaching people to play this traditional instrument.

The Institute for the Study of Chinese Music has collected a great many works and scores of *chin* music. In addition to 67 works and scores recorded within the last century, 70 unknown and hitherto unrecorded works have been discovered. Now we have about 3,300 scores of more than 560 compositions dating from after the Han dynasty, as well as directions for the fingering of more than 1,100 scores from the Southern and Northern dynasties (317–581 A.D.) onward. Research carried out under the guidance of the Chinese Musicians' Union have enabled eight experts to reconstruct the ancient compositions *The Lonely Orchid* and *Kuanglin San,* which have not been played for several centuries. All these old *chin* scores and directions for fingering have been embodied in two encyclopedias of 2 million characters, which make it possible for us to rediscover and play again tunes forgotten since ancient times. In the past, lute-players without access to such material found that the scores more than three centuries old incomprehensible. Today they are exulting because, under our socialist system, we can collect and study materials from all over China to revive the fine old traditions of *chin* music.

Today, in addition to solo *chin* recitals, not only have we revived *chin* and *hsiao* duets and *chin* accompaniments to singing, but there have also been fresh innovations. Many old music lovers in local groups and clubs are helping the daily increasing number of new amateur musicians to learn this ancient art and practicing hard to improve their own playing. Some old compositions have been adapted for performance with other instruments in orchestral concerts. Three years ago, the *chin* could be used in concerts only for three or four traditional tunes; now the standard of performance has been greatly raised and the repertoire extended. Today lute-players can give a recital of *chin* music lasting for two or three hours.

Thousands of old instruments are being collected by lute-players, organizations of musicians, and museums. These old *chin* are refurbished with pegs and strings and used again: Indeed a number of museums are even lending their *chin* for musicians to use. The Chinese Musical Instruments Factory in Soochow is now manufacturing *chin* on a large scale and they are selling in hundreds. The cooperative in Soochow that produces *chin* strings has taken on new apprentices. The reforms made in other traditional instruments have encouraged lute-players to experiment with the *chin*. Thus the Central Conservatory, the Institute of Musical Research, the Chinese Musical Instruments Factory in Soochow, and other craftsmen have produced four types of improved *chin* with a larger sound volume, which have been used in concerts. Experiments of this kind are still going on.

So, within a few years of the establishment of the People's Republic of China, this traditional art with its history of more than 2,000 years has been carried to a new stage. And this is just the beginning. Such a development is no accident. The old musicians can see clearly that only under the socialist system is it possible to have a genuine renaissance of the best traditional arts.

WHAT KIND OF MUSIC FOR CHINA?
HO LU-T'ING

The items that received the greatest attention at the four-week music festival in Peking last summer were the traditional tunes played on Chinese instruments and songs and local-style opera arias performed by folk-singers from different regions. New works —choral, instrumental, and orchestral—also occupied a considerable part of the programs. But our ancient heritage, as the festival showed, is still the best aspect of China's musical culture. Musicians all agree that it must be preserved and enriched. A more controversial problem, however, and one of quite long standing, is how to set about creating a new national music, expressive of the spirit and sentiment of modern China.

FROM Ho Lu-t'ing, "What Kind of Music for China?" *China in Transition* (Peking: China Reconstructs, 1957), pp. 377–79 and 380–82.

Now it is my opinion that a national music, like a nation itself, is formed over a long period of history—and that it is not formed in isolation. Musicians of various European countries, in the past three or four hundred years, influenced one another to such an extent that terms like the baroque period, the rococo, the classical, or the romantic can be applied to Western music as a whole. But did this have the effect of submerging national characteristics? On the contrary, it produced in the nineteenth century such unmistakably national composers as Grieg, Chopin, Debussy, Smetana, Dvořák, and Russia's "Big Five."

In China, too, one of the great flowerings of music occurred in a period when musical culture was being assimilated from abroad, from India and Central Asia, during the Sui (589–617 A.D.) and T'ang (618–906 A.D.) dynasties. Professor Yang Ying-liu wrote in his *Outline History of Chinese Music:* "The secular music of the T'ang people was a kind of creative combination of pure Chinese and *hu* [foreign] music."

As for folk songs and local operas, their different styles are closely related to the speech, customs, natural surroundings, and social life of the respective regions. But these operas did not take shape in isolation either; they, too, were affected by external influences. When an outside form first clashes with a local one, some kind of incongruity is inevitable, and immature works result. After a time, however, the outside influence is assimilated and becomes part of the mainstream.

Among our musical instruments, for instance, we now regard the *hu chin* (two-stringed fiddle), the *p'ip'a* (a fretted guitar-like instrument), and the *sona* (a horn) as Chinese. But all three originally came from what were then the foreign countries of the "Western Regions" (now Kansu and Sinkiang) and still retain their foreign names.

In Europe, from the seventeenth century onward, there was a great vitality in the arts and sciences as the various countries moved away from feudalism and modern society arose. But China, under the rule of the Ch'ing dynasty (1644–1911), experienced no basic social change and remained stubbornly aloof from outside contacts. One result was that her musical culture stagnated until after the turn of the present century, when Western influences began to impinge on it.

That clash, when it came, was a sudden one, and Chinese music entered a very chaotic period. On the one hand, there was the deep ocean of our musical heritage—consisting mainly of folk songs, local opera, and narrative ballads, along with the traditional orchestral and instrumental music. On the other hand, there was modern European music, an idiom entirely new to the Chinese people, both in its formal aims and its technique of composition. The collision of these two widely differing forms produced conflict and argument that has been going on ever since. And the recent music festival again debated the old issues: between "foreign" and "domestic," between "scientific" and "backward." This debate continues. Professional and amateur musicians, ordinary music-lovers, all are taking part in it.

Nobody has been heard actually to deny that China's traditional music has any artistic value. But it is looked down on and regarded as backward by some people, who are accustomed to the Western musical tradition only. Others, on the contrary, take a narrow national view and repudiate anything Western. In the discussions at the music festival, I heard this opinion: "The leading musical authorities these days are all trained in the Western way: they talk about creating a national music, but there is danger that they may strangle traditional music under the slogan of enriching it with Western elements." And some people asked jealously: "What percentage of the music played at the festival was Western and what percentage national?"

What do such people mean by "national"? To their ears, only songs sung in the folk style and music played on traditional instruments was national; everything else seemed Western. Therefore they reached the conclusion that Western music dominated the festival. But were not all the works performed there written by Chinese composers? We have far too few musical theorists and highly trained composers, so perhaps some of the works were immature. Nonetheless, they certainly represented a genuine attempt at modern national style.

Groups of musicians have been traveling around the country, going into the villages and into national minority areas. They have collected songs and musical scores, written down tunes and lyrics, made tape recordings, and interviewed traditional ballad singers and local musicians. Much of the material they gathered was subsequently arranged for concert performance, and some of the adaptations have been very popular with music lovers both at home and abroad.

But success in this direction is still comparatively rare. On the whole, as the music festival revealed, folk songs often lose much of their original flavor and feeling after professional musicians have gone to work on them. Why? I think it is because we have been taking these matters too lightly. The arranger must have a thorough understanding of the nature and style of every single folk song he tackles, of its pattern of development, and its relation to the people among whom it is sung. Otherwise he cannot avoid damaging its integrity or spoiling the original style. To be able to write pretty accompaniments is not enough; a musician must also know what a folk song is and how it is born. . . .

To create a modern national music, I think, we should study Western technique and apply it to traditional Chinese music. We can certainly adopt the Western system of notation. And since any traditional Chinese music can be played on Western instruments, we can use them all. We should also study their essential characteristics so as to improve our own instruments.

In such things as harmony and counterpoint, Chinese and Western music have the same basic principles. But only we ourselves can devise our own national style and enrich the texture of our music.

In relation to form, we can also recognize the same general principle in the two traditions. For instance, the sequence of movements in a Chinese musical work—"the introduction, the elucidation of the theme, the change to a fresh viewpoint, and the summing up"—is essentially the same as the Western three-part song form (AABA). But the Western form has gone on from there to more complex manifestations, such as the fugue and the sonata. We can compose traditional-style music in these forms. Some of our musicians have already attempted it.

When I say we should study Western techniques, I do not mean that we should imitate them or refashion Chinese music to make it accord with Western models. I think a knowledge of Western technique, theory, and experiences should help us to seek out our own pattern of development and to build up the necessary theories so that we can create forms suitable to our purposes. Such a new national music, composed according to a new technique and played on improved Chinese instruments, will be different from the traditional music played on the old instruments. But it will still be national in form and intensely Chinese.

During the period when the Chinese people were fighting for their freedom, we needed songs that would encourage and inspire. The traditional Chinese melodies, we must remember, were not adequate for this situation. Except for a few North Shensi ballads, our folk songs generally lacked a fighting spirit and rhythm. A

whole range of new, fighting, patriotic songs came into existence
during the anti-Japanese war, most of them in march time, with
a strong Western influence in their melodies. Among them was
Nieh Erh's *March of the Volunteers,* now China's national an-
them, and Hsien Hsing-hai's famous *Yellow River Cantata,* written in a modern choral form. It is difficult to imagine that, if
either of these composers had stuck entirely to traditional forms
and melodies, their work would have been so stirring, so apt for its
time, so right for the people.

Now, as our country moves into a new historical period, we
must create songs for our own generation, with new elements that
broaden the scope of our traditional music rather than detract
from it.

Argument has also arisen as to whether more stress should be
put on the development of the traditional orchestra or the symphony orchestra. Some people are for "coexistence" but hold that
the traditional orchestra should receive the main emphasis. I agree
that we must give special attention to organizing and training
more traditional orchestras, because this will help to spread understanding of music and delight in its performance. Traditional
instruments are simple in structure, easy to master, and inexpensive to buy. Factories, farms, and schools can all afford to have
them. So I think our composers should write more works for such
orchestras and that the Ministry of Light Industry should get
some experts to study how to improve the traditional instruments,
standardize their pitch, and so on.

Having said this, I still consider that the symphony orchestra
should be the main point of emphasis in forming China's new
musical culture. What we call "Western" musical instruments
have been developed to a very high degree of perfection by musicians and craftsmen in the different countries. The potentialities
of a symphony orchestra are far greater than those of the Chinese
traditional orchestra. A symphonic ensemble can play both Western and Chinese works, and give the latter a richer tone and color
than ever before.

China has an astonishingly rich variety of local opera styles. It
is neither a simple process nor a short one for each style to be
formed and perfected. Why then do our musicians often look
down on the folk artists? It may be because many of the latter
cannot read music and have had little general education. But it is
necessary to remember that the folk musicians have attained their
artistry after long years of arduous training, and the music they

perform is the fruit of hundreds or even thousands of years of tradition. Local operas are a composite art. Our musicians, most of whom are trained in the Western tradition, must themselves learn the elements of Chinese literature, drama, dancing, art, and history—as well as Chinese traditional music—before they can take an effective part in adapting or improving local operas.

As for the folk artists, all the educational opportunities they used to lack are now open to them. They should therefore study modern music, or at least learn to read it, so they can work with the composers to collect and edit our rich musical heritage.

WHAT PITCH SHALL WE SET?

ANONYMOUS

Liu Hsi-jung, a new soldier in the drama-and-song group: When I was studying at home, my favorite instruments were the *erh-hu* and *san-hsien* because it seemed to me most romantic to pour out one's feelings through their strings. Whenever I played the *erh-hu* or *san-hsien*, I liked to pitch the key as low as possible and play tunes like "Rain on the Plantain" or "Wang Chao-chun Leaves the Pass." To me these were "pleasing to the ear" and "enchanting." In the army, however, the songs I spent all my time playing, like "Always Prepared to Fight" struck me as dry and insipid. So when not accompanying songs, in my spare time or at evening concerts, I enjoyed playing these "enchanting" tunes "pleasing the ear" like "Rain on the Plantain." After hearing them, many of the comrades asked: "What on earth are you playing, Young Liu? Gloomy, spineless stuff, with not a militant note in it." Although I said nothing at the time, I was not really convinced by these criticisms.

After studying Chairman Mao's *Talks at the Yenan Forum on Literature and Art* again, I understood. I realized that the tunes you like or dislike are not just a matter of personal taste. The tunes you play and the pitch you set will depend on the sort of ideas you have. The reason I liked a low, soft key was that I myself did not appreciate the "smell of gunpowder" popular with all revolutionary fighters, but instead I liked the light music popular

FROM "What Pitch Shall We Set?" *Chinese Literature*, 12 (Dec., 1966), 102–3.

with the bourgeois intellectuals. Such a preference inevitably results in letting decadent bourgeois ideas infiltrate our minds through the medium of the *erh-hu* and *san-hsien*, to corrupt our soul and weaken our fighting resolve.

Chairman Mao has taught us that our purpose is "to ensure that literature and art fit well into the whole revolutionary machine as a component part, that they operate as powerful weapons for uniting and educating the people and for attacking and destroying the enemy." So we revolutionary fighters must pitch our key high to express revolutionary vigor and convey the courage of the proletariat and the heroism with which it forges fearlessly ahead. We must transform martial revolutionary songs into strength to kill the enemy! To do this, it is necessary to eradicate the influence of the old bourgeois culture and really establish a proletarian world outlook. Otherwise, no matter how many revolutionary airs we play, they will not express the feelings of a revolutionary fighter!

IX

Painting and the Arts

1. THE DILEMMA OF MODERN CHINESE PAINTING

If history and literature were the pillars of Confucian culture, painting was its chief adornment. With the disintegration of the cultural entity that produced it, China's great tradition in painting has faced acute problems. The general cultural dilemma—how to remain true to national tradition and yet depict a new modern reality—has confronted all modern Chinese painters since at least the 1920's. Some have ignored it either by continuing to paint purely traditional subjects in the traditional style or by switching completely to European styles and methods. More interesting have been the attempts to find a synthesis of the two traditions, one which maintains a Chinese style but could break the fixed traditional forms to depict the modern world. The purely technical problems (Chinese painting is essentially colored-ink drawing in contrast to European oils) have been formidable, not to mention more basic cultural and aesthetic differences. It is thus not surprising that distinct Chinese and Western schools of painting have maintained a largely separate existence.

The People's Republic has continued this division, despite its official policy of encouraging a new national school of socialist realism. Painting is one area of the cultural legacy where Communist distaste for feudal culture has not been able to overcome national pride in one of China's greatest artistic traditions. In the following selection, Michael Sullivan describes Chinese-style painting in the People's Republic.

CHINESE ART IN THE TWENTIETH CENTURY
MICHAEL SULLIVAN

In the basic question of media, it may be said that on the whole the tendency is deliberately to foster traditional methods, to the extent of using not only traditional forms such as the hanging scroll and the handscroll but also the Chinese brush, ink, and water color. While this may be partly due to a scarcity of imported oil colors, it seems more likely to stem from genuine regard for China's own traditional techniques as such. Oil painting is reserved chiefly for portraits and large official commemorative canvases executed for some office or public building. Almost without exception, these works are painstaking, insensitive, and dull, completely lacking in the traditional Chinese aesthetic virtue of "rhythmic vitality." Inevitably, great use is made of the woodcut and strip cartoon for propaganda purposes, to show, for example, the benefits of work teams and cooperatives; they are all much of a pattern, without the slightest individuality or distinction of style, their sole purpose being to instruct. Handbooks for cartoonists have been issued, showing the correct manner in which to draw a peasant (heroic and smiling), an American imperialist (rampant, with dollar bills), the moth-eaten British lion, and so on. More significant, however, is the use of the long narrative handscroll as an instrument of popular enlightenment. The works of Hsiao Ting . . . used the traditional form of the handscroll for the purposes of the cartoon; now, however, the handscroll form is reunited with a technique that first reached China from India at the end of the Han period, namely the method of continuous narration. It has been most effectively used in a long handscroll illustrating the story of how land reform came to a country village in North China. This is in style no more realistic than the traditional long scrolls illustrating festivals (such as Ch'ing-ming) and village life, which we know from historical texts to have been a fashionable genre as early as the Six Dynasties. Moreover, the artist has not hesitated to employ in the landscape of this scroll elements, such as the tree . . . which are thoroughly traditional and formalized in style and might have been taken straight from the volume

FROM Michael Sullivan, *Chinese Art in the Twentieth Century* (Berkeley: University of California Press, 1959), pp. 79–83. Copyright © 1959 Michael Sullivan. Reprinted by permission of the University of California Press and Faber and Faber, Ltd.

on trees in *Mustard Seed Garden*. If this example is typical, then it may be said that "realism" in art under the new order is capable of a certain latitude of interpretation. The precise pictorial style that the artist should employ is not laid down too rigidly; what matters is that his attitude should be correct.

Looked at from another point of view, the ideal of pictorial realism upheld by current doctrine in China is not altogether new in Chinese art. The insistence . . . that the artist should above all be accurate has its echo in countless stories of academic painters throughout Chinese history—stories in which beasts and birds were painted with such prodigious realism that they terrified the beholder or took wing before his astonished eyes.

There was at first no place for pure landscape painting in the new order. This great tradition, in which China has enshrined her loftiest concepts, was attacked not only because it smacks of abstraction, of bourgeois formalism, but even more because of its traditional association with a small and highly privileged class of scholars and officials. The insistence on figure-subjects, while good Communism, also carries the gratifying merit of an appeal to a Chinese pictorial tradition that is far older than the art of landscape painting and, in fact, goes back into hallowed antiquity, when artisans in the employ of the Ch'in and Han emperors decorated the walls of palaces and temples with frescoes composed largely if not entirely of human figures. At the same time, painters of the old scholar class who, at the expense of the toiling masses, enjoyed infinite leisure for the delights of painting and calligraphy are now discredited; there is no place for them in the new society. While the new regime likes to cultivate the impression abroad that the traditional styles and themes are being carefully fostered, in fact it is generally the work of one or two painters which is repeatedly reproduced in the foreign-language magazines—notably that of Ch'i Pai-shih. This remarkable man to the age of ninety-six serenely went on painting his crabs and shrimps, every now and then pausing to sign a peace manifesto or to produce another in a curious series of paintings in which the peace movement is celebrated in terms of Picasso's dove, translated into liquid washes, and set about with a riot of deftly painted flowers. Ch'i Pai-shih's unique position, however, stemmed less from his extreme age, which would in the past have been enough to guarantee him veneration, than from the fact that he was no long-nailed aristocrat but the son of a carpenter, a man of the people.

But Chinese art today cannot be profitably discussed in this piecemeal fashion. Force and the tide of history have integrated it so closely with other human activities that it can only properly be judged as a social activity in the broadest sense, and we will get a clearer picture of the situation by taking a brief glance at the position that art now holds in China. This position is determined by two factors. The first is the Marxist ideology itself, which lays down the theoretical principles by which all forms of human activity are integrated. This needs no further discussion in a book of this kind, beyond the general observation that the artist in China today, provided of course that he is productive and shows a socially healthy attitude, is guaranteed not only security but also prestige. At first, it appears, efforts were made to subject painters to complete bureaucratic regimentation. Pictures were assigned, like piece work in a factory. But more recently, according to the 1953 report of the Ministry of Cultural Affairs, this policy has been abandoned. The report states frankly, "We have changed our arbitrary administrative way of assigning the production of works of art: We have modified our rude manners to art workers." Local cadres have been warned that "actions in violation of discipline and rude manners toward art workers must be corrected." It is, however, too soon to see whether this pronouncement will be followed by a real relaxation of the dictatorship of arts and letters; indeed, in Communist China, as in Soviet Russia, official policy oscillates with such rapidity that predictions made on the basis of any single pronouncement are generally worthless.

The second factor in the present situation is perhaps less evident on the surface but may in the end emerge as the more powerful of the two; this is the Chinese sense of history. At every point, we see China's new masters seeking, and finding, sanction for their policies and acts in history, as did her rulers since the time of Confucius. Ai Ssu-ch'i, for instance, calls for a search for evidence of dialectical materialism in traditional Chinese philosophy, and, as is well known, Kuo Mo-jo has been the spearhead of a movement proclaiming ancient Taoism as a revolutionary protest against reactionary, feudal Confucianism. There is in this certainly an element of chauvinism, an instinctive tendency to reject any foreign ideas, even Marxism, unless they can be found to be Chinese ideas also. It is also understandable that the new epoch should seek to reinterpret history according to its own lights, for this is a universal historical phenomenon. What is not so obvious or explicable, in Marxist terms, is the importance to the regime of past history as such. A remarkable feature of the activity of the past seven years has been the energy with which archaeological exploration and excavation and the conservation and restoration of ancient monuments have been carried out. Sensational discoveries have been made of the art and archaeology of central China before the Han dynasty, of paleolithic and neolithic sites in Manchuria, of Buddhist cave temples in the northwest. When one considers that all this has been accomplished immediately after the revolution, and some of it in the midst of a major war, the results compare very favorably with those achieved by the Kuomintang in any similar period of time. No branch of Chinese art history has been neglected on ideological grounds: Buddhist art has not been neglected or destroyed as was Christian art in Russia but has, on the contrary, become a source of national pride.

However, lest one might be led to think that this enthusiasm stems from a love of art for its own sake, the regime has been careful to formulate the correct ideological rationalization. It is claimed that the great arts of China's past (with the exception, of course, of the painting and calligraphy of the *literati*) were produced by the people for their feudal rulers; now, therefore, it is the duty of the Chinese Government to preserve and restore this great heritage and hand it back to the people who created it and to whom it rightly belongs. Even if this obscures the importance of aristocratic patronage in the inspiration of this heritage, this is no ignoble aim; and if we are to judge it simply by results, it has had the immensely beneficial effect that now, perhaps for the first time in Chinese history, there is a feeling on the part of the people that the art that they have created belongs to society as a whole and must therefore be cherished and protected by everyone. This is a considerable advance on the old laissez faire attitude, which allowed the treasures of China's past either to pass into the hands of foreign museums and collectors or simply to crumble away through neglect.

Thus, just as Marxism seeks to influence history, so does history itself work upon Marxism. Soviet Russia, with no such counterbalancing force as is instinctive in the Chinese outlook, has subjected her arts almost wholly to the central ideology of the class struggle. China, on the other hand, has inherited a sense of history that she cannot shake off. She may rationalize her devotion to archaeology and reinterpret her history, but her devotion to history and to archaeology remains. Her historical sense is thus at every turn confronting Marxism with the fruits of her cultural achievements. The archaic bronzes, the Buddhist frescoes, and Sung paintings cannot be explained merely in terms of the devoted craftsmanship of those who made them and to whose descendants they are now being restored. They speak another language, more subtle perhaps, but also more universal. So long as they are cherished—for whatever official reason—there seems little doubt that, sooner or later, their voices will be heard and their message understood.

2. THE VITALITY OF PAINTING IN THE CHINESE STYLE

After its partial eclipse of the early 1950's, painting in the Chinese style (including the most traditional landscapes, bamboos, and flowers) again grew to be very much in vogue by 1957. It suffered some reversals during the Great Leap Forward, but, instead of neglecting the Chinese style, the Communists made intensive efforts to shape it to directly serve socialist construction. Misty landscapes bisected by new highways, dams, and backyard steel furnaces are typical examples of this effort. By 1960, when the ideological pressure had eased, flowers, birds, and bamboos returned to favor, although attempts to portray approved socialist themes in a national style continued. As one looks at some of these paintings, however, he is struck by the fact that appraisals by Communist art critics often seem to contain far more ideological content, socialist realism, and appreciation for bold new techniques than do the paintings themselves. Most of the paintings look far more Chinese than socialist.

The following selections show the enthusiasm that greeted the revival of Chinese-style painting, a revival extending to the art of calligraphy of scholars-aristocrats.

NEW DAY FOR CHINESE PAINTING

ANONYMOUS

With a fanfare of trumpets, drowning the cries of the prophets of woe, Chinese traditional painting is making a triumphal come-back.

On May 14, after a year's preparatory work, the Peking Academy of Chinese Painting opened its doors. It is under the direct care of the Ministry of Culture. Its president, Yeh Kung-cho, is a well-known collector and artist specializing in the painting of bam-boos, orchids, and rocks in the style of the old *wen-jen hua*, the "scholar's style." Its vice-presidents are Ch'en Pan-ting, a famous painter of flowers; Yu Fei-an, a painter of flowers and birds in a rich, decorative style, and Hsu Yen-sun, a well-known painter of figures and genre subjects. Ch'i Pai-shih, the ninety-seven-year-old master, is its honorary president.

The academy is one of the fruits of the movement to "let a hundred flowers bloom, a hundred schools contend." It will serve as a center for painters of the Chinese school of painting, fostering its various styles and tendencies and organizing discussions on their creative and other problems. It will give a helping hand to painters when needed, whether members of the academy or not.

The academy will take a certain number of students. Teaching will be along traditional lines with some innovations and mainly on an individual basis. Students will be attached to a particular master.

The academy will also undertake an intensive study of the theory, methods, and history of Chinese painting through the ages and make a comparative study of Western painting. . . .

The ravages of time, wars, fires, and floods have taken a terrible toll of the vast number of paintings both on paper and on silk that must have been created by the ancient masters over the centuries. What remains today may not exceed a fifth of 1 per cent of the total. The pictures now exhibited in the Peking Palace Museum, one of the biggest collections in the country, represent only a tiny fraction of China's pictorial legacy.

It is high time, therefore, that a determined attempt was made to compile a systematic record of Chinese painting and revive

FROM "New Day for Chinese Painting," *People's China*, 12 (June, 1957), 36–37.

this art which has been steadily declining during the last four or five decades. This is no easy task, and it is regrettable that it did not receive the attention due to it in the early years after liberation.

It was actually the case, in fact, that certain people holding leading positions in the world of art had scant respect for our national heritage and took a very supercilious and high-handed attitude in regard to traditional Chinese painting. They described it as a product of feudal society, an outmoded form of art that was no longer adequate as a means of artistic representation in our modern society. They held forth on the fact that the themes of Chinese painting are limited to landscape, old sages with lute-carriers, flowers, birds, and so on, all subjects connected with the leisured life of the upper class in feudal society, that Chinese painting by its very nature cannot serve the interests of the working people and should therefore be replaced by Western methods of painting. This sectarian approach has seriously hampered the development not of Chinese traditional painting alone but of Chinese pictorial art as a whole.

This by no means represented the policy of the Chinese Communist Party and the People's government, which was to preserve and develop the nation's cultural heritage. Painters in the Chinese style, too, stanchly treasured their art, and, in 1949, with the help of the People's government, they organized the Association for the Study of Chinese Painting with 286 members. Many have been trained by some of the foremost artists of the last generation. Chu Chen, the woman painter of flowers and birds, for instance, learned her art from her father, Chu Chao-lin, who was president of the Ju-yi Kuan (Hall of Felicity), an institute of painting attached to the court during the latter part of the Ch'ing dynasty. Along with their artistic activities, the members of the association initiated a systematic study of Chinese painting. To break new ground and get away from the habit of working exclusively in the studio, the association also arranged for its members to get out to factories, villages, farms, and historical sites—to work *en plein air*. Meetings were usually held on the return from such outings to discuss the practical problems of how to use and adapt the traditional means of painting to the representation of modern themes. Actual experience has drawn many of these painters to recognize the force of the realistic art theory propounded by Ku Kai-chih, the great fourth-century genius who exhorted painters to "copy nature and draw from inner experience."

These efforts have borne fruit. A noticeable ferment is at work in the ranks of the traditional artists and some noteworthy and interesting new paintings have appeared. Many well-attended exhibitions of their paintings have served to revive popular interest in the art and educate popular taste.

When the Hundred Flowers policy was launched, the State Council decided on the establishment of academies of Chinese painting both in Peking and Shanghai to carry on and expand the work of the association. Premier Chou En-lai and the Minister of Culture, Shen Yen-ping, both spoke at the opening of the Peking Academy and promised wholehearted support for its work. The art world of China feels that this new departure marks another stage in the renaissance of our ancient art.

MODERN CHINESE CALLIGRAPHY

ANONYMOUS

The Chinese Calligraphic Research Association recently took over one of the pavilions in Peihai Park, Peking, and in this setting of latticed windows, trees, and lake that seemed so eminently appropriate hung about 200 examples of writing by 150 calligraphers of Peking, Shanghai, Canton, Nanking, and other cities. In eleven days the exhibition attracted more than 20,000 visitors.

Penmanship is, of course, held in high esteem in many countries, but calligraphy occupies a truly unique place in Chinese art. As in Japan, it is regarded as an independent branch of the fine arts. Chinese homes usually treasure some pieces of fine writing mounted on scrolls or framed on the walls like pictures. Many painters, such as Ch'i Pai-shih, are proud to be known as calligraphers. A Chinese painting is nearly always inscribed with a colophon in the handwriting of the painter himself or some admirer. At famous beauty spots, it is traditional for well-known visitors to leave examples of their writing expressing their sentiments on viewing the scene. Sometimes they write on handy rocks or cliffs and craftsmen carve out the characters in low relief. Even daily household things, such as chopsticks, bowls, plates or teapots, often have writing on them as a decoration side-by-side with or instead of pictorial ornaments.

FROM "Modern Chinese Calligraphy," *People's China*, 10 (May, 1957), 35–36.

The reason for this esteem for calligraphy, of course, is that Chinese writing is essentially pictorial. Furthermore, the writer uses the same technical medium as the pictorial artist, the same flexible brush, the same ink and absorbent paper, with all their vast possibilities for expression. A single character may have many gradations of tone in its blackness; it can show the swift rush or graceful flow of the brush, the hesitation at a point, the onward sweep.

Historic remains—inscriptions on bone, shell, or stone carvings—show that 4,000 years ago China already possessed a relatively well developed written language. In succeeding centuries, it underwent many changes. These divide up roughly into four stages. The earliest form, still used by calligraphers, is called the *chuan shu* or "seal characters," dating from perhaps 3,000 years ago. These direct descendants of the ancient pictographic characters are composed of lines of similar thickness. They trace the lines of the ideograph with a sort of primitive strength and awkwardness and cannot be written quickly.

Later on there appeared the *li shu* or "official characters." They first appeared between 221 and 210 B.C., when Ch'in Shih Huang-ti, the first emperor of a united China, was carrying out his reforms to bind together his empire. The strokes of the seal characters were streamlined for convenience in writing. It is a workaday-looking script, not pretending to much elegance, but evidently a boon to the growing imperial bureaucracy.

By the first century of our era, the *li shu* characters had been polished till they achieved the greater elegance and flow of the *k'ai shu* or "pattern style" two hundred years later.

During the western Han dynasty (206 B.C.–24 A.D.) the scholar artists began to develop a style of writing called *ts'ao shu* or "grass characters." Here the number of strokes in a character is greatly reduced to flow into each other to facilitate speed and spontaneity in writing. The disadvantage of this style is that the arbitrary simplifications make the characters very difficult to decipher, and, in the "wild grass style," this fault is accentuated even more. Thus, for all practical purposes, the regular *k'ai shu* style continues to be generally used. This formed the basis for the printed characters of the Sung dynasty, which are in use to this day.

Calligraphy in all these styles is shown at the exhibition. There are reconstructions of the seal characters, riotous "wild grass" characters, and many variations of the *k'ai shu*.

3. THE WORK OF CHINESE PAINTERS

The rather dry accounts of exhibitions and announcements of new schools may be important for following official policy toward Chinese painting, but they give a poor picture of what China's artists are actually doing. Much better for this is the work of the artists themselves. Here are descriptions of two highly approved painters working in the traditional style. One is the distinguished veteran P'an T'ien-shou, an artist of considerable reputation before 1949. The other, Shih Lu, is one of the new painters mainly trained in the People's Republic who made a reputation as a woodcut artist before turning to painting in the traditional style. Both of them do interesting work; the appraisals of their work are no less interesting.

P'AN T'IEN-SHOU'S ART

KAI HSIEH

There was quite exceptional interest in the recent Peking exhibition of paintings and calligraphy by the Hangchow artist P'an T'ien-shou. Now sixty-five years old, this southern (Chekiang Province) artist paints landscapes and flower-and-bird scrolls in the traditional Chinese manner with equal facility, whether he is using his brushes or fingers. A poet and calligrapher as well, he is an adept at "melting poetry, calligraphy, and painting in one pot." In this, he follows the best classical tradition. Even more: He is also an expert seal-carver. The seal always occupies an important place on a classical Chinese scroll painting, so his artistry in seal-making enables him to produce the classical ensemble of painting, inscribed poetic colophon, signature, and seal in a particularly accomplished way.

All this, however, was known before. P'an T'ien-shou's work has long been known and admired in Peking. But in these latest works of his, a new artist has emerged. He has achieved a new boldness

FROM Kai Hsieh, "P'an T'ien-shou's Art," *Peking Review*, 47–48 (Nov. 30, 1962), 37–39.

of artistic conception reflected in his compositions, the freshness of his brushwork, and new color harmonies. It is the general consensus of opinion that these new elements in P'an's work breathe the spirit of the time. This has aroused the liveliest interest among critics and especially among the landscape and flower-and-bird painters of the traditional school, because this problem of infusing new, contemporary themes and content into works in these genres is one that many have been trying to solve now for many years and especially in recent years.

P'an T'ien-shou takes his subjects from the ordinary things of everyday life: a mountain view, details of brushwood and flowers, a lonely pine, a corner of a lotus pool, a cluster of bamboos. At first glance, he seems sometimes simply to splash his ink on the paper with brush or finger and the painting is done. But then you discover that these "splashings" have a new rhythm, that he has infused a new content into these ordinary objects, and one is not surprised to learn that, before he actually put brush to paper, he has made careful preparations, including studies of his subject, composition of the lines of verse for the accompanying colophon, the placing of the signature, and the design of the seals on the scroll.

Fleet Transports Sail the Misty River is a notable example of his new work. Most of the picture space is taken up by a massive shoulder of a mountain and a vigorously painted pine bough. Behind and far below that gnarled limb, you glimpse the river flowing from left to right; it is dotted with sails. A handsomely written colophon in seven character lines says: "Within the thousand mountains lie infinite riches of iron and coal. Fleets of sailing-boats, full-loaded, busily ply the misty river."

In the European tradition, a title is like a grace note to a painting: possibly delightful or expository but not essential. In traditional Chinese painting, as practiced by P'an T'ien-shou, painting and colophon (title) are one: In this scroll, he creates a visual and poetic image which conjures up, as an extension to itself, a great world of natural beauty, rich resources, and buoyant people absorbed in building socialism.

P'an T'ien-shou delights in the laconic metaphor and symbolism typical of classical Chinese poetry and painting. His scroll *To a Rich Harvest* pictures a rock and a frog and three lines of verse which read: "The southern fields are well watered. Loud croak the frogs, singing paeans to bumper crops in the years to come." Some may object perhaps that this is too succinct, too concise, but to those familiar with rural life in our southern lands, it is surely enough. Those few lines and the picture they complement speak volumes and speak in truly Chinese tones.

P'an T'ien-shou brings a sense of the new even to old subjects done in the traditional style. His *Landscape in the Style of the Mi School* is executed with the typical dot strokes of that school of painting, but, by using steely white space instead of the traditional light ink wash to represent the mists and fogs clouding the waist of the mountains, he succeeds in giving the picture a metallic note which is emphasized again in the colophon as "The thousand mountains after rain look like fresh cast iron." The same is true of his *Landscape in the Style of Ni Yun-lin* (a great landscape painter of the fourteenth century). This has the little isolated pavilion and the scrawny tree we have grown accustomed to seeing in such paintings. But the composition and the new handling of the brushwork certainly leave us with no sense of chill or desolation. It is as if a new invigorating wind has blown over the scene. It is indeed "in the style of Ni," but with a difference.

P'an T'ien-shou achieves special effects by unorthodox methods of composition. In some scrolls, such as his *Sleeping Cat*, he places his main subject in one corner while leaving the central part of the picture space empty. In his *Ink Orchid*, the few leaves run almost horizontally toward the bottom edge of the scroll; close to the right-hand side rises a thin stem topped with an orchid flower. In this unusual composition, he avoids the danger of monotony by painting the leaves of the orchid in dark ink and with a rich variety of forms and by giving prominence to the flower. This done, he has balanced the whole with an interestingly inscribed four-character signature on the left-hand side.

P'an T'ien-shou is a diligent student of the techniques of such Ming and Ch'ing masters of the sixteenth to late nineteenth centuries as Hsü Wei, Pa Ta Shan Jen, the monk Shih Tao, and Jen Po-nien, and the influence of these painters is still discernible in his paintings. But he is no slavish imitator. He has evolved a style peculiarly his own, and it is not difficult to see the close connection between his brushwork in painting and calligraphy and his style of seal-carving. In a recent discussion on P'an T'ien-shou's paintings arranged by the Union of Chinese Artists, several Peking artists noted that "he studies the techniques of the old masters deeply but never allows himself to be limited by them" and that "he is a deep student of but not a slave to nature."

His art was also extensively discussed in the press. The reviews were exceptionally warm. Writing in *Jen-min Jih-pao*, the artist-critic Pan Chieh-tzu made a bold comparison between P'an T'ien-shou's work and that of the late great master Ch'i Pai-shih:

> I used to think that, with Ch'i Pai-shih, the *hsieh-yi* ["idea-writing" or the "free-hand"] style of painting had reached its summit. His remarkable ability to capture the spirit of the object painted, his strong, superb brushwork, and his great versatility not only in painting but in poetry, calligraphy, and seal-carving, all combined to make him a great master hard to rival. P'an T'ien-shou's paintings, however, have shattered my unquestioning faith in this belief. As painters, Ch'i and P'an each excel in his own way. I have no intention of venturing on rash comments here. All I want to say is that I feel I must revise my ideas about this.

Speaking at the Artists Union discussion, the flower-and-bird painter Wang Chu-chiu paid tribute to the power and strength of P'an's brushwork. "In this, I should say that P'an is along with and in some respects even ahead of the late modern masters Wu Ch'ang-shih and Ch'i Pai-shih," he said.

Pan's unflagging creative energy has been much discussed too. Most of the ninety-one paintings on view were done in the last few years since 1958 and most of them in the last two years. Once he used to sign himself "The Lazy Old Chap," but his diligence, shown in the big pieces done in the last year or two especially, has proved that he has completely done away with his "laziness." The new spirit he has injected into his works also makes one doubt the aptness of that epithet "old." A buoyant and flourishing spirit has banished the melancholy and nostalgia that were often found in his works before liberation. The seething life he has seen and sensed around him, the dynamic spirit of socialist construction, has inspired him. The new development in his art is born of this urge to reflect our times.

THE PAINTINGS OF SHIH LU

HUA HSIA

Last autumn, six artists from Northwest China made a tour of different parts of the country which resulted in a number of new

FROM Hua Hsia, "The Paintings of Shih Lu," *Chinese Literature*, 1 (Jan., 1962), 91–92 and 94–97.

paintings and sketches. These have recently been exhibited in Peking. And the work of Shih Lu in particular has aroused wide interest, owing to his technical virtuosity and freshness of artistic conception.

Shih Lu, slightly over forty this year, belongs to the traditional school of Chinese ink painting, and his development is eagerly watched. He passed his childhood at the foot of Mount Omei, in the magnificent scenery of Southwest China, and his early love of painting often sent him up into the mountains to practice his art. The resistance to Japanese aggression in the 1930's made him leave his tranquil home to go to Yenan, the revolutionary base in the Northwest. Since then, the Northwest has become his second home, and some of his best works have been done on the loess plateau.

In the past, Shih Lu was known chiefly for his genre paintings dealing with the revolutionary struggle; but several dozens of his paintings in this recent exhibition are landscapes, while relatively few are genre scenes and still life. Some of these landscapes are based on his recollections of life in Yenan; others show villages in North Shensi today, the forests and fields of the loess plateau, construction work along the Yellow River, and the life of the people on its banks. All breathe a sense of freshness but a freshness developed from the traditional techniques of Chinese painting.

Traditional Chinese painting attaches importance to artistic conception, poetic feeling and spirit, and artists pursue the abstract rather than the concrete, choosing to suggest truths rather than point them out and striving to achieve a musical rhythm. From the characteristics of objects in real life, the old masters evolved a "conventionalized" technique, one example of which is their use of strokes known as "wrinkles" for hills and rocks. They even used extraordinary forms and exaggeration to convey their ideas and moods. This is a special feature of Chinese painting. Shih Lu, after studying the traditional approach to artistic conception and composition, the question of form and brushwork in Chinese painting, as well as their interrelationship, has created something new. He does not devote all his attention to one single aspect like brushwork. While adopting the traditional techniques, instead of following the old rules rigidly he probes for the laws which govern the art and produces original work. . . .

One of Shih Lu's favorite themes is the Yellow River. His paintings of this make up one symphony inspired by the mighty river. *The Yellow River* shows hardy boatmen shooting the rapids under beetling cliffs. *Towing a Boat* presents sure-footed towmen pressing confidently over rocky, difficult terrain. In *Rolling Waves*, we see fishermen calmly and cheerfully hauling in their catch, while the angry current rushes irresistibly on. In other words, these paintings are not so much a tribute to the Yellow River as to the people living by it, the fearless, resolute boatmen and fishermen. These scenes make a strong impact on all who see them, stirring their hearts or compelling admiration.

Shih Lu's work is significant not only because of his loftiness of conception but also because of its freshness and originality. An artist of great sensitivity, he sees the significance of what is new in our life. His portrayal of the lamplight in a loess cave in *The Approach of Dawn* seems simple enough, yet this sums up the deep impression made on him by his long stay in Yenan. Recalling those days, he has said,

> When dusk fell lights began to appear in the caves, and by these lights people were working or studying hard. Those lamps and the people silhouetted against them were a reflection of life in those revolutionary years. And memories like these linger. . . . Every minute of the night brought fresh changes in Yenan, and the lamp in Chairman Mao's cave stayed on all night. . . . These are things I shall never forget.

Shih Lu makes sparing but most telling use of artistic images. In *Horses Drinking by the River Yen*, only a few horses are depicted. Instead of expressing outright praise of Yenan, the cradle of the revolution, by painting a few horses resting there for a while before going back to the front, he conveys the idea that Yenan served as a haven of rest for revolutionaries as well as their starting point. *The Approach of Dawn* shows not the man working by lamplight but just the lighted window, leaving the rest to our imagination. The freshness of a work's artistic impact depends largely on the subtlety with which the artist conveys his ideas. Shih Lu generally succeeds in combining an original conception with skillful evocation of atmosphere. Again, the achievement of good, original work depends to a great extent on the composition, images, and brushwork. The composition is determined by the central theme. In *The Approach of Dawn*, it is determined by the requirements of the images, which in turn depend on the artistic conception. It is very important here to convey the sense of dawn's approach, and this is done by means of specific shades of ink and the whole composition. It is fitting that this painting should induce a sense of breadth and space, avoiding any feeling of restriction. By making the tree in the middle spread wide its branches, Shih Lu suggests a radiation of strength, and this does much to reinforce the sense of spaciousness.

Shih Lu's technique is bold and varied. The mountain in *Golden Waves Below Mount Chungnan* is painted with large, heavy blobs of ink, contrasting with the finer strokes laid on with a dry brush at the foot of the mountain and thereby increasing the interest of the painting and giving it a sense of rhythm. The fields of millet here seem a rolling sea, whereas the maize in *Autumn in North Shensi* is drooping, suggesting movement in the first case and tranquillity in the second. These different effects produced by the angle of the lines and the density of the ink show Shih Lu's skill in the language of expression.

An artistic conception achieves vitality only if allied to a suitable technique. Some painters have original ideas but cannot convey them, often because their technique is at fault. A new form of brushwork does not mean that we can dispense with tradition. The new technique must grow out of the old, for only so will it retain a Chinese style. On the other hand, if we merely rely on tradition without evolving new techniques, we cannot satisfy the new demands. Good artists of every period have to a greater or lesser degree improved upon or added to tradition. Shih Lu's brushwork suits the needs of his subject matter; he studies tradition and introduces innovations according to these needs. In paintings like *Rain on the Mountain Peak, The Winter Hills Are Asleep,* or *Golden Waves Below Mount Chungnan,* the composition, forms, and "wrinkles" on the rocks are all basically traditional. So is the method of painting the ripples in the water in *Rolling Waves,* except that here there are some variations and additions to suit the subject matter.

To convey the atmosphere and rugged solidity of the loess plateau, Shih Lu uses a variety of strokes with a wet and dry brush, painting first with a wet brush and then drawing the contours with a dry one, or vice versa. He does not stick to one way. His brushwork, then, is based on tradition, but he is so flexible in his use of techniques that we cannot tell which particular one he is using. Sometimes he combines several traditional methods; sometimes he evolves a new one from the old. Thus he used the traditional brushwork to paint ripples, but to show the eddies of the Yellow River he introduced a greater realism, giving us a truer impression. When he painted *The Approach of Dawn,* to suggest the mistiness of early dawn he evolved a method calculated to produce a more sculptured effect. In a mist, the leaves of distant trees are invisible; only the branches can be seen. So instead of depicting the trees too meticulously or making them too distinct, he aimed at a rather "blunt" and chunky effect. This is something quite unusual in Chinese painting and was a new departure by Shih Lu, based on the needs of his subject. In this painting of his, the tough, wiry date tree and the morning mist clinging to the distant tree tops convey the contrast between the incoming dawn and the receding night, lending vigor to the whole scene. There is a just correspondence here of the brushwork with the objects depicted; traditional techniques are not used for their own sake. This characteristic of all Shih Lu's painting, the integration of form and content, accounts for the strong appeal his work makes to the public.

4. THE INTENSIFIED DRIVE FOR
SOCIALIST CONTENT

Just as the theater changed drastically in the period leading up to the Cultural Revolution, painting also reflected the increased pressure for ideological purity. Here, too, the emphasis on serving socialism and countering revisionism has become overwhelming.

Thus, the traditional themes of Chinese painting (landscapes, birds, and flowers) are once again not in demand. But there is one essential difference between the last few years and the period immediately after 1949. Then Chinese-style painting was generally ignored in favor of Soviet-inspired oil painting; now there is a determined effort to make the Chinese style serve socialism. As with the new Peking Opera, one may wonder if the results are still meaningfully "Chinese." It is noteworthy, however, that the regime still insists on a national style.

The first selection here, by the eminent painter Li K'o-jan, is significant for several reasons. First, it describes the increased emphasis on positive, modern subject matter. Second, it shows the tense political situation that could lead a sensitive and talented artist of the Chinese style to debase his aesthetic judgment so flagrantly. Third, it presages the massive entry of the army into cultural spheres. The description in the second selection of the permanent display of Chinese art completes our picture of what now is fashionable in Peking.

SOMETHING NEW IN TRADITIONAL PAINTING
LI K'O-JAN

The Third Art Exhibition of the People's Liberation Army gives a most exciting display of works of art, many of which attracted me immensely. As a painter in the traditional style myself, I spent most of my time in the hall of traditional painting and learned a great deal from the stimulating exhibits, which provided much food for thought.

The traditional paintings in the exhibition far surpass the previous works of this kind which paved the way for them. An intrinsic change seems to me to have occurred in our time-honored traditional style of painting, resulting in splendid new works in conformity with the spirit of the socialist age.

As soon as one enters the exhibition hall, one is impressed by the strong flavor of contemporary life and revolutionary fervor and cannot but be inspired by the noble qualities and heroic deeds of the People's Liberation Army. My first impression of such pictures as *Ou-yang Hai Gives His Life to Save a Train*, *The Slaves Have Stood Up*, *Hsieh Chen, a Model in Serving the People*, *Heroes of the Sea*, *Red Heart in Turbulent Waves*, and *The Landscape Here Is Beyond Compare* was that these are not "diversions with brush and ink" to pass the time for scholars but art for the masses which will play a militant and inspiring role in our great socialist revolution and construction and in the struggle against imperialism and revisionism.

On display were some works by professional artists in the PLA, but more than half—and the ones I admired most—were by amateurs, ranging from ordinary soldiers to generals and combat heroes. Drawn from their own rich experience of life, these are mostly realistic and moving works, for the artists have shown boundless revolutionary enthusiasm and a creditable mastery of technique. *Ou-yang Hai Gives His Life to Save a Train* by Yang Sheng-yung is a painting which drew a great crowd. A horse loaded

FROM Li K'o-jan, "Something New in Traditional Painting," *Chinese Literature*, 10 (Oct., 1964), 80–85.

with a heavy gun is crossing the railway track, while an express is fast approaching. Disregarding his own safety, Ou-yang Hai shoves with all his might and pushes the horse off the track just in time to save the train from being derailed. He gives his life heroically to save all the lives and property on the train. The artist's vivid presentation of that fleeting, stirring moment is a fine depiction of the hero's courage, the horse's panic, and the speed of the express. . . .

General Chien Chun's portrait of the soldier Chang Nien-hsing who distinguished himself in his first battle makes an equally powerful impact. The general has inscribed this painting as follows:

> The new sword has its first testing,
> Glittering it slashes through iron.
> The young soldier in his first battle
> Shows invincible courage against the enemy.

The soldier is portrayed standing erect, shouldering his rifle, and wearing a big red commendation rosette. His gallant bearing and the honest frankness and fearless optimism apparent on his face are indeed typical of the fine soldiers of the age of Mao Tse-tung, the true sons of the Chinese people. I noticed many paintings on different themes which give a truthful picture of our splendid soldiers, by means of telling touches. Those like *Little Tiger*, *Bright Lamp*, *Reaping Every Grain*, and *A Pause During the March Through the Snowy Plain* filled me with admiration and elation, for I recalled that some artists of the traditional school used to find it difficult to present workers, peasants, and soldiers. They said soldiers were particularly hard to present and did not "fit into paintings" because they looked so much alike. Although some of them attempted to paint soldiers, the result was often a "model" in the uniform of a soldier, sailor, or airman. Others turned out men with rough features, the personification of abstract ideas. In one way or another, they failed to present the spirit and outlook of the People's Liberation Army men. In this exhibition, however, I feel that many artists have overcome this difficulty and, through a series of penetrating depictions, are gradually developing a new style, majestic and powerful but rich in delineation. Certain artists not only have something significant to say but have found suitable artistic forms of expression, as in the case of *Fountain* by Han Yueh, *Little Tiger* by Hu Chin-yeh, and *I'll Carry Chairman Mao's Works Wherever I Go to Read When*

I've a Moment to Spare by Chang Pei-chu. I studied these paintings very carefully and found them so vivid and real that even the cap, uniform, belt, and army boots have a style and rhythm all their own. These works are not only moving but extremely attractive as well.

Other outstanding pictures with fine content and good forms of expression include Lang Cho-hung's *Eyes of the Motherland*, showing a sentry post on the coastal front. A few soldiers stand on the high cliffs of an island, their eyes on the distant sea, vigilantly watching the activities of the enemy and safeguarding the country. A landscape in appearance, this is not an ordinary picture of scenery. The artist has put revolutionary feeling into his representation of our new age. Although painting the landscape in the traditional style with Chinese ink and water-colors, instead of applying the "rock wrinkle" technique in the rigid conventional way, he further developed it to blend the brushwork harmoniously with the content, achieving a rare spontaneity and realism. A *Pause During the March Through the Snowy Plain* by Mei Hsiao-ching depicts two young soldiers busy mending their shoes, which have already been stitched and patched numerous times. It gives us an idea of the Liberation Army men's persevering spirit as they tramp over hill and dale as well as of their simple, frugal life.

I stood long before these paintings on exhibition and felt that they had taught me a great deal. It came home to me that the need to present magnificent new themes in our traditional painting is bound to result in a tremendous development of the forms of expression, which certainly cannot be fettered by ancient traditional conventions or techniques introduced from abroad.

PERMANENT DISPLAY OF MODERN CHINESE ART
ANONYMOUS

The art lover in Peking can now, for the first time, conveniently get a fairly complete view of Chinese art from early times to today. The first part of that view has long been available at the Palace Museum, the nation's biggest and richest collection of ancient

FROM "Permanent Display of Modern Chinese Art," *Peking Review*, 13 (March 25, 1966), 30–31.

art. The second, contemporary, part is now being presented by the new permanent exhibition at the Museum of Chinese Art.

When completed, this new exhibition will include representative work from the time of the May Fourth Movement in 1919—the beginning of China's New Democratic Revolution—through to the present time of socialist revolution and construction.

At the moment, it contains 302 traditional-style Chinese paintings, oil paintings, water colors, graphic art, and sculpture. All are from the fine collection of contemporary work which the museum has built up by purchases from the major exhibitions held in China since 1949. In this first selection, only works done since 1949 is shown, half of them in the last three years. Cartoons, book illustrations, and other branches of art will be added later. From time to time, certain works will be retired and replaced with others from the museum's ample store.

A steady stream of visitors has passed through the galleries since they opened last October, and the selection has aroused lively comment. It gives an excellent opportunity to review the current art scene.

In creating this new socialist, national art which serves the cause of revolution, which reflects the people's life with greater understanding than ever before and is loved by the masses, artists are critically assimilating not only their own national artistic heritage but also that of other lands.

New themes and subject matter, new content, have given rise to changes in artistic form and style. But the spirit of the new age is intimately blended with the national style of Chinese art. You will not find copies of T'ang or Sung paintings here nor simple transplantations from foreign art. You will find creative works which break through the established styles of old and adapt foreign forms to the characteristics of socialist Chinese art.

Such traditional-style paintings as *News of the Tiger's Defeat, Bringing Food on a Snowy Night, Two Lambs,* and *Lienyun Harbor* are by veteran painters as well as by young artists. The veterans are shown here as to have turned away from outmoded artistic interests and sentiments and developed bolder, freer brushstrokes to depict today's life and people. New compositional means, new color harmonies, are emerging. The dominant note is a fresh, new look at things. Stereotypes are out. These works show that when an artist sincerely endeavors to remold his world outlook, then his style and technique—the form of his art—undergo a fundamental change. His ideological remolding progresses in the course of his artistic practice. For an artist who has determined to work for the working masses, artistic practice is the means of helping to bring about the revolutionary transformation of his consciousness, his ideology, and his art.

The younger painters of the traditional Chinese school were brought up under the five-starred red flag. Their brushstrokes are animated by a revolutionary spirit that gives their paintings a new vitality and realism, yet there is no lack of traditional Chinese flavor in them. In the field of graphic art and especially in their New Year pictures, this characteristic of the young artists is displayed with particular force. The New Year picture *Heroes of Our Age* successfully represents the people who are now masters of their own destiny. *To Be Worthy Successors* shows the eagerness of the younger generation to become worthy successors to the revolutionary cause of their fathers. The colored woodcut *The First Bumper Harvest* depicts the happiness of the emancipated Tibetan serfs reaping a bumper harvest; while *Turn Shackles into Swords* lauds the revolutionary heroism of the fighting African people. Youthful patriotism and internationalism, revolutionary hatred for imperialism and revisionism, have inspired these successful pictures. Naturally, there is some artistic immaturity, but their keenness to plunge themselves into the heat of the struggle, to identify themselves with the working masses, and their diligence in their art give assurance for the future. What is decisive here is their determination to serve the people.

5. THE "SMALL" ARTS

If painting was the glory of China's artistic tradition, it was not its sum total. There were also the products of the numerous "small" arts or handicrafts such as porcelain, jade and ivory carving, lacquerware, and embroidery. By the standards of the scholar-literati, they had been "small" arts because they were the work of craftsmen, not expressions of the gentleman's individual character. Those standards hardly apply in the People's Republic, of course, when the "people's" character of these arts has been a mark in their favor. Thus, although they too express themes from the

Ch'i Pai-shih, until his death in 1957, was Communist China's most celebrated painter.

Two Prawns by Ch'i Pai-shih.

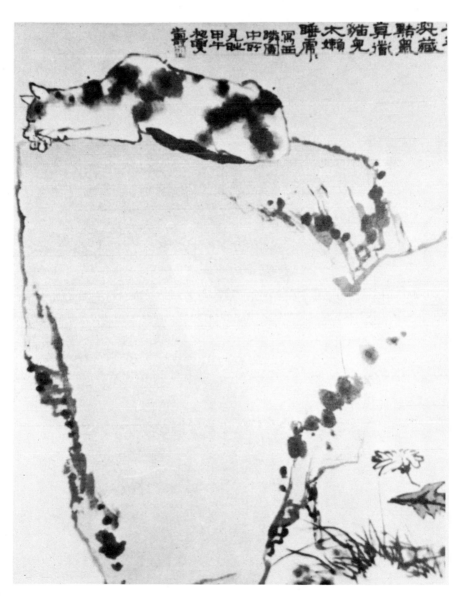

Cat Asleep on a High Rock by P'an T'ien-shou.

The Approach of Dawn by Shih Lu.

Mei Shan Reservoir by Chang Wen-chun shows socialist construction in a traditional Chinese landscape.

The collective painting *Victory Report at the Plant* typi-
fies the use of traditional stylistic techniques in portraying
contemporary life.

Ou-yang Hai Sacrifices His Life to Save the Train is a "Chinese-style" painting produced during the Cultural Revolution.

Handicrafts on traditional and revolutionary themes:

Jade carving—*Beauty Teasing Parrot.*

Stone carving—*Workers of the World Unite!*

Traditional towers top the new Peking Railway Station.

The graceful Chaochow Bridge was built early in the seventh century.

feudal past, the handicraft arts have been actively promoted. But, for obvious reasons, they have not been excluded from the recent drive for new themes in the old art forms.

HANDICRAFT ARTISTS MEET
ANONYMOUS

At the end of July, Chinese handicraft artists—465 representatives of 13 nationalities from 27 provinces, municipalities, and autonomous regions—held a national conference in Peking and brought with them the latest examples of their work for exhibition. They came from 106 different trades in this field. A few of the representatives were artists and professors who had long collaborated with the craftsmen and made their contribution to the development of handicrafts.

The exhibition was housed in two spacious halls. There was cloisonné from Peking, lacquerware from Fukien, embroidery from Hunan, sculptured ivory from Kwangtung, pottery from Yihsing in Kiangsu, porcelain from Chingtehchen in Kiangsi, fine silver wire ware from Szechuan—a collection of valuable and beautiful objects.

The Chinese handicraftsman's art has a long and honored tradition which we take great pride in nowadays. But, in Kuomintang times, it fell on evil days. The craftsmen found it harder and harder to make a living. Many of them had to give up their trade altogether, and some had to live as vagabonds, with the result that many famous handicraft arts were forgotten and lost. After liberation, the Party and government came to the rescue, and they have gradually been restored and some progress made. Old craftsmen who had been driven out of business came back. Goods which had gone off the market reappeared. During the great socialist transformation of 1956, the craftsmen, helped and encouraged by the government, flocked to organize themselves into cooperatives. This has had a remarkable effect in both raising output and improving quality. In the eight years since liberation, the craftsmen have begun to live far better than ever before and have been respected by society. The conference was called to review achieve-

FROM "Handicraft Artists Meet," *People's China*, 17 (Sept., 1957), 38–39.

ments, exchange experience, learn from each other, and so stimulate the development of the handicraft arts.

It is impossible to do more than comment on one or two of the 2,800 exhibits which so brilliantly demonstrated the genius and originality of the Chinese craftsmen.

There were, for instance, among the more valuable pieces, a sailing-vessel carved from ivory, with the sailors hoisting a bellying white sail; two running horses carved from two pieces of red-flecked white jade; a piece of coral worked by clever fingers into the form of a beautiful maiden who leans against a tree, teasing a parrot on a perch hanging from a branch.

But you need not work in costly materials like ivory, jade, or coral to show yourself a consummate artist. More often, in fact, they use quite common materials like pieces of rock, grasses, straw, bamboo—even a sheet of paper or a handful of clay or dough.

Chinese painters, poets, and craftsmen have always loved the bamboo. In South China, where it is abundant, baskets, mats, curtains, and other things in daily use are commonly made of bamboo. But Kung Yu-chang, an old craft artist from Szechuan, brought to the exhibition a wonderful bamboo *objet d'art*—a fan, not more than a foot in diameter, woven of thousands of transparent hair-like bamboo fibers. It was as thin as the finest silk, with kingfishers and water chestnuts woven into it, all in the style of traditional Chinese painting.

Lang Shao-an, the artist in dough who visited London last year, brought a figure of Ch'u Yüan, the famous poet who lived more than two thousand years ago. It was at this meeting that he met his old master, Chao Kuo-ming, who taught him his craft and whom he had not seen for eighteen years. Chao is now deputy-director of the Shanghai Handicraft Arts Studio. The meeting of master and apprentice was a moving moment for the onlookers. Who could have guessed that during their eighteen years' separation fate had driven them to give up their trade and earn a living by selling sweet potatoes or pulling rickshaws?

There were, too, Uighur *dombras* (a kind of mandolin) and embroidered caps, Mongolian horse-headed fiddles, saddles and delicately carved silver sheaths, embroidery worked by the Miao people in Kweichow, cross-stitch embroidery by the Sanis of Yunnan, elegant Tibetan carpets. . . .

Never had China known such a gathering of Chinese handicraft artists. The conference reaffirmed the future course of their art—socialist in content and national in form. Artists, scientists,

and commercial and industrial circles now recognize the importance of the handicraftsmen and will give them all the support and
help they can. We are confidently looking forward to a new
flourishing of our handicraft arts.

NEW THEMES IN OLD CRAFTS

ANONYMOUS

Chinese handicraft art incorporates the skills and wisdom of
the working people distilled over five millennia. The tradition
stretches back over the ages. Highlights spring to mind: neolithic
pottery of red clay painted in purple and black; sonorous bronze
bells, elaborate ritual cauldrons, and delicate jade wine cups of
Shang and Chou times; silk weaves and brocades of the Han
highly prized in ancient Rome; T'ang and Sung porcelain and
Ming cloisonné. . . . In the countryside, the ingenuity and industry of peasant artisans produced a vast assortment of homespun
miracles in decorations, ornaments, and toys, embroideries and
dyed work, straw and bamboo articles, wood and earthenware.

This handicraft art has been polished and perfected by genera
tions of folk masters. New China, inheriting the legacy, has developed it and made it shine with greater luster than ever before.

New themes from the revolutionary past and present-day life
now appear in Chinese handicrafts side by side with traditional
motifs from history, mythology, and legend. A recent exhibition
in the Round City of Peking's Peihai Park showed some of the
best of these new works made in the last two years. A number of
them are of a high ideological as well as technical standard.

From the minute peach-stone carving of a boatload of Liberation Army men to the life-size portrait of Chairman Mao embroidered in wool, the 200-odd exhibits showed how well traditional
techniques are being adapted to new themes. On the stone
of an ordinary peach 1.5 centimeters high by 2 centimeters wide,
the veteran artist Kao Kung-ching of Weifang, Shantung, has
carved a boatload of a dozen or more PLA soldiers fording the
Yangtze during the War of Liberation. He catches the men in
various fighting postures that realistically bring out the suspense

FROM "New Themes in Old Crafts," *Peking Review*, 31 (July 30, 1965),
22–23.

and heroism of the crossing. The anchor chain, about two-thirds the length of a line from this column, is made up of fifty links. This alone indicates the unbelievable delicacy of the work.

The 2-x-3-meter embroidery of Chairman Mao standing smiling under the pine boughs looks like a stereoscopic photograph. Many visitors are tempted to try a careful touch to make sure the Chairman's woolen scarf and coat were not three-dimensional. Shanghai embroiderers used wool threads of 1,700 different colors and millions of stitches to make it.

The Peking ivory carving *Sisters of the Grasslands* recalls the incident of the two children of Inner Mongolia who, for a day and a night, fought to protect their commune's sheep from a sudden blizzard on the pastures. It shows the two girls at the height of the storm. Their Mongolian-style coats and scarves wildly flying, one clutches a frightened lamb to her chest as the other leads the way in pursuit of the flock. It is a glowing image of Chinese children.

The Red Army Crossing the Great Snow Mountains is a good example of new Shoushan stone-carving. An oblong block of milky stone with a strand of red cutting across its middle has been cleverly chiseled into a precipitous icy mountain with a thin line of Red Army men making their way across its flank during the Long March.

The newest developments in Hsi-wan painted pottery figurines are typified by *Arise!*—a figure of a stalwart African fighter, one hand holding a rifle, the other raised high as he gives a call to battle. There is realism in the new, more rational composition and body proportions, while the traditional exaggeration of posture and facial expression—the glaring eyes and open palm with outstretched fingers, for instance—give it power and symbolic meaning. . . .

There were also an idyllic Tientsin clay figurine of a fat boy tending to a commune sheep; an illustration to Chairman Mao's poem *Ode to the Plum Blossom* made entirely of black and white bird feathers; a series of poker-work pictures on wood depicting, among others, Dr. Norman Bethune among his Chinese friends and a Vietnamese fighter single-handedly destroying a U.S. tank.

The exhibition could not fail to impress. It showed that Chinese handicraftsmen are not resting on their laurels. Mobilizing their vast technical skills, they are coming to grips with the problems of depicting contemporary life.

6. A GASTRONOMIC FOOTNOTE

No account of China's cultural legacy would be complete without at least a passing glance at its fabulous cuisine. Indeed, it may be confidently stated that only the Chinese and the French have raised the pleasures of the table to the level of great art. But can this art survive in an atmosphere of mass egalitarianism and socialist austerity? Peggy Durdin, writing as much in sorrow as in anger, answered negatively from Hong Kong as she watched the effects of commune mess halls on Chinese cuisine. But her eulogy may have been premature. As the second selection indicates, by 1962 there was a lively interest in promoting culinary arts along with other traditional arts. And there is also the satisfied testimony of many Western visitors to Peking, like Phillip Bonosky, that all the gastronomical glory has not yet departed.

MAO'S "GREAT CRIME" AGAINST CUISINE

PEGGY DURDIN

No civilized person who enjoys the basic gifts of life can view with equanimity Mr. Mao's efficient campaign to make the world's best, most richly diversified cuisine taste progressively like a single brand of fodder. The Communists are reprehensible enough when they destroy the art of conversation through forced tattling and a web of spies; when they make everyone simultaneously write "poems," swat flies, mouth identical slogans, "love the army," or join in a spasm of hatred for America or support for Cuba. But let them quit tampering with, and destroying, one of the greatest pleasures of every Chinese—food—improved, refined, and varied over the centuries.

The Chinese have long valued their superb cooking as an art. Like all really civilized peoples, they have loved to eat—and eat well: to plan and cook a dinner with care for the flavor, texture,

FROM Peggy Durdin, "Mao's 'Great Crime' Against Cuisine," *New York Times Magazine* (March 19, 1961), pp. 62 ff. Copyright © 1961 by The New York Times Company. Reprinted by permission.

and order of the dishes; to savor and celebrate with friends a special seasonal dish; sometimes to dispose of a meal with hearty gusto and sometimes to reach for only a few of the tastiest morsels with ivory, silver-tipped chopsticks at the languid pace of the experienced connoisseur.

There will be no attempt here to discuss today's drastic food shortage in China, rooted less in "natural" disasters than in a decade of deliberate, dogmatic Marxist-Maoist neglect and sacrifice of food for heavy industry. As Confucius did *not* say, man does not live by bread alone; he lives by the way that bread is prepared.

It is quite a job to wreck the cuisine of a huge nation. But Mao did it with the flick of a finger; more exactly, by speaking three simple words just two years ago last August: "Communes are good." Almost overnight this remark abolished individual and private kitchens, stoves, and meals in rural areas; almost overnight it organized, throughout China's countryside, groups eating in what might be called the world's largest and worst chain of government-run cafeterias. Today, these messes, still unpopular with most of 550 million peasants, are being extended to the 100 million or so Chinese in towns and cities.

Chinese food requires longer preparation and more elaborate cooking than French cuisine. It bears no relationship to dishes that can be prepared quickly and easily in quantity or to our "short-order" meals such as hamburger or sandwiches. Besides, today there still are very few Chinese cooks trained to produce meals for more than a single family, and large, mess-size stoves and cooking utensils are in short supply.

As Chinese eat their rationed dole of inferior and diluted rice or bread, with perhaps a dish of salted vegetable, they must find it bitter to remember that only a decade ago every province in China, often even a single city or district, had its own delicious, famous culinary specialties.

Can anyone who once lived north of the Yangtze River, and who is now eating cakes of starch, potato, and corn flours, ever forget all the breads of the area? The varieties of round, thin pancakes of unleavened wheat flour in which one wraps and eats various meats and vegetables; the salty sesame-seed biscuit; the steamed roll called Silver Whirls because it is fashioned of many slim strands of dough; the *yu-t'iao*, multiple fingers of batter fried in deep oil, sizzling hot and fragrant, and cooked for breakfast right before the customer's eyes by street venders?

How greatly the Chinese used to enjoy their superb seafood

dishes! At Chungking up past the great Yangtze gorges, one ate a fine river fish cooked whole, with bean curd, in a highly flavored sauce in which either red peppers or small, tasty, black beans predominated. From nearer the mouth came the Yangtze River shad, so delicate in flavor that, fables say, new brides were tested by their ability to cook it.

The old canal-laced city of Soochow was famous not only for China's most beautiful women but also for steamed fresh water crab. When this dish came in season, good friends used the occasion to gather, chat, reminisce, joke, and play for hours a complicated "fingers game," in which the loser always had to down his cup of warm rice wine at one gulp.

There were the countless permutations of fish, lobster, and shrimp of many sizes and flavors, in Kwangtung Province, bordering Hong Kong; the fishtails and eels of Shanghai were flavored with some of China's finest sauces. In famous restaurants along the lovely lake at Hangchow, shrimps were so fresh and delicate that connoisseurs gathered there to eat them raw. And one should never forget the tiny, dried shrimp almost anyone could once afford. Gourmets used to argue endlessly over the comparative merits of China's innumerable shrimp and lobster dishes.

No European diet includes the great number of vegetables once used by the Chinese. Nor can even a Parisian chef prepare vegetables better than did the run-of-the-road Chinese peasants ten years ago. Sometimes, with proper sauces and condiments, they were cooked alone, like Chinese spinach; sometimes together, like the dish which contrasted—in appearance, texture, and taste— ivory-colored, crisp, young bamboo shoots with huge, soft, black mushrooms.

Today's almost meatless Chinese must think sometimes of the many dishes of pork, beef, and mutton which, combined in exactly the right ways with vegetables, make American cooking seem a product of unimaginative children.

One could write poetry about Chinese soups intelligently served not to begin a meal but to allow a pause during one or to finish it. Americans know a westernized version of some of these: the "potage" cooked and served in a melon; birds-nest soup, made of the saliva that swallows use to build their nests high up in crevices of tremendous Borneo caves; Szechwan's vinegar-pepper soup and clear Yunnanese broth that is the distillation of slowly steamed chicken. Some of my favorites were made by my childhood nurse; as far as I knew, they had no names, but they are still unforgotten.

Who cares—or dares—in China today to carry on the aged, endless argument over which is more superb: the force-fed Peking duck whose crisp brown skin is the only portion eaten, or the Szechwan duck, fried in deep fat so that under the crisp skin the brown-colored meat is so tender it leaves the bones at the slightest touch of chopsticks?

My Shanghai friends generally preferred their own city's Eight Jeweled Roast Duck, stuffed with rice and eight other delicious ingredients. My Hangchow friends liked Beggars' Chicken, a fattened fowl salt-spiced, wrapped in great fragrant leaves, enveloped in a thick coat of mud, baked very carefully, carried from the kitchen in a great shovel, and broken open by the chef in the customer's presence.

In the North at least, dishes of the poor were simpler but, I thought, often as good as those of the rich, cooked as carefully, and eaten with as much enjoyment. Give me inexpensive North China noodles to pasta any day. Each part of China prepared the versions of the cheap, once universally available, high-protein bean curd, and steamed or fried dumplings stuffed with meat, vegetables, or both were one of the best, least expensive foods in China, as well as a reliable test of anyone's cooking.

Then there were the exotic delicacies—paw of bear, for instance, which had to be cooked for a week; or, served in wine, the galls of living, writhing snakes (afterward the snakes were made into soup). There were the foods forced on the ingenious Chinese people by poverty or famine: many weeds Americans scorn; locusts and silkworms (in their worm-like chrysalis stage) fried in deep oil—both of which I found delectable when I was a child.

With communes spreading, and restaurants, even in cities, being closed, one by one, all this food, even the simplest, has become steadily less available. Anyway, like sentimental love between the sexes or undue attachment to the family, indulging in good eating is almost a sin against Marx and Mao in China.

It is all very confusing, especially, one supposes, to China's citizens to whom Mao, for decades, promised all good things. Communist China's "beloved Chairman" comes from Hunan, a province of such hearty eaters that their rice bowls are bigger, their chopsticks longer, than anywhere else in China. In Hunan, the practice of eating violent red peppers has failed to deaden the taste buds; Hunanese cuisine is among the best in the country.

So Chairman Mao knows fine cooking. And he is perfectly aware how much it has meant, for centuries, to his fellow countrymen.

Yet, for the time being at least, the huge portrait of Chairman Mao in the mess hall has replaced one of China's most ancient deities, the Colorful Kitchen God that presided over the household stove.

I have always found the Chinese, however illiterate, to have long memories. Someday they may forget the Communists' cruelties; they may become numbed to the total prohibition of individualism. But it is possible that, just as they have spit for centuries at the name of Ch'in Shih Huang-ti, the emperor who tried long ago to destroy their books, so someday will they abhor Chairman Mao Tse-tung's name for destroying their incomparable cuisine.

On the other hand, if events continue to take their present course, in another fifteen or twenty years the new generation of Chinese will never have tasted their own galaxy of superb dishes. China will have forgotten them. Perhaps then all that will remain of the world's best cooking will be the "chop suey" restaurants of New York and San Francisco, where the food, by some inexorable law, always becomes less and less Chinese. Perhaps, by then, the chefs themselves will hardly recollect the origin of the tasteless, hybrid, and homeless dishes they are cooking.

A SCHOOL FOR CHEFS

CHANG CHIANG

Every part of China has a style of cooking distinctively its own, according to the varying farm products, natural conditions, and ways of life of the different regions. It is said that people in the South prefer their dishes sweet; in the North, salty; in the East, sour; in the West, hot. In Soochow where I live, just south of the Yangtze River in Kiangsu Province, we like richly flavored food, slightly sweetened, and cooked until very tender. As the town is surrounded by lakes and streams, fish play an important part in our diet. Some of the well-known dishes are savory turtle, eel casserole, and shrimps in Chinese cabbage.

Soochow cooking is one of the most famous of China's many styles. Soochow pork, pot-roasted in soya sauce until it is tender, is said to have been praised in a verse by Su Tung-p'o, the great

FROM Chang Chiang, "A School for Chefs," *China Reconstructs*, 11, 9 (Sept., 1962), 41–43.

Sung-dynasty (960–1279 A.D.) poet, and is now known by his name. The meat, with shiny, deep brown skin, fat as white as jade, and pink, glossy lean, when attractively arranged in a golden-brown sauce along with fresh green spinach and ivory-white bamboo shoots, has all the "color, aroma, and flavor" characteristic of the Soochow cuisine.

This style of cooking is also known for its pastries: steamed filled dumplings, crisp shortcakes, rice-flour dumplings, and especially the "boat tidbits." These tiny rice-flour cases made in the shapes of birds, multi-colored goldfish, insects, and fruit and filled with minced ham, date paste, walnuts, sesame seed, or rose petals are served on the brightly painted pleasure boats which ply Soochow's waterways.

In recent years, as the people's living standard improved, chefs able to do Soochow-style cookery have been in demand in many parts of the country. As a public service, the Kiangsu provincial department of commerce has opened many schools and classes to train them, and in March, 1960, our own school was set up.

For entrance, we require only that applicants like to cook and that they possess the equivalent of a primary school education. The 157 students who enrolled in the first class were workers from restaurants and pastry shops in 41 counties of the province. Expenses for tuition, room, books, and cooking materials are paid by the municipal government. Students continue to draw their regular wage while in school.

We offer two classes, a one-year course in the fundamentals of cooking for those who have had little experience and a six months' advanced course. Students in the former begin by learning the characteristics of different types of stoves, the correct way to use kitchen utensils, and how to kill and dress poultry and clean fish. They learn how to select the best materials and vegetables—peas, Chinese cabbage hearts, bamboo shoots, tomatoes, chestnuts, or others in season—to go well with each other or in combinations with fish, meat, or fowl.

Half the time is spent in practical work in the kitchen learning to make the easier dishes and pastries. The rest is at lectures or demonstrations. The students also make some study of nutrition and methods of preparing foods to get the most value from them. An example is the famous Soochow dish "squirrel" Mandarin fish, which is sautéed slowly with a little oil until it is a flat golden brown crisp and the tail curls upward like that of a squirrel: Prepared in this way, the fine bones of the fish can be eaten. A sweet-sour sauce made with vinegar helps soften the bones and aids gastric absorption of their phosphorus calcium.

Most of the students in the advanced class have had three years or more of cooking experience, so they can already prepare the basic dishes. They study the theory of Soochow cooking, preparation of the most famous dishes and desserts, and arrangement of menus for banquets.

One of the things that gives Soochow cookery its distinction is the care with which the materials are selected to suit the special requirements of each dish. The cooks learn, for instance, that the best duck is one from T'ai-hu Lake, which, properly cooked, will be so tender that the meat falls from the bones at the touch of the chopsticks.

A student who enters the elementary class and completes the advanced class a year and a half later will be able to make more than 300 meat or vegetable specialties and 20 kinds of famous desserts as well as 150 everyday dishes. He will have studied eight ways to prepare a duck and ten different ways to cook one kind of fish. His skill is tested in the restaurant run by our school. The day's cooking lesson becomes the day's menu for the diners, who offer criticism on the way the dishes have been made. Students often go to factory or office canteens to pass on what they have learned to the staffs. In the past two years, they have taught methods of preparing more than 120 ordinary dishes to about 140 different cooks. In this way they also get practice working independently, calculating costs, and applying in everyday situations the techniques learned for famous dishes.

While a few among our first group of graduates were offered jobs in famous local restaurants or workers' rest homes, most of them have gone back to their old restaurants or pastry shops where they are raising the quality of service. Sometimes they themselves conduct classes to teach their new skills to fellow-cooks in their towns.

Many old chefs tell us that our trainees have learned more in our course than a cook would have in five or six years' apprenticeship before the liberation. They say that even chefs with long experience might not have such a grasp of the theory of Soochow cookery and its key problems and would not be able to prepare so many dishes or be experts at meat and vegetable dishes as well as desserts.

The reason our students can learn so much in this short course is that they are taught the best skills of many experienced masters.

Besides the seven regular teachers on our staff, more than twenty famous chefs and pastry cooks come in to give special classes. Most of them have nearly a half-century of experience and excel at making certain dishes. Each is distinguished in some aspect of cooking, like organizing the kitchen work, knowing the exact time and heat for certain results, or preparing and arranging cold plates. Without reservation, these veterans share all they know with their students. In the past, they used to guard these professional secrets from all but members of their families. . . .

Once, while our experts were chatting, Chang Kuei-fu, who is now more than seventy, recalled that when he was young he used to hear his master boast about a banquet of Han and Manchu delicacies the latter had prepared for the Ch'ing-dynasty court. After much thought, Chang was able to recall most of the dishes and piece together information he had gleaned on how they were made so that he could re-create the food of the banquet for us.

The secrets of Soochow cooking, widely scattered in the past, are now being collected, and books of its recipes and techniques are in preparation by the Municipal Department of Commerce. In this way, our school is making a contribution to better living.

DRAGON PINK ON OLD WHITE (II)

PHILLIP BONOSKY

This day that ended with Peking duck was a day never to be forgotten. With some writers I drove to Great Concentrated Morality Restaurant for its Peking duck—a gourmet's delight. The ducks are raised on a special diet, literally stuffed with grain for weeks before eating. The guests choose the particular duck, which the chef holds before them—its glossy, almost pink skin glowing— and then it is roasted right there and then for some forty-five minutes. While we waited, we sat around a circular table and sipped shao-hsing wine, ate "dragon's eyes," and talked. The waiter set the table as we talked, putting down dishes of soya bean sauce and leek and dishes of unleavened flat pancakes.

When the duck was ready, it was brought in once again for our approval—held up by the chef, a golden-glowing bird, glazed from the molasses in which it is roasted. Then strips of skin are cut off

FROM Phillip Bonosky, *Dragon Pink on Old White* (New York: Marzani and Munsell, 1963), p. 32. Reprinted by permission of the publisher.

first, which I spread—I following their lead—on the pancake; over this we placed strips of leek and dipped it all, rolled into a tube, in the sauce. It was indescribably delicious, as the rest of the duck was; and we chose savory portions which we gripped between our chopsticks and ate until we could eat no more. Cool custard was served at the end—just after a soup made of the bones of the duck was eaten.

Chinese culture and civilization were at their most exquisite.

X

Architecture

Probably no area is so important for maintaining the Chinese character of China's rural and urban landscapes as architecture. The Communists have not been insensitive to this, and conscious efforts have been made to preserve elements of traditional architectural style in new construction. The classical-revival school led by Professor Liang Ssu-ch'eng has taken the lead in promoting a national style of modern architecture, but as we see in A. C. Scott's critical appraisal, not with unqualified success. The problem of finding an architectural style that is both functionally modern and stylistically Chinese has apparently not been solved. Chai Li-lin poses the problem in its sharpest form: "It is said that socialist content cannot be expressed except through national form. But what of a national form into which the uses of socialist life will not fit?" His question could be transposed to any element of the cultural legacy.

CHINA'S ARCHITECTURAL HERITAGE
AND THE TASKS OF TODAY
LIANG SSU-CH'ENG

The architecture of the Chinese nation forms a distinct system of its own among the great architectural systems of the world. In this system, a skeleton of wood is first built on the stylobate in order to support the weight of the upper part of the building. Walls are in fact only "screens" forming the interior and exterior.

FROM Liang Ssu-ch'eng, "China's Architectural Heritage and the Tasks of Today," *People's China*, 21 (Nov. 1, 1952), 31–36.

Complete control is thus achieved in the arrangement of the position and size of windows and doors, so that this system of architecture can be adapted to suit any climate. It is, in fact, distributed over a very broad area, ranging from the subtropics of South China to the cold climate of the Northeast. This method exactly conforms with the principle of the modern use of a steel and reinforced-concrete skeleton and provides an excellent foundation for the adaptation of modern materials and techniques to the characteristic features of Chinese architecture.

Based on the experience of generations in the use of wood, the architects and craftsmen of ancient China developed the method of using tiers of cantilevers on top of the columns forming sets of brackets or *tou-kung* to support the beams and overhanging eaves of the roof. The *tou-kung* and the majestic roof they support are particularly remarkable characteristics of Chinese architecture. The ancient craftsmen also made dexterous use of wood-protecting paints. Their beautiful decorations successfully control the boldest combinations of colors. The designs on ceilings and friezes seem endless in their variations. They also often replaced plain tiles with colored glazed tiles and achieved magnificent effects. Although the Chinese builders are bold in their use of color, the over-all effect produced is one of harmony. Their classical ornamentation has splendid qualities of simplicity and displays great powers of control of all architectural elements. In Chinese architecture, every visible structural element is at the same time a decorative element. An ornamental element is a structural element which has had additional artistic treatment. Decoration and structure in Chinese wooden architecture are in most cases completely unified. . . .

Chinese architecture, whether in wood or in masonry, has preserved throughout several thousands of years a distinct, continuous, and uniformly consistent national character. But China's architects have been adept at absorbing outside influences on the basis of their own tradition. They have thus enriched their art and yet not lost their basic characteristics. The Buddhist and Muslim architecture of China clearly exemplifies this point. But when the imperialists invaded China, and the peaceful and natural interflow of culture was replaced by relations based on brute force, the situation changed completely. The aggressors indiscriminately transplanted into China their own architectural forms. Their buildings, like their gunboats, dominated the larger cities along the coast and the Yangtze River. In their arrogance, they looked down upon and destroyed the original style and setting of

Chinese cities. Architecture in China lost its independence and individuality. Ideologically and artistically, it was degraded. Although new techniques of construction were acquired and new materials mastered, for several decades mostly Western-style buildings were built in large cities. Chinese architecture was deprived of its chances for lively development.

Liberation brought about a revolutionary change in the status of architects in China and in the whole direction and content of their work.

Today, all architects, whether in the field of economic or cultural construction, are without exception active participants in the assertion of the ideology of the new China, the New Democracy in architecture. They have shouldered this great responsibility with great earnestness. It is an inspiring task.

The full significance of their new tasks, however, was not immediately realized by all architects. Because of past habits, they at first saw only the vast increase in the amount of building as so many opportunities for showing off their abilities and asserting their pet theories. But soon more serious questions were brought to their attention. The appearance of such great numbers of new buildings will alter the appearance of all Chinese cities. What materials should be used? What kind of structures, styles, and forms should be adopted? All these are momentous questions. Laissez faire and unplanned development cannot be permitted. The cultural and educational policy of the Common Program adopted by the Chinese People's Political Consultative Conference has, however, provided them with a working guide.

This policy is the same new-democratic cultural and educational policy enunciated by Chairman Mao Tse-tung. Brilliantly analyzing the new culture in his "On New Democracy," he writes that China's new culture is, and therefore China's new architecture must also necessarily be, "national. It opposes imperialist oppression and upholds the dignity and independence of the Chinese nation. It belongs to this nation of ours and is imbued with our national characteristics." New China's architecture naturally must also . . . "have its own form, namely, a national form. National in form, new-democratic in content—such is our new culture today." . . .

Our architects gained confidence from such clear directions. They will enable us to stride boldly forward and overcome our defects.

The architectural profession in China has been for so long subjected to the semicolonial conditions of the so-called treaty ports that the architects became strangers to our finest national traditions, which were most regrettably rejected and cast aside. The priceless skill of experienced artisans was allowed to degenerate through disuse. The architects of New China are faced with no small task in re-acquainting themselves with the great artistic traditions of the motherland and making the very great adaptations needed in order to bring those traditions to serve the needs of today and tomorrow and in preserving and developing our national artistic characteristics in architecture while new techniques are being absorbed. These tasks are especially difficult since the tempo and scale of construction work in our country is increasing with such rapidity, and our architects' time is already so overburdened.

The Chinese people have every confidence that New China's architecture will play a useful role in peaceful construction throughout the country, that the quality of architectural design will be significantly raised by absorbing the special features of China's own traditional art. With the use of new techniques and materials, a glorious new architecture will be developed, a new-democratic architecture that is "national, scientific, and of the broad masses," "loved by the Chinese people," and worthy of Mao Tse-tung's era.

ARCHITECTURE AND SCULPTURE

A. C. SCOTT

When the Communists came to power in 1949, they inherited a negative architectural policy and a complex crop of problems. The years of war had left every major planning and constructional need in the country unfulfilled. The difficulties were enormous and continue to be so. The Communists have tackled some of them with characteristic energy and startling results. The bridge over the Yangtze River is a case in point. It has been described as China's

FROM A. C. Scott, *Literature and the Arts in Twentieth-Century China* (New York: Doubleday Anchor Books, 1963), pp. 116–22. Copyright © 1963 by A. C. Scott. Reprinted by permission of Doubleday and Company, Inc., and George Allen and Unwin, Ltd.

finest achievement in the first Five Year Plan, although the Russian engineer Konstantin Silin must take a great share of the credit as the real genius behind the project and the inventor of a new method of sinking piers. Opened to traffic in October, 1957, the bridge has a 3,800-foot span over the water and is a double-decker, with a six-lane traffic highway on the upper level and a double rail track below. A verse by Mao Tse-tung inscribed on a banner that floated over the girders on the opening day ran "A bridge from North to South: an insuperable natural barrier becomes a thoroughfare." Certainly it is an engineering feat of the first magnitude, but, as an example of architectural design, it is open to some criticism, particularly in the eternal problem of combining Chinese and Western forms. The Chinese-style bridgehead pavilions are unsuitable in their setting, and the bridge itself has the nineteenth-century heaviness that is associated with so much Soviet design and, by implication, Chinese design today. In the matter of evolving a contemporary style, the Communists have not yet proved any more successful than their predecessors, and, in their Western-style architecture, they have become imitators of Soviet neo-Communist classicism, at any rate in the public buildings of Peking, which must be regarded as the architectural showpiece of the nation.

In a regime as bombastically nationalistic as the Communists were in their first year of power, it was perhaps inevitable that immediate architectural instincts were to promote the "national" style in all its glory of glazed tile roofs and replicas of past greatness. An example was the Government Ceremonial Hall and Guest House in Chungking, built between 1951 and 1954. The central feature of this ornate construction was a replica of the Temple of Heaven in Peking, which dominated a building whose lavishness and cost were afterward hotly criticized for their impractical extravagance. This came at the end of a period in which the apostles of the "national" style had been given a free hand.

In February, 1955, *People's Daily* (*Jen-min Jih-pao*) published a cartoon showing the Empress Dowager patting a present-day architect on the shoulder and saying: "You certainly know how to spend the money. I never thought of using glazed tiles for the kitchen when I built the Summer Palace." This marked the end of the architectural honeymoon with "curved roofs and high walls," which were now declared bourgeois in principle. Meetings were held by the Ministry of Building, and there was a spate of architects' confessions and repentances. Ideas were forced into line with prevailing Soviet dictates and a Moscow campaign to negate luxury and extravagance in public buildings.

So far as replanning Peking went, the traditionalists never regained control. The many new buildings erected since the mid-1950's are either unabashed imitations of Soviet styles pure and simple, or, if they do make concessions to Chinese traditions, use towers, the ubiquitous tiled roofing, superimposed columns, and replicas of the old-style brackets for staying eaves. The new Peking railway station is an example of this kind of mixture. The twin towers at the entrance are fussy and pointless, while the Chinese design elements are irrelevant to the general façade. The interior of the station drops all pretense of being Chinese, and the escalators, rest rooms, and waiting halls make it a far more spacious, efficient, and functional center than the inadequate old terminus it replaced. But everything about the interior is redolent of the heavy hand of Soviet "classicism"—and this also applies to a majority of the new buildings, whatever their façades pretend to the contrary.

The new National Agricultural Exhibition Center in Peking is an example of all that is worst in the attempt to blend sham tradition with imported ideas. The arrangement of the buildings is supposed to be reminiscent of Chinese garden layout, although the realistic and muscular group of statuary standing in the main approach to the Center is imitative only of the monumental mason school of sculpture favored in controlled societies. A description from a contemporary Chinese account gives the best clue to the real nature of the Exhibition Center:

> The General Agricultural Hall, around which the others are grouped, is particularly majestic. On its roof stand seven turrets glistening with green tiles and yellow walls. The broad granite steps in front of the entrance and the balustrades on either side are carved with designs of grapes, cotton bolls, and wheat ears. The floor of the main hall is red marble. Eight pink columns are capped with a fretwork of golden flowers. At the center of the hall stands a large statue of Chairman Mao Tse-tung chatting with peasants, symbol of the flesh-and-blood relations between the Party and the peasants.

Other contemporary public buildings in Peking include the Center for Returned Overseas Chinese, a dull construction in yellow brick and grey stone of a characterless kind to be found in any large city in the West, and the Chinese People's Revolutionary Army Museum, a blatant piece of second-hand Sovietism down to the last brick in the tower and the red star which surmounts it.

The use of heavily ornate lamp standards is a feature of all the new architecture in China. Those in the T'ien An Men, Peking, are typical. Ostentatious and top-heavy in design, their chandelier form is sadly out of keeping with the spaciousness of their setting and the dominating pile of the old Imperial Gate, if well-suited to the pillared façade of the Great Hall of the People flanking the Square. The auditorium of this building, which seats 10,000, is, incidentally, characteristic of the scale of architectural planning in contemporary China.

The doyen of the traditional school of architecture is Professor Liang Ssu-ch'eng (1901–   ), son of the famous Liang Ch'i-ch'ao, a prominent figure in the reform movement at the beginning of the century. Liang Ssu-ch'eng was educated at Pennsylvania and Harvard universities. From 1931–46, he directed the Institute for Research into Chinese Architecture and led a number of field expeditions to study various styles and periods. He is regarded as the leading authority on his subject. An architectural historian rather than a creative artist, he is today dean of the architectural department of Tsinghua University, Peking. He came under heavy criticism for his ideas in the early years of the regime but made his peace with the Party in 1957. During 1961, a series of architectural forums held in Peking, Harbin, and Canton focused attention on the professor's theories again. In June of that year, he was interviewed by the *Kuang Ming Daily* in Peking and made a long statement on architecture as an art.

Harping on the theme that architecture is the reflection of ideology, particularly class ideology, Liang climaxed a long exposition with the following precept:

> we should not criticize a building by divorcing it either from its historical background or from the needs of today. We should not, furthermore, take it apart and analyze each architectural element as if it were an independent thing. We should differentiate between heritage and tradition. The only criterion for analysis is what Chairman Mao has pointed out, political standards in the first place and artistic standards in the second place.

Soviet Russia's official attitude has been the condemnation of contemporary Western architecture as "modernism for modernism's sake." In determining what was most applicable to Soviet ideas, the classical styles of Greece and Rome were selected as fundamentally "civic" and therefore social in aspiration. Gothic and oriental architecture were coupled with mysticism and feudalism, while twentieth-century functional styles were regarded as the product of decadent capitalism. Such Russian "tail chasing" has posed some aesthetic problems in Peking which are reflected in three ways in the new Chinese architecture. First there is pure imitation of Soviet models; second, an uneasy fusing of Soviet and Chinese ideas; and third, a frank return to the prewar "national" style as exemplified in the recently completed Peking Art Gallery.

THE QUESTION OF ARCHITECTURAL FORM
CHAI LI-LIN

For some years after the liberation in 1949 . . . building in China showed a tendency toward crude constructivism and cosmopolitanism. This tendency was not checked until 1952. After 1953, the influence of cosmopolitanism was shaken off, and the national style in building began to prevail.

That was a change for the better, but soon a new erroneous tendency appeared, a proneness to extravagance, impractical emphasis on form, and lordly disregard of cost. This was done at the insistence of a group of architects typified by Professor Liang Ssu-ch'eng, who wanted to apply the palace and temple architecture of feudal China, unaltered, to our hospitals, schools, hotels, halls, theaters, and even factories. The forms they adopted, such as ancient pavilions, terraces, and towers, and the elements they used, such as painted beams with gold decorations, big artistic roofs, stone lions, etc., were all very expensive. They employed legions of artisans to paint complex decorations for the purpose of ostentation. They stressed beauty of form to such an extent that practicality and economy were virtually disregarded. Their buildings were often quite unsuited to their function, and vast government funds were unproductively wasted. In some cases, the decorations alone mounted to 30 per cent of the entire cost of construction.

FROM Chai Li-lin, "The Question of Architectural Form," *People's China*, 14 (July, 1956), 30–32.

Huge "artistic" roofs were regarded as *de rigueur*. But in using them, these architects did not ask themselves how they had arisen in ancient times. The reason was this. Owing to the fact that the walls of old-style buildings were made of clay, projecting eaves were necessary to protect them from the weather. And since such eaves tend to keep the light out of the rooms, they were curved upward. That is how the characteristic Chinese roof came about. The high stylobate—the continuous raised basement—also had its good reason, for while wooden columns were used as supports, it was necessary to protect the bases of the columns from damp-rot and from being eaten away by alkaline soil. The chief elements of the old Chinese style were thus functional in origin, though they were, of course, elaborated on by feudal rulers who wished to parade their prestige and wealth.

From any point of view, the spending of huge sums to reproduce these elements in New China's buildings was unnecessary and unjustified. The architects who did it did not consider function. One hostel built in Peking imitated the old solid foundations with a false stylobate having a basement inside. Unwilling to spoil the external view they left out many side windows so that in the basement the electric light had to be kept on day and night. In another case, a building was reconstructed at a cost of 18 yuan per square foot of floor space. Two years later, an ornately tiled palace-style roof was added at the cost of 37 yuan per square foot. But the building had been in full use before the roof was put on. Clearly the roof contributed nothing at all to its function.

After discussion, it was concluded that the greatest mistake these architects made in their search for national style was the arbitrary separation of form from content. In all genuine architectural advances, the content or function is basic; the form derives from it. It is said that socialist content cannot be expressed except through national form. But what of a national form into which the uses of socialist life will not fit? It can only be an abstraction, without meaning or life. So the trouble with the classical revivalists was that they did not see form and content in their proper relation. That is why their lead was finally rejected by other Chinese architects.

XI

Science in the Cultural Legacy

Almost everything about the cultural legacy that we have discussed so far has had to do with art, literature, philosophy, and other humanistic studies. Architecture is a possible exception, but there, too, our discussion of cultural legacy has mainly been concerned with aesthetics and national style. The Chinese cultural tradition, for all its predominantly humanistic or scholastic bent, however, has not been devoid of great achievements in natural sciences and technology. And, in modern China, science is a highly prized commodity. It is not surprising, therefore, that modern Chinese have taken far more pride in China's ancient scientific discoveries, from mathematical calculations to the invention of gunpowder, than their ancestors themselves ever did. But it has been difficult to find very much in the legacy that could contribute directly to the modern scientific world. Two elements valued not just as historical achievements but also for present-day relevance are described next. In his article on bridge construction, Mao Yi-sheng makes it clear that ancient Chinese engineering experience can be "used widely to serve the needs of the people" —today's people. Even more striking, as shown in the second article, are the claims for traditional Chinese medicine and the effort that has gone into its preservation and development. Beyond any doubt, it is the showpiece for scientific value in the cultural legacy.

THE STONE ARCH: SYMBOL OF CHINESE BRIDGES

MAO YI-SHENG

When did the stone arch bridge first appear in China? In *Annotated Water Classic* (written during the northern Wei dynasty, 386–534 A.D.) there is this description of the Traveler's Bridge: "It is situated six or seven li from the Loyang Palace and built entirely of stone. It rises round above the water, and large vessels can sail beneath it." This bridge, completed in 282 A.D., was probably the first of its type. A stone arch has been found, however, dating back to 250 B.C. It is the entrance to a tomb of a certain Lord Han buried in Loyang and shows that such a structure was in existence five or six hundred years earlier.

Although they are most numerous south of the Yangtze where the land is heavily intersected by rivers, canals, and creeks, stone arch bridges are found in nearly all parts of the country. Local annals always include a special section on bridges, the number of which is often amazing. One such record of Soochow County near Shanghai, published during the early Ch'ing dynasty (1644–1911), lists the names of 397 bridges, many of which are described as of the arch type.

There are several reasons why stone arch bridges are so popular in China. First, the material is plentiful in all areas where there are rivers and mountains; second, the people have a long tradition for excellent stonework as shown in the many existing palaces, towers, city walls, and large tombs; third, after centuries of study and experience, bridge-builders became extremely expert and had worked out many unique methods, especially in the erection of the stone arch type.

The main structure of the bridge is the arch itself, made by the laying tightly together of carefully cut stones. In addition to semicircular arches, segmental, semi-elliptical, and pentagonal ones were produced by the ancients through the adoption of various devices. Most commonly a wooden "centering" was set up in the river so that the upper surface of the framework conformed to the outline of the under surface of the arch to be built. The stone blocks were then fitted on the frame by either the "longitudinal" or "transverse" method of lining. In the former, the

FROM Mao Yi-sheng, "The Stone Arch: Symbol of Chinese Bridges," *China Reconstructs*, 10, 11 (Nov., 1961), 18–21.

stones were built up row by row from both end supports of the arch until they met at the crown. In the latter, complete arch rings were built side by side in a series until the required width of the bridge was reached. Later builders sometimes combined both methods.

The ancient bridges were built on such sound scientific principles that many of them have been found capable of carrying heavy trucks after a smooth road surface has been laid. The arch ring can bear a greater load than the modern stress analysis of the arch alone would seem to justify, because the abutment wall, together with the filling of the spandrel, forms a buttress producing "passive pressure" on the arch which increases its strength and rigidity. This, however, is often neglected in the design of an arch even today, but it was a feature unique to the old Chinese arches.

To erect an arched bridge so that it will keep its shape intact against mechanical and weathering effects is a real technical problem. Traditionally, this was achieved by giving the wooden centering a little "camber" so that when the frame was removed the stones would sink slightly on their own weight and become pressed together. Such practice is common in modern bridge construction, but what is remarkable is that it was done so early in China.

Another important feature is that ancient bridge-builders ground their stones smooth and placed them together dry—without mortar. This prevented distortion of the arch through expansion and contraction of the mortar joints, which would have happened following contact with water.

The Lukouch'iao Bridge near Peking was first made famous by Marco Polo, who described it in his *Travels* as "a very handsome bridge of stone, perhaps unequalled by any other in the world. Its length is three hundred paces, and its width eighty paces, so that ten mounted men can, without inconvenience, ride abreast. It had twenty-four arches . . . built with great skill." He went on to give details of the roadway, parapets, and carved lions which formed "altogether a beautiful spectacle." This continuous-arch bridge, built in the amazingly short time of four years (1189–92), was considered a rare accomplishment in its day. The design is notable for its economy; each abutment serves two arches so that the load on any one span is shared by all the others.

Marco Polo was astonished by what he saw at Lukouch'iao but he did not know that there were many other older and even more impressive structures in China. One of these is the Chaochow

Bridge, about 300 kilometers from Lukouch'iao, built in the Sui dynasty between 605 and 616 A.D. Probably the most perfect example of its type, it consists of a single arch. The design is surprisingly scientific; the building technique shows immense inventiveness and the appearance is distinctly national. Although it is still serving the Chinese people after 1,350 years, from a photograph it can easily be taken for a modern arch bridge built just yesterday.

At a time when there was neither steel nor construction machines, the span of the arch, built up with limestone blocks, was 37.5 meters long, which was more than double the usual length. Generally the height of such bridges is equal to the radius of the arch, but in this case the arch is a segmental arc, making the bridge low and long with the crown of the arch rising only 7.23 meters higher than the abutments. Technically, this presented a much more difficult problem than the semicircular design, but it had the advantage of giving the bridge a much more gentle slope.

The builders devised many ingenious methods for its construction. "Transverse lining" was used for the arch, and the width of the roadway was obtained by placing together 28 separate narrow arches. The advantage was that, if one of these were to collapse, the bridge would still be safe for traffic. It also allowed for a great saving in timber, since the building was done with a very narrow centering, moved as each arch was completed. The stones were cut of equal thickness but those used at the haunch of the arch were slightly wider than those at the crest. This gave the bridge an almost imperceptible "waist" at the center which adds to its grace and beauty.

The most remarkable feature, however, is the four small arches, two at each shoulder of the main arch, which help to support the roadway. They serve to lessen the earth pressure on the main arch and act as spillways when the river is in flood, reducing water pressure on the bridge. This design is what today is known as the open spandrelled arch, which became widely used in Europe only after the middle of the nineteenth century. The Pont-de-Ceret Bridge in France was the first of this type known to be built outside China. It was erected in 1321—700 years later.

Recognizing the tremendous scientific and cultural value of the bridge, the People's government in 1952 appropriated funds for its renovation and preservation. The group of workers responsible made careful investigations, and, through the unearthing of lost stones and general research into the sources of ancient rivers, weathering and relaxation of rocks, and the gathering of hydrological information, collected valuable historical data. Renovation was completed in 1959.

The building skill and fine features of the stone arch bridge have accumulated throughout the past 2,000 years. Today, such structures are used extensively in the construction of both rail and highway bridges.

In any engineering project, it is a great advantage to be able to construct with materials available on the site rather than having long haulage. A stone arch bridge is practically finished once the arch is built, and this itself only calls for a simple centering and the laying of the stones. With modern machines, the work involved in quarrying, shaping, polishing, building arch supports, and lifting the stones into place greatly reduces the labor formerly required, thus removing some of the old disadvantages of this type of bridge. If steel is used for the centering instead of wood, the span can be made much longer.

Experience gathered from ancient engineers has been applied in the building of many stone arch bridges since the liberation. The Yellow Tiger Ridge Bridge over the Li River in Hunan Province, completed in 1959, is one such example. In this instance the arch has a span of 60 meters, which is considered quite large for such structures.

China's legacy in bridge construction is an exceptionally rich one. In addition to the stone arch, many other types have been built since very early days, often showing amazing structural invention. As early as 270 A.D., a pontoon bridge was erected over the Yellow River in Honan Province; a cantilever bridge in Kansu Province dates back to 410 A.D., an imposing 1,200-meter stone girder bridge in Fukien Province to 1053; and one of the world's earliest movable bridges at Ch'aochou, Kwangtung Province, to 1100. From the fourteenth century on, suspension bridges of bamboo, rattan, cable, or iron chains became common in the southwestern provinces. To construct these involved knowledge of many complicated questions, such as how to lay foundations under water, how to solve the structural problem in each case, and how best to coordinate land and water communications. To follow the process by which these problems were solved provides a fascinating history of man's conquest of nature. The experience gained by our ancestors from the battle is today being further developed and used widely to serve the needs of the people.

CHINESE COMMUNIST ATTITUDES TOWARD
TRADITIONAL MEDICINE

RALPH C. CROIZIER

Most foreign visitors to Communist China have commented upon the paradoxical position of traditional Chinese medicine in the People's Republic. Finding venerable herbalists practicing alongside modern doctors, seeing acupuncture in the wards of the largest hospitals and millennia-old medical texts in the classrooms of medical colleges, they have wondered why so militantly modern and scientific a regime has taken such pains to preserve, encourage, and develop an ancient and obviously prescientific medical system.

The paradox here goes beyond the foreigner's limited understanding of a strange and different culture. For, in terms of Chinese history itself, we find that only a few decades earlier the first generation of Chinese Marxists bitterly opposed Chinese medicine. In common with the other young modern intellectuals of their day, they had no use for traditional Chinese medicine— or anything else traditionally Chinese for that matter. Medicine, however, because of its scientific associations, was a particularly noxious part of the old culture to a generation who saw "Science" as the panacea for China's many ills. Thus, Ch'en Tu-hsiu, the father of the Chinese Communist Party, condemned Chinese medicine for its "nonsensical beliefs and reasonless ideas." And later, in the 1920's and 1930's when a movement developed to preserve at least the core of Chinese medicine as part of the "national essence," the main figures behind it were prominent in the right wing of the Communists' main enemy, the Chinese Nationalist Party.

How, then, has the Communist leadership reached its present policy of supporting traditional medicine, insisting that its integration with modern Western medicine not sacrifice the key practices and concepts of the indigenous Chinese medical tradition? If we look at their experience in the guerrilla areas before 1949, we see that—cut off from modern medical supplies and with very few modern trained doctors—the Communists sufficiently modi-

FROM Ralph C. Croizier, "Chinese Communist Attitudes Toward Traditional Medicine," *Asia*, 5 (Spring, 1966), 70–76. Copyright © 1966 by The Asia Society, Inc. Reprinted by permission of The Asia Society.

fied their aversion to "feudal medicine" to allow them to make pragmatic use of traditional herbs and herbalists. In 1944, Mao himself warned the medical cadres that pressing immediate needs made it necessary to unite with and make use of the large number of traditional doctors despite their scientific shortcomings. It was the Western-style doctors' responsibility to "help, stimulate, and reform" their traditional colleagues.

In the first few years after their rise to national power, this policy was essentially continued. The half million or so traditional practitioners with their modern counterparts were organized into "health-workers unions," were given some training in basic sanitation and preventive medicine in short term "improvement classes," and were generally set to work in the vast countryside where medical needs could have swallowed the small number of modern trained doctors with scarcely a ripple on China's total health picture. Traditional medicine was not attacked. Official policy was to integrate the two systems. But with modern trained people in control of the Ministry of Health and traditional doctors being re-educated in the rudiments of Western medicine, this integration clearly indicated an eventual assimilation of useful specifics from the indigenous system into the body of modern, scientific "Western" medicine. Chinese medicine, as a distinct medical tradition, apparently would not survive its immediate usefulness as a stop-gap until sufficient numbers of modern medical personnel could be trained.

By 1954, however, all this began to change. First, more and more statements praising the "medical legacy of the Chinese people" appeared in the press and periodicals, accompanied by increasingly sharp criticism of the public health authorities for slighting Chinese medicine. By 1955, this criticism had grown into a major campaign to criticize modern doctors' bourgeois prejudice against their own national heritage. Throughout the nation, meetings were held to drive home this lesson and to correct the modern medical profession's erroneous ideas acquired from a predominantly foreign-style education. Two high officials in the Ministry of Health—Wang Pin, Director of Health in Manchuria, and Ho Ch'eng, First Deputy Minister—were singled out as special targets for criticism, and both were purged.

Apart from words—words of criticism for modern doctors, words of praise for Chinese medicine—the reappraisal of the role of traditional medicine in the new China was apparent in concrete actions as well. For one thing, the curriculum of the "Chinese-style doctors' improvement classes" was revised to "correct the past prejudice in favor of Westernizing educational methods." Simultaneously, the government began to build new clinics and hospitals for the practice of Chinese medicine, to employ traditional doctors in the health services, to invite them as consultants into large hospitals and medical centers, and to set up special wards in those hospitals for Chinese medicine. In 1955, the Chinese Medicine Research Institute with a large staff of modern and traditional specialists was established in Peking. In contrast to earlier research on specific elements in the native *materia medica*, research now was to respect the principles behind traditional methods and to find the scientific rationale for them. In other words, Chinese medicine was to be investigated as a complete system which had valuable lessons to offer the modern world. The goal was its synthesis with (not assimilation by) Western medicine in order to produce a new medicine, both scientific and unmistakably Chinese in origin—a distinctly Chinese contribution to world medical science.

Thus, on the theoretical level, official policy had become an equal-value synthesis; on the practical level, it was to raise traditional practitioners to equal status with their Western-style colleagues. The most important signs of the earnestness of the Communist Party's intent have been in the field of medical education. This, I might add, has been the crucial field in effecting any real revolution in the state of medical care for the vast majority of the Chinese population. And here the Peking government has made great strides in training large numbers of modern doctors, reportedly 200,000 by 1966. But while the major emphasis has gone into training modern physicians, the state has also devoted considerable resources to training new Chinese-style doctors. It has not, as foreign observers might have expected, been content to let the old-style practitioners gradually die out. There are now twenty-one colleges for traditional medicine, with a total of 10,000 students. More important for maintaining the ranks of Chinese-style doctors, the traditional disciple system has been maintained and encouraged. A *People's Daily* editorial in 1958 admitted that this was an "artisan system," hardly appropriate for the socialist society's attempts to break down these particularistic relationships in favor of universal standards. Yet it rationalized continuation of this venerable means of medical training as necessary in order to preserve the scattered and unsystematized precious elements of the native medical tradition. Recently it has been claimed that since 1949 no less than 600,000 students have been trained, or are being trained, in this way. This would mean that the total number of Chinese-style doctors has been increased substantially.

Even more significant, however, is the role Chinese medicine has been given in the education of modern-style doctors. From the mid-1950's, large numbers of modern medical personnel—doctors, nurses, technicians—were required to take spare-time courses in Chinese medicine as part of reshaping their unpatriotic bourgeois medical attitudes. The medical colleges also incorporated courses in Chinese medicine—its theory and practice, not just medical history—in their regular curricula. Most important of all, in 1956 the government launched a pilot project of withdrawing 400 young, well-qualified modern physicians from active practice to undertake a program of three years' full-time study under traditional doctors. The end-result would be a new type of doctor, versed in both the Chinese and Western systems of medicine. Out of their ranks, it was hoped, would come the theoreticians who could effect the desired medical synthesis. In late 1958, at the height of the Great Leap Forward, it was decided to expand this program to include 2,000 modern-style doctors. Since then, several classes of these dual-type doctors have been graduated. The Westerner is struck by the "waste" of a significant number of critically needed modern-trained physicians. If the government's policy is interpreted as making use of Chinese medicine only as an interim measure, such a diversion of scarce medical resources would be pointless. It makes more sense as evidence of the Communist Party's sincere belief that there is real value in China's own medical system.

Admittedly, the most extravagant praise for Chinese medicine and the strongest ideological criticism of modern doctors occurred during the late 1950's. It is easy to see how this policy coincided with the emphasis on home-grown methods and playing down technical expertise during the fervor of the Great Leap Forward. Since then, the claims for Chinese medicine have been somewhat muted, and it no longer plays a prominent role in the ideological rectification of bourgeois tendencies in the medical profession. While there is less fanfare, Chinese medicine continued to maintain an important and an honored place in the nation's medical picture. Since 1959, the de facto integration of medical practice—that is, the two types of doctors working side by side in the same clinic or hospital—has become a reality.

What I have described so far is a matter of historical record.

When we try to probe beyond this record for the motivating factors behind such a policy, we find ourselves on the more slippery ground of conjecture. Most foreign visitors, especially medical people, have tended to stress practical factors. The Communists had to use what was available, so the argument runs, and they have done so. The greater emphasis on native medical resources after 1953 perhaps could be explained by the regime's fully realizing the magnitude of China's health problems after the unexpectedly high census returns that year. This has a certain plausibility, but I think it does not explain all the measures the Chinese Communists have taken in the field of traditional medicine. As I have suggested before, too many of these steps do not make sense in terms of using Chinese medicine as a stop-gap until it can be replaced.

Of course, there is the possibility that the Communist Party, carried away by its own propaganda about the virtues of Chinese medicine, took measures which it originally had not envisioned. This has happened in other areas. But, in any case, it would suggest a strong sympathy for China's own medical tradition which I would like to stress.

First of all, I would note that the reappraisal of Chinese medicine coincided with a general re-emphasis on distinctively Chinese cultural elements after the brief period of slavish imitation of everything Russian in the early 1950's. This can be seen in fields as disparate as painting, the theater, and architecture, where official policy began to be redefined as "Chinese in form, socialist in content." There is also a strong note of national pride running through the Chinese Communists' pronouncements on Chinese medicine. After all, it is a Chinese achievement—the only area in the whole scientific realm where the modern Chinese can find something of value in his own national tradition. This sentiment is fully shared by non-Communist or even anti-Communist Chinese, and the Peking government has prominently displayed to the overseas Chinese communities of Southeast Asia its solicitude for the national medical tradition. Chinese medicine also has been given a fairly important role in Communist China's cultural diplomacy. Both Sukarno and Ne Win reportedly have been treated by Chinese doctors, and recently a team of traditional doctors visited Pakistan to discuss the development of "Eastern medicine." Acupuncture also enjoyed a brief vogue in the Soviet Union but lately seems to have become another casualty of the Sino-Soviet split.

Apart from national pride and foreign policy, how have the Communists reconciled their ardent commitment to science and progress with the old society and old culture? This has been psychologically possible, I believe, mainly because so much of that old society and culture has been broken. The millennia-old force of tradition which faced earlier revolutionaries is a visible protagonist has largely been routed and smashed, at least as an integral force, so that the Communist leadership, securely in power, has been able to select and rehabilitate isolated fragments of the traditional culture as part of the Chinese peoples' national heritage. Medicine—because of the Confucian literati's lack of esteem for it as a tradesman's calling—has been relatively easy to identify with the healthy elements of the popular culture. Moreover, as we have seen, it has been useful in fighting the evident threat of bourgeois ideological influences. Since "imperialism," not "feudalism," is now the number one enemy, the present leadership in Peking has been able to adopt a more tolerant stand toward elements of the Chinese tradition which were anathema to social revolutionaries a few decades earlier. This does not mean that China's leaders have come full circle—from attacking traditional medicine to accepting it again. On the contrary, what we have here is not another cycle of Cathay. It is precisely because so much of China's total social, political, and cultural situation has changed that Mao and company—new men, not Confucian mandarins in Peking—have been able to cast Chinese medicine in a new positive role in the new China. That role, stressing synthesis and scientific improvement, is no more traditional (for all the high praise for China's own medical heritage) than is Marxism-Leninism in China.

Epilogue

Chinese Culture in the Cultural Revolution

1. BACKGROUND AND DEVELOPMENT OF THE CULTURAL REVOLUTION

Western analysts have been prone to give scant attention to the word "culture" in Great Proletarian Cultural Revolution. After all, "proletarian" seems to refer to any loyal supporter of Chairman Mao; "cultural" seems to refer to proper ideology and spirited dedication. Political maneuvering, social upheaval, and international repercussions have engaged most of the China-watchers' brigade.

There is good justification for this tendency. Shaking the entire political and social fabric of the People's Republic, the Cultural Revolution has indeed gone far beyond art, literature, and scholarship. But it started there, and it started with the cultural legacy.

In almost every one of the preceding chapters, we have seen strong tensions over the cultural legacy developing after 1962. Most intellectuals, badly burned during the various thought-reform campaigns of the 1950's, were not likely to express much open appreciation for bourgeois-contaminated Western culture. National culture, the cultural legacy, seemed much safer. Moreover, throughout most of 1959–62, the Party apparently approved of work on the cultural legacy as a manifestation of patriotism. Gradually, however, suspicions began to arise about the motivations of China's academic and artistic elite in so ardently cultivating the cultural legacy. Material from the past began to seem less innocuous in the new society than had been imagined.

The whole situation—the underlying rationale for the series of sharper and sharper political-academic debates during 1962–64—is perhaps best caught in the controversy over ghosts on the Peking Opera stage. During the relaxation after 1956, elements of the supernatural, banned earlier for propagating superstition, crept back into many famous old plays and even into some new ones. There was, in fact, a lively debate around 1960 over whether these stage ghosts were harmful to socialism. The eventual verdict, handed down by the Party, was affirmative; these relics of feudal superstition were indeed harmful. After fifteen years of socialism, ghosts from the past were still to be feared. Why?

The answer seems to be that the Party, or rather some key persons high in the Party, had become seriously worried about the ideological reliability not just of the upper intelligentsia but of the entire country. They were no longer so confident that fifteen years of Communist rule and education in the thought of Chairman Mao had immunized the Chinese people against bourgeois influences from the West and revisionist tendencies within socialism itself. With this confidence shaken, there was also less tolerance for feudal elements in the cultural legacy. The faith was in danger, and all culture, including the cultural legacy, had to be bent to its defense. When, on the eve of the Cultural Revolution, Maoists began to lump together "feudal and bourgeois influences" (both representing a less than total dedication to the Maoist goal of an unselfish collectivity), the cultural legacy was deep in trouble. Ideas and values the Party had thought long dead—ghosts from the past once thought laid safely to rest behind museum walls—were abroad in the People's Republic. In league with the specter of revisionism, they called for the most drastic kind of exorcising. The Cultural Revolution has been that process of exorcism.

In the following selections, we see the background and development of these aspects of the Cultural Revolution. Donald J. Munro, writing just before the Cultural Revolution hit full swing, shows how humanistic values from China's cultural legacy haunted the guardians of the new orthodoxy. Joseph R. Levenson, writing in the midst of the Cultural Revolution, stresses its cultural and intellectual significance. He sees China's past being "demuseumified" and once again treated as a living protagonist.

DISSENT IN COMMUNIST CHINA

DONALD J. MUNRO

Ever since the intensive response to the year of liberalization began in the late spring of 1964, the charges of seeking a class-transcending human nature and of advocating "humanitarianism" or "class reconciliation" have dominated the polemics. This can be found in the 1964 attacks on the aesthetic theories of Chou Ku-ch'eng, who wrote that art should reflect the spirit of a whole society at a given time (something transcending the spirit of an individual class). It is found in the criticism of the elderly philosopher at the Higher Party School, Yang Hsien-chen. His dialectical theory (another unorthodox product put forth first in 1961), emphasizing "combining two into one" instead of "dividing one into two," was said to be equivalent to stressing class compromise rather than class struggle. It is found in the condemnations of the popular philosopher Feng Ting. His biologically based attempts to derive a common human nature in terms of the "instincts" (e.g., for self-preservation) common to all men is said to represent a typically capitalistic idealization of individual "survival," as opposed to the proletariat's willingness to sacrifice for the collective interest.

The intensity of the anti-intellectual campaign has risen considerably since the beginning of 1966. Again one finds these same charges laid at the feet of the new targets. Three playwrights (Wu Han, T'ien Han, Meng Ch'ao) are condemned for having promoted bourgeois humanitarianism in their plays which appeared in July and August, 1961. For example, Wu Han's play, *Dismissal of Hai Jui*, concerns the problems faced by a high official in the Soochow area during the years 1569–70 in returning land to the peasants from whom it had been confiscated by retired officials. Hai Jui strove to ignore class favoritism in handling peasant grievances in the courtroom. His efforts led to conflicts with the landlords and ultimately cost him his post. Wu Han is said to have advocated "humanitarianism" because he has portrayed Hai Jui, the official, as "loving the people" and demonstrating this love

FROM Donald J. Munro, "Dissent in Communist China: The Current Anti-intellectual Campaign in Perspective," *Current Scene*, 4, 11 (June 1, 1966), 7–10.

in his acts, which were in *their* interest rather than in the interest of his own class. Wu Han's fault is to pretend that there is such a class-transcending love of man and to portray an "honest and incorrupt official" in the service of the peasantry, rather than actually having only the interests of the landlords at heart. He is said to have substituted the internal contradictions between landlords for the antagonistic contradictions between members of the landlord class and the peasantry.

Now an extremely important point about these attacks on the theory of human nature and "humanitarianism" is that they have occurred not just during the period 1964–66 but with greater or lesser intensity every year since the Communists assumed power. The previous period of greatest intensity was 1957–60, during and after the antirightist campaign. The focal point of many of the criticisms then was Wang Jen-shu (Pa Jen). In an article "On Human Feelings," he stated that all humans share the same basic needs, likes, and wishes and that these common sentiments— found in all men regardless of class—should form the soul of art works. Intellectuals such as Pa Jen continually charged that the "Communist Party spirit" liquidates human nature. They have especially opposed the demands that relatives inform on each other to the authorities.

Why does this charge of seeking to discover human nature and of advocating humanitarianism keep cropping up? The answer is simple. It represents without question the strongest legacy from the past in China today. Chinese philosophy since the period of the Warring States (403–221 B.C.) has occupied itself with the study of human nature (*hsing*) and with the "love of humanity" (*jen*), which is innate to that *hsing*, more than with any other topics. In the Sung dynasty (960–1279 A.D.), the "love of humanity" was turned into a metaphysical principle.

Periodic denials of the fact that humanism is a Chinese product appear in the Chinese Communist journals. They claim it is a capitalist import which made its way into China during the May Fourth Movement (1917–21). Western humanism, which goes back to the Age of the Enlightenment, has been antitheistic in essence, stressing that the goal of life is to increase man's happiness on earth rather than his bliss in heaven. Certain ideas associated with it were introduced to China during the May Fourth period.

But the form which "humanitarianism" has taken in China in

the 1950's and 1960's, with its exclusive emphasis on seeking the sentiments common to all men and on preaching a love of humanity, affirms its indigenous origins.

Dramatic restatement that this is a Chinese product came in a series of radio broadcasts made by a former Communist and a founder of the Fukien People's Government (early 1930's) who is now the leading anti-Communist theoretician in Taiwan. In 1960, Hu Ch'iu-yüan aimed his radio broadcasts at intellectuals on the mainland. Hu decried the attacks on the theory of human nature and on humanitarianism made there. He stated that these are *Chinese* conceptions and that the condemnations of them, plus the despotism which violates not only human nature but also the love of humanity, are alien Russian incursions.

He called on all Chinese intellectuals, because the tradition is so strong, to band together against such mouthpieces of the non-Chinese ideology as Mao Tse-tung, Chou Yang, and Lu Ting-yi and remold them instead of being remolded by them. It is interesting that he did not condemn Communism *per se* as running counter to Chinese humanism, for he tries to prove that the founders of the Chinese Communist Party (Ch'en Tu-hsiu and Li Ta-chao) were within that tradition. It is these other men whose attacks on the theory of human nature demonstrate an alien policy.

There are three basic explanations for the tremendous opposition of the Chinese leadership to "humanitarianism."

First, the Chinese Communists have a real awareness of the contradiction throughout Chinese history between the honor given to the humanitarian ideal that "all men are brothers" and the practice of social responsibility which stopped with the family. They realize that when Chinese speak of common human sentiments, they have in mind, before anything else, the innate affection all individuals are supposed to feel for their own kin. They realize, too, that the call to love all men has often been a sop which covers up the limited range of responsibility actually felt by the individual. Understanding that no modern state can function if responsibility does not extend to larger units and ultimately to national and international problems, they feel the urgency of removing any such sham and of cultivating responsibility for specific, public goals.

Second, the Communist leaders are mindful that in the past the appeal to "common human sentiments" has been an ineffective substitute for concrete action. Thus, Peking's methods are large-scale, intensive campaigns against internal class enemies and a militant stance against international enemies. The Chinese do not believe the opposition can be won over by merely speaking of improvements made in the human condition under the Chinese Communist regime.

These are two long-term reasons for the Chinese opposition to this aspect of the Chinese legacy. The third explanation is based on a consciousness of what the legacy may mean in the immediate future. At the start, it is necessary to bear in mind the Chinese Communist terror at the thought of resurgent capitalism (or revisionism, as its form would be) in China. Their orthodoxy in this matter stems in part from the youthfulness of their revolution but even more from the fact that capitalism is identified in their minds with China's period of international humiliation. A resurgence of capitalism is identified with a resurgence of that humiliation. It is for this reason that they continually depict the "degeneration" of Yugoslavia and Russia into revisionism as paired with their "degeneration" into dependencies of the United States.

AN EXCHANGE ON CHINA

JOSEPH R. LEVENSON

In China, the Great Proletarian Revolution is quite clearly a political event, and so in his essay "What Is Happening in China" [*New York Review of Books*, October 20, 1966] Franz Schurmann is right, I think, to see questions of war and peace bound up in it. There is Aesopian language, certainly; animadversions about Western culture and traditional Chinese culture mask comments about political conditions. Nevertheless, cultural issues are really issues to the Mao behind the mask. "Cultural Revolution" means something in its own right: It *relates* to politics; it is not merely another term for politics. Instead of saying "for *culture*, read *politics*," we need to keep culture firmly in mind.

In other words, a little less gossip would do no harm. Hong Kong and all the other tracking stations are buzzing with old-fashioned Chinese speculation about "factions." Who was the real, the political target behind the hapless "cultural" Wu Han,

FROM Joseph R. Levenson, "An Exchange on China," *The New York Review of Books*, 7, 12 (Jan. 12, 1967), 31–32. Reprinted with permission from *The New York Review of Books*. Copyright © 1967 The New York Review.

the author, historian, and Deputy Mayor of Peking who was the object of an attack which now seems to have signaled the beginning of the Cultural Revolution? Why was Chou Yang, the leading Party propagandist and cultural commissar, the object of a "cultural" attack? (It could not happen to a nicer guy, is the general preamble, but what friends of his are they *really* after, and who are *they?*) Still, there are other questions. Why should a Communist movement that once had cosmopolitan associations become so especially nativist now—not just politically prickly (no problem there), but culturally so anti-Western? And, why, just now, should a nationalist movement be so harsh with the national culture, the heritage of the past?

To take the last questions first. Partly it is a matter of balance: The very intensity of the anti-Westernism compels a corresponding antagonism to traditional Chinese forms. Otherwise, it would be merely xenophobia, a throwback to the antiforeign Boxer revolutionaries of 1900. And, while the Communists grant an honorable place to the Boxers, it is a place in history only. The Boxers are harbingers, not prototypes, of the Communist fighters for Chinese independence. For Boxer xenophobia, while commendably anti-imperialist in political intent, was reactionary in its defense of "feudal" culture. Chinese Communists are Marxist enough to see history as a linear process—it is evolution through revolution, the *past* does not revolve.

Yet, the problem of today's special iconoclasm remains. Early twentieth-century radicals, living in a world they never made, were generally hostile to the old values, and Chinese anti-Communists have always seen their enemies as destroyers of Chinese culture. But once in power, the Party seemed to confound them. Iconoclasm was not a prerequisite of revolution. Restoration was not a counterrevolutionary prerogative. The Communists themselves were "restoring" (in a way), not scuttling the past. Their way was the museum way. The restoration—of imperial palaces or classical reputations—was not a restoration of authority but of a history which the Chinese people (under *new* authority) could claim as its national heritage. Their historicism enabled the Communists to keep the past passé: The Communists owned the present and would preside over the future.

Today, however, the museums, literal and metaphorical, are being ransacked. The old books, once assumed to have been sterilized by history of the power to do harm, are disappearing. All kinds of relics are being treated as ominously significant for the

here and now; they seem no longer safely dead or simply historically significant. Even as they threw off the hand of the past, the
Communists for a time retained the priceless advantage of con-
serving traditional culture, to better effect than the modern conservatives did. Why has Peking now thrown the traditional game?

It is because the modern game is a tricky one to play, especially
now. Especially in China, where the Confucian amateur-ideal was
uncongenial to science, the advancement of science has had revolu
tionary implications. It has led to specialization, the cultivation of
experts. But these are suspect in Communist China—which nevertheless, unlike Confucian China, is absolutely committed to the
celebration of science.

It is not just that "scientific socialists" can hardly condescend to
science as literary people do. Marxists trade on the prestige of science, and they know quite well that in everyone's modern world
(quite unlike Confucian China), in "bourgeois" countries and
antibourgeois alike, science has prestige. When the Chinese Communists put scientists down, they acknowledge that prestige, they
do not impugn it; its very universality, its apparent transcendence
of ideology, is a threat to the masters of ideology. Science must be
mastered by the ideologues, or their own occupation would be
gone. In a world where science cannot be gainsaid, mere experts,
practitioners of science, have to be bent to Marxist authority, or
Mao, the latest Marxist in line, would lack authority himself.
Ideology, the correct ideology, must dominate the ostensibly non-
ideological expert. Politics must take command. For, as Mao proclaimed in his *Problems of Art and Literature*, the very profession
of ideological unconcern ("art for art's sake") is a classic product
of bourgeois ideology.

In spite of all the common "generalism" of the Communist
cadre and the Confucian official, the latter never believed what
the former holds as an article of faith: that one of the reasons for
demeaning expertise is the need to erase the distinction—a crucial
Confucian distinction—between mental and physical labor. Just
as the Confucianist, with his amateur ideal, had displaced the old
aristocracy and then taken on an aristocratic aura (with license to
condescend to the technical professional), so the professional in
the modern world, having broken the amateur ideal, has the status
pride of the aristocrat today. Therefore, the Party must trim him
down, to vindicate its own version of autocratic rule.

It is this that creates the impression of a willful cultural pro-
vincialism today. The experts are China's "rootless cosmopolitans"

—rootless, since the peasants are the roots (whence the Red Guards, as a counterweight to the urban, university types), and cosmopolitan, since, with universal science, the experts may see their associations with professional colleagues on the other side of national and ideological walls. And so the climate becomes wintry for the cosmopolitan scientists. Yet the armies and industries need them, after all. The ones who are really blasted by the anticosmopolitanism are the expendables in the arts, dispensers of English literature, French music, Hong Kong haircuts.

Yes, the armies and industries need the fruits of science, maybe to throw at the Americans. But the armies and industries might be hostages to science and technology, as well as beneficiaries. A war with America now would certainly ravage the scientific complex, and exclusively "expert" advisers would have to counsel peace. Does the deep freeze of the experts, the coldness toward Western culture (which was the source of the expertise), mean that the risk of war is going to be accepted, that merely prudential, technical-expert arguments are going to be overruled? Then the old spirit of the Long March and the Yenan days, when the stronger battalions were on the other side, would naturally be invoked, as now they are. Not senile nostalgia, nor a general taste for spiritual athletics, but a conviction of present crisis may be driving the train of events. If the weight of weapons is against China, and yet the weapons may come into play, man's spirit (a good Maoist antiexpert shibboleth), not weapons, will have to be decisive.

For spirit, read ideology, the fantastic drenching in ideology that China is taking now. It comes from a sense of danger, the danger of a war that cannot be left to experts, because they would not choose it and could not win it with their expertise alone. And it is this danger that gives the Cultural Revolution its dual targets, the two cultures, Western and traditional. The concurrent attack on the latter confirms danger as the source of attack on the former, on the cosmopolitan spirit which the experts represent. For the tendency to make a museum of the past, instead of rooting it out, belonged to the age of self-assurance. It had not been there in the early days of struggle, when the Communists had the passion of engagement, and it vanishes now in an embattled age of possible destruction. The god of history is a hidden god again. Relativistic historicism, coolly accounting for one-time foes by giving them their proper niches, is out of fashion. The dead are no longer monuments but "ghosts and monsters" to be slain again. When they had confidence in historical progress (confidence in their own success in moving from strength to strength), Communists could patronize their Chinese cultural past. But if the pastness of the past is not so certain, because the future is so uncertain, if regress seems possible, then the Communists will cease to be patrons, encouraging curators to restore the past; they will be at action stations instead, finished with contemplation for a while. And regress is the specter, regress seen as furthered by Russian example ("revisionism"). If the essential Marxist notion of progress is not to be abandoned in a general failure of nerve, revolutionary voluntarism, not evolutionary determinism, must be brought to the fore again, and the past be not relativized but seen as all too possibly present. Absolutes take command. Impending crisis puts the expert under the gun, with the foreign cultural borrowings that made him. And crisis, too, strips the native cultural heritage of its protective historical color. The Chinese are not listening much to ancestral voices now. But someone in China is prophesying war.

2. HISTORY AND THEATER IN THE ORIGINS OF THE CULTURAL REVOLUTION

In retrospect, an article by the then-obscure Shanghai critic Yao Wen-yüan has been hailed as the opening shot of the Cultural Revolution. It was directed against the historian and playwright Wu Han for his new Peking opera Dismissal of Hai Jui, *produced in 1961. Donald J. Munro has already referred to the ideological objections raised to Wu Han's portrayal of the good official. Yao Wen-yüan also insinuated the political charge that Wu Han was using historical figures as an analogy to the present. The return of land to the peasant, the dismissal of a loyal official for opposing wrong policies, sycophantic and corrupt courtiers—was this a reference to the difficulties besetting the Party after the collapse of the Great Leap Forward? Yao Wen-yüan preferred the charge and, after some sharp debate late in 1965 and early in 1966, it became clear that the verdict the Party wanted was guilty.*

Obviously, if the past could be called on to bring such devastating criticism to bear on the present, it was indeed dangerous. Nor was Wu Han's case an isolated one. In the spring of 1966, a succession of other celebrated exposés occurred involving Peking operas, historical dramas, movies, and historical commentaries. These escalated from Wu Han to T'ien Han, a leading playwright and Vice-Mayor of Peking, to Teng T'o a Secretary of the Party's Peking branch and a close associate of Politburo member P'eng Chen, the Mayor of Peking. The gravity of the charges also increased, as we see in the following indictment of Teng T'o for his veiled counterrevolutionary threats in the column "Evening Talks at Yenshan." The reliance on historical analogies and literary references in these "Talks" is striking. As old as Confucius himself, it is the Chinese scholar's technique of criticizing political authority. The outrage at seeing the technique turned on the Party and Mao Tse-tung himself is obvious. Soon afterward, the Cultural Revolution moved beyond the cultural and intellectual world to attack many of the leading political figures in Communist China—P'eng Chen, Lo Jui-ch'ing, Teng Hsiao-p'ing, and Liu Shao-ch'i. Interestingly, political-cultural crimes, such as opposing the reform of Peking Opera, continued to figure in their indictment.

ON THE NEW HISTORICAL PLAY
DISMISSAL OF HAI JUI

YAO WEN-YÜAN

In this historical play, Comrade Wu Han makes a perfect and noble character of Hai Jui. Hai Jui was portrayed as "a person who had the people in mind in every place" and "was a savior of the oppressed, bullied, and wronged people." In his person, you simply cannot find any shortcoming. It seems that he is the ideal

FROM Yao Wen-yüan, "On the New Historical Play *Dismissal of Hai Jui,*" *Jen-min Jih-pao (People's Daily)* (Nov. 30, 1965). Translated in American Consulate General (Hong Kong, B.C.C.), *Current Background*, 783 (March 21, 1966), 2, 4, 9, 12, and 14–16.

character of the author. He not merely was the "savior" of the poor peasants in the Ming dynasty, but is also an example for the Chinese people and cadres of the socialist era to learn from. . . .

In this play, only Hai Jui is the hero. The peasants can only air their grievances to their lord, beg "their lord to make decisions in their favor," and entrust their own destinies to the "Honorable Hai." In order to make the image of Hai Jui stand out against all other feudal officials, all the principal officials in the play are portrayed as bad characters. Hai Jui's wife and family dependents are wise people who want to protect themselves, and only his mother backs him up. Hai Jui goes it alone in making a great economic and political revolution.

After seeing this play, people strongly feel that this heroic image as molded by Comrade Wu Han is much greater than the image of Hai Jui which was portrayed by many operas and novels of the feudal age in the past. Although Comrade Wu Han has especially written some explanatory notes for inclusion in the play, published in a single volume, and has extracted a number of historical data from the story of *Dismissal of Hai Jui* itself in an attempt to give people the impression that he has written the play in complete accordance with historical facts, yet people still cannot help asking: Was there really such a hero among the ruling classes of the feudal society? Is this "Honorable Hai" just an artistic version of the real Hai Jui in history or just a fictitious character coined by Comrade Wu Han?

We are not historians. But according to the data we have read, the historical contradictions and the class stand taken by Hai Jui in handling such contradictions—as portrayed in this play—are in contravention with historical realities. The Hai Jui in the play is only coined by Comrade Wu Han to give publicity to his own point of view.

By comparing these historical facts with the Hai Jui in the play *Dismissal of Hai Jui*, it is not difficult to discover that the latter is a fictitious character. It is a character remolded with the bourgeois viewpoint. . . .

A historical play needs to be processed artistically and recreated. We do not expect a new historical play to agree with history in every detail, but we do expect that the class stand and class relationship of the characters portrayed therein should agree with historical facts.

Comrade Wu Han has said that a historical play "must make

every effort to bring itself in greater conformity with historical facts, and there is no room for distortion and hypothesis." However, facts speak louder than words. The image of Hai Jui in this play has already nothing to do with rational imagination or typical generalization. It can only come under the category of "distortion, hypothesis, and making veiled criticism of contemporary people with ancient people."

We hope that Comrade Wu Han will compare the image of Hai Jui which he has molded and the viewpoints publicized through this image with the Marxist-Leninist viewpoints which Comrade Mao Tse-tung has explained again and again. It will not be difficult to discover that he has actually replaced the Marxist-Leninist concept of the state with that of the landlord class and the bourgeoisie and the theory of class struggle with the theory of class reconciliation. What is he driving at in publicizing today the antiquated viewpoint which has been played up by the landlord class and the bourgeoisie for hundreds and thousands of years? And who will reap the benefit? It is necessary to distinguish right from wrong. . . .

It is not a matter of no significance if, in the course of writing a historical play, we can really follow the principles of historical materialism, scientifically analyze such historical data, eliminate what is false, retain what is true, and mold the character of Hai Jui according to his original features—thus enabling the audience to see what is his class essence and to know the class features of historical characters from the viewpoint of historical materialism. It will acquire a positive significance in eliminating the undesirable effects spread by many old novels and plays which sing praises to Hai Jui.

However, Comrade Wu Han not only runs counter to historical facts and adopts—in whole and without any change—the standpoint and viewpoint of the landlord class and its data to sing praises of Hai Jui, but he even goes to the extreme of molding Hai Jui as the "savior" of the poor peasants and a victor in the struggle for the interests of the peasants. He wants the people of today to follow his example. This is total departure from the correct direction. . . .

Comrade Wu Han unambiguously calls upon others to learn from the Hai Jui molded by him. What are, after all, the things we can "learn" from him?

The "return of the land"? The socialist system of collective ownership has been realized, and great people's communes have been established in our countryside. Under such a circumstance, who is required "to return the land"? Do we want the people's communes "to return the land"? Can it be said that the 500 million peasants who are pushing forward with resolve along the socialist road should be required to "learn" such "return of land"?

Or to learn "the redressing of grievances"? Ours is a country in which the dictatorship of the proletariat has been realized. Speaking of redressing of grievances, with the proletariat and all oppressed and exploited classes breaking out from the darkest hell in the world, smashing the shackles of the landlords and the bourgeoisie and becoming the masters of their own destinies—have not the grievances been redressed the most thoroughly in the history of mankind? If we are required to learn "to redress grievances" today, we must ask: What are after all the classes which have "grievances," and how can their "grievances" be "redressed"?

If we are not required to learn the return of land or the redressing of grievances, what then is the "realistic significance" of *Dismissal of Hai Jui?*

Perhaps Comrade Wu Han would say: Granted it is wrong to learn Hai Jui's return of land or redressing of grievances; we can at least learn his spirit as "a great man" who "stands on the earth with his head reaching to the sky" and to "oppose today's bureaucratism as he opposed the hypocrites in old days." Have I not said in the synopsis of *Dismissal of Hai Jui* that this play "lays emphasis on Hai Jui's uprightness and refusal to bow to brute force" and his "determination"? Do we also need such a "he-man" to handle our internal relationships today? The play has saliently portrayed Hai Jui's opposition to "licorice root" and his attack on the hypocrites and has also molded Hsü Chieh as a typical "hypocrite."

It is necessary to oppose bureaucratism. As a matter of fact, the Chinese Communists have never slackened their struggle against bureaucratism. However, we know that the existence of bureaucratism in the socialist society has its social origin and root cause in ideology, and it is necessary to wage a protracted struggle before it can be extirpated.

As to "uprightness," "great man," "he-man," and "opposition to hypocrites," it is first necessary to determine their class content: For what class do they work and against what class are they directed? These concepts are interpreted by different classes in different ways, and we cannot discard their class content and regard them in the abstract. "Uprightness" or "great man" has its specific class meaning and basically cannot be mixed with the revolutionary or militant character of the proletariat.

As is known to all, China in 1961 encountered temporary economic difficulties because it was attacked by natural calamities for three years in succession. With the imperialists, the reactionaries of various countries, and the modern revisionists launching wave after wave of attacks against China, the demons and spirits clamored for "individual farming" and "reopening of cases." They played up the "superiority" of "individual farming" and called for the restoration of individual economy and the "return of land." In other words, they wanted to demolish the people's communes and to restore the criminal rule of the landlords and rich peasants. The imperialists, landlords, rich peasants, counterrevolutionaries, undesirable characters, and rightists who were responsible for numerous grievances of the working people in the old society had lost their right to manufacture more grievances. They felt that it was "wrong" to overthrow them and vociferously clamored for "the redressing of their grievances." They hoped that someone who represented their interests would come forward to resist the dictatorship of the proletariat, redress their "grievances," and "reopen the case" for them so that they might be returned to power.

"Return of land" and "redressing of grievances" formed the focal point of bourgeois opposition to the dictatorship of the proletariat and the socialist revolutionary struggle at that time.

The objective existence of class struggle will necessarily be reflected in this or that form in the ideological sphere or through the pen of this or that writer. Regardless of whether this writer is conscious of it or not, this is an objective law which is independent of one's will. *Dismissal of Hai Jui* is a form of reflection of such class struggle.

TENG T'O: BIG CONSPIRATOR
AGAINST THE PARTY AND SOCIALISM
HSIAO CH'IEN

LI HSIU-LIN

TUNG HSIN-MIN

FANG KO-LI

The socialist Great Cultural Revolution is rapidly, forcefully, and penetratingly moving forward. The main forces of the Great Cultural Revolution—the masses of the workers, peasants, and soldiers—holding high the great red banner of the thought of Mao Tse-tung, have directly joined this battle. Their fighting spirit is strongest and so is their fire power. The front of the proletariat and of the thought of Mao Tse-tung have never been so strong as now in the cultural sphere.

The anti-Party and antisocialist demons and spirits have been and will be exposed one by one and group by group to broad daylight. This is a colossal victory. The exposure of the anti-Party and antisocialist plot of Teng T'o and his ilk, and the exposure of the criminal activities of the *Ch'ien-hsien* and *Pei-ching Jih-pao*, which have done their utmost to cover and shelter Teng T'o and other villains and have looked for a way to beat the threat and shelter themselves, constitute an important component of this victory.

From 1961 through 1962, the class enemies at home and abroad swept up a black wind against our Party and the socialist system. When this black wind was blowing, Teng T'o, as a Secretary of the Secretariat of the CCP Peking Municipal Committee, made use of his important post to launch a rabid attack against the Party and socialism in the Peking forum.

Apart from running himself a store, which dealt in narcotics, called "Evening Talks at Yenshan," he also set up in partnership with Wu Han and Liao Mo-sha the "Three Family Village" store to deal in narcotics. Teng T'o transformed the *Ch'ien-hsien, Pei-ching Jih-pao,* and *Pei-ching Wan-pao* into the sales departments of this joint-stock company; the propaganda machines of this

FROM Hsiao Ch'ien, Li Hsiu-lin, Tung Hsin-min, and Fang Ko-li (of China People's University), "Teng T'o: Big Conspirator Against the Party and Socialism," *Jen-Min Jih-pao (People's Daily),* (May 18, 1966). Translated in American Consulate General (Hong Kong, B.C.C.), *Current Background,* No. 792, pp. 45–47.

company plotted to overthrow the leadership of the Party and the socialist system.

Comrade Mao Tse-tung taught us: In the socialist society there still exist the struggle between classes and the struggle between the socialists and capitalists.

In the fierce and complex class struggle, the proletariat continuously sums up its revolutionary experience and the bourgeoisie also continuously sums up its counterrevolutionary experience. The historical experience of the proletariat shows that the restoration of capitalism always begins with ideology and the superstructure with theory, learning, literature, and art and other things of the spiritual aspect, which create public opinion and pave the way.

Capitalism was restored in the Soviet Union by the Khrushchev revisionist group in this way. The counterrevolutionary resurrection of Hungary in 1956 was also engineered by a group of revisionist and bourgeois writers, artists, and intellectuals who formed the Petofi Club and served as the vanguard for the restoration of capitalism.

Teng T'o and his ilk—with their reactionary class sensitivity and drawing political nourishment from international counterrevolutionary restoration—also vainly wanted first to make a branch in the cultural ground of the proletariat and lead China on to the evil road of capitalist restoration.

As Teng T'o saw it, the political situation around 1961 was "early spring" for the intellectuals, the general situation was rather unfavorable for socialism, Marxism was not so much in vogue, and the time was ripe for their group of anti-Party revisionists to take over. Therefore, "Evening Talks at Yenshan" and "Notes from the Three Family Village" opened their doors to business.

When "Evening Talks at Yenshan" was open to business, Teng T'o hung out the signboard, "Welcome to 'Miscellaneous Scholars,'" to beckon to his friends and birds of a feather and to recruit supporters. In the name of promoting "broader knowledge," this article highly lauded the "miscellaneous scholars" of ancient times who "made integrated use of the teachings of Confucius and Mencius and the schools of logic and law" and "the celebrated scholars of old days." It especially publicized that the "miscellaneous scholars" of today were of "great significance" not only to "scientific research work" but also to "various kinds of leadership work."

Teng T'o who considered himself a "miscellaneous scholar," was so exalted that he called on the big and small anti-Party and antisocialist "miscellaneous scholars" to usurp "various kinds of leadership work." This was the vital part of Teng T'o's plot.

Who are the "miscellaneous scholars" welcomed by Teng T'o? They are the demons and spirits. Miscellaneous scholars are Jacks-of-all-trades—men of many-sided abilities who are wholly opposed to the Party and socialism.

Comrade Mao Tse-tung said: "There may be many sects and schools in various branches of learning. But so far as the world outlook is concerned, there can be only two schools in the modern world—that is, the proletarian school and the bourgeois school."

The "miscellaneous scholars" who "made integrated use of the teachings of Confucius, Mencius, and the schools of logic and law" in ancient times were not above classes. In realistic class struggle, what Teng T'o described as "miscellaneous scholars" naturally also could not be above classes but could only be of the bourgeois family and anti-Party and colonialist experts.

Teng T'o welcomed the "miscellaneous scholars," because he plotted to mutilate the Party guideline of letting a hundred flowers bloom together and a hundred schools of thought contend and to change it into the policy of bourgeois liberalism and to encourage the demons and spirits to come out from hiding in a hurry. He openly called on the anti-Party and antisocialist demons and spirits to occupy first the cultural ground, "to shed radiance in the ideological field," and then to usurp "leadership in various kinds of work" so as to realize completely the fond dream of restoring capitalism.

Comrade Mao Tse-tung told us: "All erroneous thoughts, all poisonous weeds, and all demons and spirits should be criticized and can never be allowed to spread freely."

Teng T'o dreaded this directive very much and hated it to the bone. He said in sharp ridicule: "There are many persons who are not very learned but fond of finding fault and making comments which are wide of the mark." He also said: "Some persons fond of finding fault often make sarcastic comments which chill the writers."

He even maliciously likened our criticism of and struggle against the poisonous weeds to Kun's use of the blocking method to control the floods. "As a result, the floods became more and more serious, and the people were dissatisfied. Later, Shun called him one of the four villains and ordered his execution at the Yü Mountain."

Audacious Teng T'o, whom do you want to kill? It has been the vain hope of your black gang that only you would be allowed to spread poison, while we are not allowed to get rid of such poison. The revolutionary people are resolved to work in accordance with the directive of Chairman Mao. They will destroy the poisonous weeds and fight the demons and spirits and will never allow the dirty water of capitalism to spread freely.

Teng T'o pinned his hope of restoring capitalism especially on the persons of the "honest, incorrupt officials" who had been relieved of their offices, the insubordinate "arrogant scholars," and other anti-Party and antisocialist elements. He exerted his utmost to laud their "deportment" of "considering themselves as the masters and refusing to serve as slaves."

He repeatedly eulogized the Tung-lin faction—the "opposition faction within the landlord class of the Ming dynasty"—and showed great appreciation for their "political ambitions." He called on the anti-Party and antisocialist elements to form a contemporary "Tung-lin faction." He urged them "not to indulge themselves in scholarly discussion" but "to show concern for politics." In order to achieve "their political aims," they must not fear "death and bloodshed" and must "steadfastly fight against the crafty statesmen in power."

Teng T'o—the "grievous scholar" who "begins with the discussion of such insignificant things as flies and bedbugs but ends in commenting on the political "situation"—has thus laid bare his diabolical features as a big conspirator against the Party and socialism.

Does Teng T'o merely want to air his grievances? No, definitely not. Teng T'o "dares to speak and to act" and "his deeds are in correspondence with his words." He means to do what he says.

He has organized the "Three Family Village" shady inn and has seized control of the publications of the CCP Peking Municipal Committee. He also wants to make friends and to organize shady clubs. He plots to form a gigantic contingent of "amateur writers" who can be summoned at any time and are able to fight. Through these relationships, he is linked with such poisonous weeds as *Hai Jui Abuses the Emperor, Dismissal of Hai Jui, Hsieh Yao-huan*, and *Li Hui-niang* and the black line of the academic, educational, journalistic, and literary and art circles against the Party, socialism, and the thought of Mao Tse-tung. This makes people sense that there is another commander above this commander, there is another "village" by the side of this "village," and that this shady club comprises more than three families.

3. THE ARTISTIC PRODUCTS OF
THE CULTURAL REVOLUTION

By any conventional aesthetic standards, the products of the Cultural Revolution have been crude, amateurish, at times ludicrous. To the ideological spokesmen behind the movement, all this is beside the point. Art and culture must serve political and social goals, directly and totally. For the cultural legacy, this has meant direct attack in some instances (physical attack in the Red Guard destruction of historical monuments), neglect in others (almost all scholarly and cultural journals have been closed down, along with the universities, since 1966), and drastic transformation of parts of the cultural legacy that have been judged suitable for carrying the proper political message. The most notable examples of the latter have been music, art, and theater. These are, of course, the art forms most readily adaptable to propaganda purposes. In saturating the arts with propaganda, the Cultural Revolution has attempted to maintain a distinctly national, even if heavily popular, style. After all, Western culture is no more in favor than feudal culture. We have seen, in earlier chapters, some of the results in music, painting, and theater. Here, an interesting letter from the distinguished English critic Herbert Read and the reply of the China Policy Study Group capture some of the main issues very well.

The principal field of cultural activity in the Cultural Revolution, however, has continued to be the performing arts, especially the reform of Peking Opera. Since her rise to political prominence in 1966, the former bit-part movie actress and present wife of Mao Tse-tung, Chiang Ch'ing, has held sway in this domain. The 1964 festival of Peking operas on contemporary themes mentioned in the seventh chapter is now listed as her achievement, as is almost everything that has happened in the arts since then. This section concludes with an anything but critical appraisal of one of the new Peking operas, which makes abundantly clear the political significance given it, and an article hailing Comrade Chiang Ch'ing's latest cultural achievement—the introduction of piano accompaniment to Peking Opera. It is a sorry note on which to leave China's cultural legacy, but it is too early to write its obituary. One suspects that long after the Cultural Revolution, Chiang Ch'ing, and

Mao Tse-tung himself have departed, China's cultural legacy will still be there.

A CRITIC OF ART IN THE CULTURAL REVOLUTION
ANONYMOUS

We have received the following letter from the distinguished poet and art critic Sir Herbert Read:

It is possible that you cannot find space for a letter from one of your readers and supporters, but it is time someone expressed doubts about certain aspects of the Cultural Revolution in China. I read Professor Joan Robinson's article on the subject with great interest: It is by far the best of many articles that I have read.

On the social and political consequences of this revolution within a revolution, I have nothing to say, but the artistic consequences are disastrous from any conceivable standard of aesthetic judgment. Since the Cultural Revolution, the contributions to the monthly *Chinese Literature* have become more and more crude and monotonous. The illustrations in this periodical, which used to include beautiful examples of the "traditional" style (ancient and modern) are now all as dreary as commercial posters in a capitalist country. I have not been to China since the Cultural Revolution took place, but at the New Year I received from Peking (as a supplement to *China Reconstructs*) a portfolio of reproductions of a large group of life-size clay figures entitled "Rent Collection Courtyard," and this is acclaimed as "a milestone marking a great epoch in sculpture born in China's Great Proletarian Cultural Revolution."

Any criticism of this "milestone" by a Western art critic would be dismissed as an expression of ineradicable bourgeois prejudice, so I content myself with a comparison. This group of sculpture is exactly like similar groups in Madame Tussaud's popular exhibition gallery in London. It becomes clear what a cultural revolution would mean in this country—the closing and perhaps the destruction of the National Gallery and the Tate Gallery and the elevation of Madame Tussaud's to national status.

I do not write this letter in anger or scorn but with feelings of intense distress. I cannot believe that the Chinese people will for

FROM "A Critic of Art in the Cultural Revolution," in China Policy Study Group (London), *Broadsheet* (Apr.–May, 1968).

long renounce their incomparable heritage of art or cease to prolong the most continuous tradition of art known to history.

We appreciate this comment and thank the writer. His view is not uncommon, but we do not share it.

In Western society today, artistic form often takes precedence over content, lack of which is regarded by many as a virtue. This absence of a general understandable content arises because of the gulf that separates the majority of the people from works of art and because of the artist's alienation from the people. Too often his work has no relevance to their lives.

In China, content takes precedence over form, but this does not mean that the latter is brushed aside. Some traditional forms of art have proved too rigid or inadequate to express the new Chinese way of life, but others are being used creatively. In China, as in the West, the great art of the past remains an inalienable cultural heritage which can enrich life.

In saying that the artistic consequences of the Cultural Revolution "are disastrous from any conceivable standard of aesthetic judgment," Sir Herbert Read flatly condemns some examples of contemporary sculpture, on the basis of photographic reproductions. He claims to have taken into account "any conceivable standard" but does not in fact seem to have considered possible new standards.

The comparison of the clay sculptures in "Rent Collection Courtyard" with Madame Tussaud's waxworks is quite inappropriate. The Chinese figures have a form that is more than photographic and a content that moves the peasants profoundly. The waxworks parade of the notable and the notorious hardly arouses any profound emotions or ideas in the viewer, but the reproductions in clay of scenes of the wickedness of the old society, seeking to catch the intensity of anguish and the spark of revolt, exemplify much of what spurs the Chinese people on to create a new and better life.

Sir Herbert Read's gloomy imaginings of what a cultural revolution would mean in Britain may be read to imply that in China today the great national museums and galleries have been closed and their contents destroyed. In reality, they were temporarily closed, and the masterpieces they contain were safeguarded against either counterrevolutionary provocation or excess of youthful enthusiasm (thus preserving them from iconoclasm such as that of Cromwell's soldiers who destroyed so much of England's cultural heritage).

But the question at issue is not the art of the past; it is the function of art in society today. "Rent Collection Courtyard," like all art, must speak to the condition of the beholder—that is, in China, first of all the workers and peasants. Of this, the best judges are the Chinese people, whose feelings about their own past are given concentrated expression in this sculpture by eighteen amateur and professional artists working together. The work exemplifies the attempt to create not only art for the workers and peasants but new artists who are themselves of the people and seek to express a new social morality.

If revolutionary artists in China today can succeed in producing truly universal art, so much the better. But China's art must be meaningful first for the Chinese. In the Cultural Revolution, they are making an effort to bridge the gap that almost everywhere in the world separates the artist from the ordinary people and are confident that they will produce a new art that will yet be seen not only as a prolongation but as an enrichment of "the most continuous tradition of art known to history."

AN ILLUSTRIOUS MILESTONE OF PROLETARIAN LITERATURE AND ART

TING HSÜEH-LEI

During the days in which the twenty-fifth anniversary of the publication of the "Talks at the Yenan Forum on Literature and Art"—the illustrious work of our great leader Chairman Mao— is commemorated with a warm heart by the proletarian revolutionaries as they beat battle drums to launch a general attack against the top person in authority taking the capitalist road within the Party [Liu Shao-ch'i], the revolutionary modern Peking opera *Taking the Bandits' Stronghold** has once again been

FROM Ting Hsüeh-lei, "An Illustrious Milestone of Proletarian Literature and Art: A Comment on the Revolutionary Modern Peking Opera *Taking the Bandits' Stronghold*," *Jen-min Jih-pao* (*People's Daily*) (May 27, 1967). Translated in American Consulate General (Hong Kong, B.C.C.), *Current Background*, 831 (July 24, 1967), 1–2, 7, and 10–11.

* Set in Northeast China late in 1946, the plot consists of a Red Army officer's infiltration of a Kuomintang bandit gang that has been terrorizing the

staged in the capital. This is a heavy blow for the top person in authority taking the capitalist road within the Party and is a great victory for Chairman Mao's "Talks."

Twenty-five years ago, Chairman Mao put forward in his "Talks" the call for orientation of literature and art to serve the workers, peasants, and soldiers. He unambiguously pointed out: "All our literature and art are for the masses of the people, and in the first place for the workers, peasants, and soldiers; they are created for the workers, peasants, and soldiers and are for their use." Two years afterward, in his "Letter to the Yenan Peking Opera Theater after seeing *Driven to Join the Liangshan Mountain Rebels*," he again issued the great call for the revolutionization of opera and for reversing the reversal of history.

For a long period of time after this, however, the top person in authority taking the capitalist road within the Party, ganging up with a handful of counterrevolutionary revisionists, including P'eng Chen, Lu Ting-yi, and Chou Yang, frenziedly opposed and resisted Chairman Mao's revolutionary line in literature and art and obstinately put into force a counterrevolutionary revisionist black line in literature and art. They turned the stage of art into a position for restoring capitalism and allowed emperors and princes, generals and ministers, demons and monsters, to exercise dictatorship over the workers, peasants, and soldiers.

Can we tolerate the continued existence of such a state of affairs? No, a thousand no's! Tolerance of such a state of affairs means the tolerance of capitalist restoration, of the "peaceful evolution" of proletarian dictatorship into bourgeois dictatorship, and of a change of political color in our socialist regime.

Under the boundless radiance of the thought of Mao Tse-tung, Comrade Chiang Ch'ing, holding high the great banner of the Proletarian Cultural Revolution, has led the revolutionary writers and artists to launch a heroic and tenacious attack first against Peking Opera—the most tenacious citadel of feudalism and capitalism—thus initiating the revolution of Peking Opera that rocks the world and starting skirmishes in the Great Proletarian Cultural Revolution with a bang. Carrying all before it and with the

---

peasants of a liberated area from its mountain hideout. This device gives the hero, platoon leader Yang Tzu-jung, the chance to appear in more colorful garb than a PLA uniform. He thus becomes an antibandit, modern proletarian hero but appears on stage in the traditional bandit costume of many old operas.

emperors and princes, generals and ministers, monsters and demons, swept away, the Peking Opera revolution has planted for the first time the great red banner of Mao Tse-tung's thought on the stage, made heroes of the workers, peasants, and soldiers, and truly implemented the orientation of literature and art to serve the workers, peasants, and soldiers.

This heart-stirring struggle to seize power carried out on the stage of art is an important aspect of the struggle to seize power on the political stage. The revolution of Peking Opera is precisely the beginning and an important component part of the Great Proletarian Cultural Revolution.

Taking the Bandits' Stronghold is one of the brilliant achievements of this great revolution. In this play, everything is brand new, bearing the vivid characteristics of the great Mao Tse-tung era. The thoroughgoing revolutionary spirit of the proletariat casts its radiance to all corners and spans the sky like the rainbow. The images of the revolutionary heroes of the proletariat armed with the thought of Mao Tse-tung stand erect with dignity and luster.

Having been reformed and given a new lease of life, the Peking Opera art is replete with the bite of revolutionary militant art. Great art must necessarily be born in this great era. The appearance of this opera and other outstanding model plays—such as the revolutionary modern Peking operas *On the Docks*, *The Red Lantern*, *Sha Chia Pang*, and *Raid on the White Tiger Regiment*, the revolutionary ballet plays *The Red Detachment of Women* and *The White-haired Girl*, the symphony *Sha Chia Pang*—has sounded the knell for capitalist, feudal, and revisionist literature and art and founded a new era of revolutionary literature and art and revolutionary culture of the proletariat. . . .

Like all kinds of old literature and art, Peking Opera had all along been under the domination of characters of the exploiting classes. The revolution of Peking Opera seeks precisely to reverse such reversal of history and to establish the image of proletarian revolutionary heroes in a big way so that they may forever be masters on the stage. This is the key to seizing leadership on the Peking Opera stage and is also the key to seizing all positions in literature and art.

Under the direct guidance of Comrade Chiang Ch'ing, *Taking the Bandits' Stronghold* has, in the course of processing and improving things, laid down a clear and definite idea in regard to creation: Everything should submit to establishing the heroic images of good characters on the stage, and, regardless of whether music, stage art, or a bad character is dealt with, it is necessary to submit to the above central task.

In the past, there was once the idea that the more blatant a bad character was, the more it could show the greatness of the good character. This is preposterous in the extreme. One of the two opposites always plays the leading role and dominates over the other. Bringing the bad character to the fore will necessarily end in weakening and even distorting the good character.

Originally, *Taking the Bandits' Stronghold* portrayed Tso Shan-tiao with the tactics of lining up men on two sides, establishing a stronghold, appointing leaders, and taking the chair in the tent in order to play up his counterrevolutionary bearing and arrogance, and supported the scene with powerful background music. As a result, the villains were most blatant, while Yang Tzu-jung and other good characters were spiritless and could hardly stand on their feet.

After Comrade Chiang Ch'ing discovered this, she sharply pointed out that this was a question of standpoint and class feeling. She personally took the lead in redesigning the scene, and, when she dealt with the bad characters, she paid attention to exposing their last-ditch struggle—but as that of "paper tigers" who were doomed.

In the Weihu Chamber scene, Tso Shan-tiao was made to sit on the side right from the beginning, and the musical effect was weakened. Ho Lao-tao and three other villainous characters were deleted in order to make more room for the portrayal of the images of three leading heroes. In order to bring the image of heroes to the fore, various artistic means, especially musical means, were employed in the play, and a series of creations and reforms were carried out in artistic form. A complete set of tunes was arranged for the heroic characters and, in the matter of music and tunes, the conventions of the old school were eradicated and new militant melodies were bravely drawn from modern revolutionary music. The prelude, end, and many important episodes of the whole play adopted "The March of the Chinese People's Liberation Army" as the basic tune. This played a vigorous supporting role in revealing the spiritual features of the heroic characters of the Proletarian Revolution. . . .

Displaying the revolutionary spirit of a proletarian statesman and proceeding from the political interests of the people of the whole country and the revolutionary people of the whole world, Comrade Chiang Ch'ing considered the revolution of Peking Opera strategically. She pointed out that all kinds of art served either the bourgeoisie or the proletariat. Peking Opera formerly portrayed the emperors and princes, generals and ministers, and was serving feudalism and the bourgeoisie. It will not do to use it to serve the proletariat in its original form. It must be reformed, and, for this purpose, there must be revolutionary and pioneering people. We must follow our own road, and our art must play its role in the world. We must be ambitious and think for the people of the whole country as well as the oppressed people in the whole world.

She called for creative work and demanded that performers exert themselves in the study of Chairman Mao's writings, go deep among the troops to learn from the Liberation Army, and realize ideological revolutionization. She called for seeking ever greater refinement with the "effort of an ox," so that *Taking the Bandits' Stronghold* might be polished and improved to become an exemplary revolutionary play. She made a scientific analysis of this play, ranging from the script, musical imagery, direction, acting, up to stage art. Things were studied all together, and a complete, fine, revised plan of proven effectiveness was put forward. She called for a high degree of unity between revolutionary political content and artistic perfection so that the heroic characters armed with the thought of Mao Tse-tung might look greater and the thought of Mao Tse-tung might be used to educate the broad audience. . . .

The growth of *Taking the Bandits' Stronghold* to maturity shows that, after the proletariat seized political power and changed and reformed the system of ownership, the bourgeoisie and its representatives within the Party necessarily will strongly exert their political influence in the sphere of literature and art and the ideological sphere. They will at all times obstinately make use of the various kinds of ideological and cultural positions they have occupied to plot for counterrevolutionary restoration and shape public opinion for launching a counterrevolutionary coup. In the final analysis, it is for the purposes of safeguarding the economic basis of socialism and the dictatorship of the proletariat and for guaranteeing that our socialist regime will never change color that we carry out the revolution of Peking Opera and the Proletarian Cultural Revolution. . . .

BIRTH OF REVOLUTIONARY CONTEMPORARY
PEKING OPERA THE RED LANTERN
WITH PIANO ACCOMPANIMENT

ANONYMOUS

The singing of the Peking opera *The Red Lantern* with piano accompaniment, a proletarian art of a new type, has been created under the personal guidance and care of Comrade Chiang Ch'ing. This splendid revolutionary news has come at a time when the people throughout the country hail the forty-seventh anniversary of the founding of the Chinese Communist Party. It is a birthday present to the Party from the revolutionary literary and art fighters. It is another blossom of proletarian revolutionary art radiant with the light of Mao Tse-tung's thought. . . .

As early as 1964, Comrade Chiang Ch'ing, following Chairman Mao's revolutionary line for literature and art, instructed that the piano should be used to accompany Peking operas with contemporary revolutionary themes. However, the handful of counterrevolutionary revisionists in literary and art circles blocked this important instruction and kept it from the revolutionary artists. The vigorous Great Proletarian Cultural Revolution has completely smashed this crime committed by this handful of class enemies. Inspired by the excellent situation in which victories have been achieved one after another in the Great Proletarian Cultural Revolution, the revolutionary literary and art fighters have displayed dauntless revolutionary initiative, broken with fetishes, and displayed the spirit of daring to think, to act, and to make revolution. Starting from the beginning of 1967, and after repeated experiments, they finally succeeded in composing piano accompaniments for the main parts sung by Li Yu-ho, the hero, and Li Tieh-mei, the young heroine, in the Peking opera *The Red Lantern*. As a result, the piano, a Western musical instrument, takes a place on the Peking Opera stage for the first time in history.

The Peking opera *The Red Lantern* with piano accompaniment retains the basic characteristics of singing in Peking Opera; at the same time, it brings into full play the characteristics of the piano— its wide range, great power, and varied means of expression. Thus the lofty and heroic images of Li Yu-ho and Li Tieh-mei are even

FROM "Birth of Revolutionary Contemporary Peking Opera *The Red Lantern* with Piano Accompaniment," *Peking Review*, 27 (July 5, 1968), 9–10.

better depicted. This successful trial in making foreign things serve China is a new creation in proletarian revolutionary literature and art. It has opened up a new road for Western musical instruments and symphonies and for musical accompaniments to Chinese operas. It has fully displayed the great vitality of the new revolutionary literature and art of the proletariat and has shown once again the immense strength of Chairman Mao's proletarian revolutionary line for literature and art.

Further Reading

As mentioned in the Preface, the English-language reader is not very well served by the existing sources on cultural activities in the People's Republic. Since the outbreak of the Cultural Revolution in 1966 and the suspension of all academic journals, the Chinese-language reader is scarcely better off. For most of the period since 1949, however, there is considerable discussion of cultural issues in both general interest magazines and newspapers (notably *Kuang-ming Jih-pao*) and in specialized journals.

Some of this, especially the more important discussions of cultural policy, is available through one or more of the various translation services. Most abundant and most usefully indexed are the translations of the U.S. Consulate in Hong Kong: *Survey of the China Mainland Press, Selections from China Mainland Magazines*, and *Current Background*. Also available are *Joint Publications Research Service* and *Union Research Service*. For summary and analysis of recent events, *China News Analysis* and *Current Scene*, both published in Hong Kong, are probably most useful. *The China Quarterly* has been the premier English-language academic journal on all aspects of Communist China, including culture, for the last ten years.

There are also numerous publications from the Foreign Languages Press in Peking. Some of the pamphlets and short books by Mao Tse-tung, Kuo Mo-jo, Chou Yang, Lu Ting-yi, and other cultural spokesmen may still be available in the United States from *China Books and Periodicals*, 2929 Twenty-fourth Street, San Francisco, California. English-language magazines—notably *Peking Review* (and its predecessor *People's China*), *Chinese Literature, China Pictorial*, and *China Reconstructs*—are much more informative and available.

As for specific fields, history in Communist China has been discussed by Joseph R. Levenson, *Confucian China and Its Modern Fate: The Problem of Historical Significance* (Berkeley: University of California Press, 1965); James P. Harrison, *The Communists and Chinese Peasant Rebellions* (New York: Atheneum, 1968); Albert Feuerwerker, "China's History in Marxian Dress," *The American Historical Review*, 66, 2 (Jan., 1961), 323–53; and Albert Feuerwerker (ed.), *History in Communist China* (Cambridge: Massachusetts Institute of Technology Press, 1968). For Chinese writings, apart from the standard translation series, the International Arts and Sciences Press (IASP) Translation Journals, especially *Chinese Studies in History and Philosophy*, are important. *An Outline History of China* (Peking: Foreign Languages Press, 1959), gives a useful summary of the accepted version of Chinese history.

Archaeology is most exhaustively covered in Cheng Te-k'un's *Archaeology in China*, 3 vols. published to date (Toronto: University of Toronto Press). Several issues of *China News Analysis* also deal with Communist archaeological work but in a considerably more critical manner. Rewi Alley's frequent contributions to *Eastern Horizon* contain an enthusiastic amateur observer's accounts of archaeological and historical monument reconstruction work in China.

Philosophy has been somewhat eclipsed by ideology in Communist China and also in Western studies of recent Chinese thought. Donald J. Munro has most closely followed formal philosophy in the People's Republic, writing a number of articles on the subject in *The China Quarterly* and elsewhere. Presently, he is writing a book, *The Concept of Man in Communist China*. Joseph R. Levenson has touched on philosophy in his studies of Chinese Communist intellectual history, especially in Volume III of *Confucian China and Its Modern Fate*. *China News Analysis* has several issues on contemporary philosophy, particularly on Fung Yu-lan. There are also translations of philosophical writings available in the International Arts and Sciences Press Translation Journals.

On religion, Holmes Welch is the only Western scholar to study Buddhism in Communist China in any depth. He has published two articles on this in *The China Quarterly*, 6 (April–June, 1961), and 22 (April–June, 1965). The forthcoming third volume of his history of Buddhism in modern China will deal with the Communist period. As for the other indigenous Chinese religions, they have largely been neglected as Western writers on religion in China concern themselves almost entirely with Christianity. Only occasional glimpses are available from the Chinese press and periodicals.

Chinese Communist literature is much better covered. A large number of modern novels, plays, short stories, and collections of poems are available in translation. There is also the usually very good English-language publication *Chinese Literature*, edited until recently by one of modern China's most famous novelists, Mao Tun. As for Western scholarship, pre-1949 Chinese Communist literature is exhaustively studied in J. Prusek, *Die Literatur des befreiten China and ihrer Volkstraditionen* (Prague, 1955). Probably the best survey is by Cyril Birch (ed.), *Chinese Communist Literature* (New York: Frederick A. Praeger, 1963), originally a special issue of *The China Quarterly*, 13 (Jan.–March, 1963). The last section of C. T. Hsia, *A History of Modern Chinese Fiction, 1917–57* (New Haven: Yale University Press, 1961) covers the early 1950's.

Specifically on poetry, there is a large section of Kai-yu Hsu's *Twentieth-Century Chinese Poetry* devoted specifically to the Communist period. Ch'en Shih-hsiang, "Multiplicity in Uniformity," *The China Quarterly*, 3 (July–Sept., 1960), 1–15, deals with the mass folk-song campaign of the Great Leap Forward. For the poetry of Mao Tse-tung himself, authorized translations are *Nineteen Poems* (Peking: Foreign Languages Press, 1958), *Poems of Mao Tse-tung* (Hong Kong: Eastern Horizon Press, 1966), and *Ten More Poems of Mao Tse-tung* (Hong Kong: Eastern Horizon Press, 1967). There is a sensitive study of his poetry in C. N. Tay, "From Snow to Plum Blossoms," *Journal of Asian Studies*, 25, 2 (Feb., 1966), pp. 287–303. The deep Chinese Communist concern for folklore is brought out in Wolfram Eberhard, *Folktales of China* (Chicago: University of Chicago Press, 1965), especially in the foreword by Richard M. Dorsan.

Chinese opera, like literature, is available through translation of new and revised plays. A brief introduction to its best known variety is provided by Rewi Alley, *Peking Opera* (Peking: New World Press, 1957). Important articles on the reform of Peking Opera and on the new operas on contemporary themes are contained in Chiang Ch'ing, *On the Revolution of Peking Opera* (Peking: Foreign Languages Press, 1968).

The leading Western interpreter of classical Chinese theater is A. C. Scott, whose writings include *The Classical Theatre of China* (New York: Macmillan, 1959); *An Introduction to the*

Chinese Theatre (New York: Theatre Arts, 1959); *Mei Lan-Fang, Leader of the Pear Garden* (Hong Kong: Oxford University Press, 1959); and a section on theater in *Literature and the Arts in Twentieth Century China* (New York: Doubleday Anchor, 1963). A splendid pictorial introduction to Peking Opera in China during the 1950's is Kalvodova Sis-Vanis, *Chinese Theatre* (London: Spring Books, n.d.).

Furthermore, traditional theater (particularly Peking Opera) has been a favorite subject for the often bemused attention of Western visitors to China. A few, however, have written on it with insight and sensitivity. Among these, I would include Peter Schmid, *The New Face of China* (London: George G. Harrop, 1958); Michael Croft, *Red Carpet to China* (London: Longman's, 1959); Lord Boyd Orr and Peter Townsend, *What's Happening in China?* (New York: Doubleday, 1959); and Phillip Bonosky, *Dragon Pink on Old White* (New York: Marzani and Munsell, 1963).

Finally, there are records available of Peking Opera performances in recent years. The dazzling *Opéra Chinois* (Pathé FCX 429), recorded during the National Peking Opera troupe's triumphant visit to Paris, is outstanding. There is also a short film of the troupe in action, *A Night at the Peking Opera*. Chinese-made records of the Cultural Revolution's new Peking operas on contemporary themes are available from *China Books and Periodicals*, 2929 Twenty-fourth Street, San Francisco, California.

The other performing arts are not nearly so well covered. There is relatively little on new plays or movies outside the specialized theater journals, except for the thunderous denunciations of subversive playwrights that have marked the Cultural Revolution. Many of those can be found translated in *Current Background*, 783 and 784, *Union Research Service*, and elsewhere. One interesting pre–Cultural Revolution product still available in English is T'ien Han's play *Kuan Han-ching*, based on the life of that great thirteenth-century dramatist (Peking: Foreign Languages Press, 1961). On puppets, there is Sergie V. Obraztsov, *The Chinese Puppet Theatre* (London: Sidgwick and Jackson, 1961).

Music is discussed by A. C. Scott, *Literature and the Arts in Twentieth-Century China* (New York: Doubleday Anchor Books, 1963) and also by Robert Offergeld, "Music: China's Three-Headed Dragon," *Diplomat* (Sept., 1966), pp. 130–36. Here, too, records are available such as *Passport to China* (Artia ALP-112) and *China in Song and Dance* (Bruno Hi-Fi 50062). Records from China currently available in the United States, however, are almost entirely products of the Cultural Revolution. (A catalog is available from *China Books and Periodicals*.)

Painting remains an aspect of recent Chinese culture that has sadly been neglected by Western scholars. There is some discussion of the Communist period in Michael Sullivan's *Chinese Art in the Twentieth Century* (Berkeley: University of California Press, 1959), but it is very brief. The only extended treatment of painters active in Communist China is that by Lubor Hajek, Adolf Hoffmeister, and Eva Rychterova, *Contemporary Chinese Painting* (London: Spring Books, 1961). However, most of the examples here are pre-1949, and none is later than 1955.

Fortunately, the English-language periodical *Chinese Literature* has published a good many excellent color plates of recent Chinese paintings, along with political and aesthetic evaluations by contemporary Chinese critics. There are also frequent reproductions in *China Pictorial* and *China Reconstructs* that are generally of much better quality than those in the specialized Chinese-language art journals. Finally, in the relatively relaxed years of the mid-1950's and early 1960's, a number of quite handsome art books, some with English captions, were published in China.

Other arts and handicrafts are also represented in the above periodicals, especially in *Chinese Literature*.

As for architecture, here we can use the camera work of Western reporters such as Emil Schulthess, *China* (New York: Viking Press, 1966), and also Chinese photographic essays such as *China: Land of Charm and Beauty* (Shanghai: Fine Arts Publishing House, 1964). Magazines like *China Reconstructs* and *China Pictorial* also give an impression of the architecture of the new China. Critical accounts relating it to China's architectural tradition are much rarer. A. C. Scott has a good brief survey of the architecture of the 1950's in his *Literature and the Arts in Twentieth-Century China* (cited previously). Observant journalists like William Kinmond, *No Dogs in China* (Toronto, 1957), Peter Schmid, *The New Face of China* (cited previously), and Felix Greene, *Awakened China* (New York: Doubleday, 1961) sometimes make interesting points.

Science has been, as I observed earlier, rather peripheral to the cultural legacy, largely an object of historical pride in past achievements. These achievements are carefully studied in Joseph Needham's *Science and Civilization in China* (Cambridge: Cambridge University Press, 1955).

An example of modern Chinese pride in the past and its great scientific names is Chang Hui-chen's *Li Shih-chen: Great Pharmacologist of Ancient China* (Peking: Foreign Languages Press, 1955). Medicine, as the showpiece of the cultural legacy in science, is examined in the last section of my *Traditional Medicine in Modern China* (Cambridge: Harvard University Press, 1968).

Principal Contributors

REWI ALLEY Emigré New Zealander, long-time resident in China. Author of numerous books and articles about life in the People's Republic, especially about literary and cultural matters.

CYRIL BIRCH Professor of Chinese, University of California, Berkeley. Author and translator of several books on Chinese literature.

PHILLIP BONOSKY American Marxist novelist and literary critic.

CH'A FU-HSI Veteran master of the Chinese lute and President of the National Association of Lute Players.

CHAI LI-LIN Professor of Architecture, Peking University.

CH'EN PO-TA Longtime close associate of Mao Tse-tung. Author, historian, and leading member of Cultural Revolution Group.

CH'ENG CH'IEN-TAN Historian of Chinese literature.

CHENG TE-K'UN Lecturer in Far Eastern Art and Archaeology, Cambridge University. Author of *Archaeology in China*, 3 volumes published to date.

CHIANG CH'ING Onetime bit-part movie actress. Wife of Mao Tse-tung. Currently leading cultural authority, especially in theater, for the Cultural Revolution.

CHOU EN-LAI Premier and one of the top Party leaders.

CHOU YANG Former Deputy Director of Propaganda Department. Chief literary spokesman of the Party until his fall in the Cultural Revolution.

CH'Ü CHUNG Chinese Buddhist lay leader.

PEGGY DURDIN American journalist and former resident in China.

FENG CHIH Poet and literary critic in Communist China.

ALBERT FEUERWERKER Professor of Chinese history, University of Michigan. Author and editor of several books on modern Chinese history.

C. P. FITZGERALD Professor of Far Eastern History, Australian National University. A distinguished historian of T'ang China who has also written several books on twentieth-century history.

Fung Yu-lan Distinguished modern Chinese philosopher and historian of Chinese philosophy. Author of *A History of Chinese Philosophy*.

Jerome B. Grieder Associate Professor of Chinese History, Brown University.

Robert Guillain French journalist. Former resident of China who has returned twice since 1949.

James P. Harrison Associate Professor of History, Hunter College, New York. Author of *The Chinese Communists and Chinese Peasant Rebellions*.

Ho Lu-t'ing Leading composer and Party member since Yenan period. Became President of Shanghai Conservatory of Music.

Hou Wai-lu Prominent Communist historian. Editor of *Historical Research*. Member of Chinese Academy of Sciences. Denounced in Cultural Revolution.

Hsiung Deh-ta Graduate of Slade School of Art, London. Works in the film laboratories of Rank Organization.

Hua Chun-wu Well-known cartoonist. Secretary-general of the Chinese Artists' Union.

Hua Hsia Painter and art critic.

Kai Hsieh Painter and art critic.

Kai-yu Hsu Professor of Humanities and Languages, San Francisco State College.

Kuo Mo-jo Historian, playwright, and poet. One of China's most versatile intellectuals.

Joseph R. Levenson Late Sather Professor of History, University of California, Berkeley. Author of *Confucian China and Its Modern Fate*, 3 volumes, plus other works on modern Chinese intellectual history.

Li Jen Party literary and dramatic critic.

Li K'o-jan Prominent painter in the traditional style.

Liang Ssu-ch'eng Professor of architecture, Tsinghua University. Foremost proponent of the national style of architecture.

Lu Ting-yi Former Director of Propaganda, Department of the Central Committee and Minister of Culture. Denounced in Cultural Revolution.

Mao Tse-tung Classical-style poet from Hunan. Chiefly known for his efforts in other fields of endeavor.

Mao Yi-sheng President of the Chinese Society of Civil Engineers. Chief Consulting Engineer for the Yangtze River Bridge at Wuhan.

DONALD J. MUNRO   Assistant Professor of Philosophy, University of Michigan. Author of *The Concept of Man in Early China* and the forthcoming study *The Concept of Man in Communist China.*

DAVID S. NIVISON   Professor of Chinese Philosophy, Stanford University. Author of several books on Chinese intellectual history.

HUGO PORTISCH   Austrian journalist. Editor of Vienna *Kurier.*

PETER SCHMID   Swiss journalist and literary critic.

A. C. SCOTT   Formerly with the British Council for Cultural Relations in China and Hong Kong. Teacher of Chinese Theater, University of Wisconsin. Has written several books on Chinese theater.

SHEN TSE-FAN   Historian of Chinese literature.

MICHAEL SULLIVAN   Professor of Chinese Art History, Stanford University. Author of several books on Chinese art.

ANDRÉ TRAVERT   French career-diplomat and student of Chinese affairs.

HOLMES WELCH   Vice-Director of the Center for the Study of World Religion, Harvard University. Author of a three-volume study of modern Chinese Buddhism, of which two volumes have appeared to date.

WU HAN   Prominent historian and playwright. Attacked in first stages of the Cultural Revolution.

WU TSU-KUANG   Director of the film "The Stage Art of Mei Lan-fang."

YAO WEN-YÜAN   Previously obscure literary critic who, since his attack on Wu Han in 1965, has become a leading figure in the Cultural Revolution group around Chiang Ch'ing.